Tap Dance for All

# Tap Dance for All

*Adapting Instruction
for Disability
and Mobility Impairment*

Victoria Moore *and*
Joan Gerrard

McFarland & Company, Inc., Publishers
*Jefferson, North Carolina*

LIBRARY OF CONGRESS CATALOGUING-IN-PUBLICATION DATA

Names: Moore, Victoria, 1962– author. | Gerrard, Joan, author.
Title: Tap dance for all : adapting instruction for disability and mobility impairment / Victoria Moore and Joan Gerrard.
Description: Jefferson, North Carolina : McFarland & Company, Inc., Publishers, 2022 | Includes bibliographical references and index.
Identifiers: LCCN 2022031086 |
   ISBN 9781476688084 (paperback : acid free paper) ∞
   ISBN  9781476647302 (ebook)
Subjects: LCSH: Tap dancing—Study and teaching. | Dance for people with disabilities. | Tap dancing—Psychological aspects. | Tap dancing—Physiological aspects. | BISAC: PERFORMING ARTS / Dance / Tap | SOCIAL SCIENCE / People with Disabilities
Classification: LCC GV1794 .M66 2022 | DDC 792.7/8—dc23
LC record available at https://lccn.loc.gov/2022031086

BRITISH LIBRARY CATALOGUING DATA ARE AVAILABLE

**ISBN (print) 978-1-4766-8808-4**
**ISBN (ebook) 978-1-4766-4730-2**

© 2022 Victoria Moore and Joan Gerrard. All rights reserved

*No part of this book may be reproduced or transmitted in any form or by any means, electronic or mechanical, including photocopying or recording, or by any information storage and retrieval system, without permission in writing from the publisher.*

On the cover: Child tap dancer wearing pink ballet leotard dances beside her gold walker mobility aid while wearing glasses and hearing aids (B Wright/Shutterstock); *inset left to right* tap students Joyce Curti and Marianne Cordes (author photograph)

Printed in the United States of America

*McFarland & Company, Inc., Publishers*
   *Box 611, Jefferson, North Carolina 28640*
      *www.mcfarlandpub.com*

I dedicate this book to the art of tap dancing,
its preservation, and all its many performers,
teachers, and students throughout the world.
—Joan Gerrard

With my deepest appreciation and gratitude, I dedicate this labor of love to my remarkable and beautiful mother, Joan Gerrard. She was and will always remain the other half of my heart, and this book is the collaboration of our combined expertise and passion for the unparalleled art of tap dance. As a prolific choreographer, an inspirational instructor, and a brilliant hoofer who could go tap to tap with the best of the best, my mother left a legacy that will live on through the joy brought to those who never thought tap dancing was something they would ever be able to experience. Thank you, Mom, for your endless encouragement, loyalty, and staunch support throughout my life. Your optimism, strength, and relentless determination were awe inspiring to witness and a reflection of your valuable contributions to the world of tap. I know you are still tapping and showing them all how it is done up there in Heaven. We will tap together again someday.
Tap expresses with the feet what words cannot.
—Victoria Moore

# Table of Contents

| | |
|---|---|
| *Acknowledgments by Victoria Moore* | ix |
| *Preface* | 1 |
| *Introduction* | 5 |
| 1. Tap: Exclusive to Inclusive | 7 |
| 2. Dance: Mind, Body, and Soul Benefits | 21 |
| 3. Diseases, Conditions, and Age Groups | 29 |
| 4. The Power of Music | 47 |
| 5. Tap Styles: Rhythmic vs. Broadway | 52 |
| 6. Choreography vs. Improvisation | 56 |
| 7. Beginning and Beginning II Levels | 65 |
| 8. Extra Combinations: (Beginning / Beginning II Levels) | 77 |
| 9. Beginning III / Intermediate / Advanced Levels | 94 |
| 10. Extra Combinations: (Beginning III / Intermediate / Advanced Levels) | 113 |
| 11. Intermediate / Advanced, Advanced Levels | 131 |
| 12. Time Steps / Time Step Breaks: (Beginning III / Intermediate / Advanced Levels) | 145 |
| 13. Professional Physically Integrated Dancers Spotlight | 157 |
| 14. The Evolution of Tap | 209 |
| *Appendix: Tap Glove / Mitten and Tap Board Instructions* | 221 |
| *Glossary* | 230 |
| *Bibliography* | 235 |
| *Index* | 237 |

# Acknowledgments
## by Victoria Moore

First, I must express my deep appreciation and gratitude to David Alff at McFarland for giving this subject matter the opportunity to make a lasting change and impact for disabled people and senior communities and for being my ever-patient editor. Thank you to everyone on the McFarland team who guided and helped me throughout the creative process.

To Ginger Lane, Mindy Kim, Lindy Dannelly, and Mary Verdi-Fletcher, thank you. These four fierce powerhouse women generously gave of their time to speak with me and graciously offered a glimpse into their differently-abled world to educate and enlighten those of us who are stand-up dancers, studio owners, and dance company directors so that we may better serve and advocate for their needs and rights. May their stories be the spark that ignites the flame of change in the nondisabled population to not only shift perceptions but also create a more equitable and compassionate world for the disabled community to live in and thrive.

I also want to give my sincere thanks to the superlative tap master Barbara Duffy for allowing me to share some of her brilliant knowledge of improvisation from her book *Tap Into Improv*. It is available on Amazon, and I highly recommend all tappers pick up a copy.

Lastly, I would like to acknowledge and thank my family, especially my son David Moore, Bill Turner, who will be my husband by the time this book is ready for print, and my brother Tim Welpott and his wife Bobbie Welpott, whose expert knowledge in diseases and conditions was an invaluable contribution. I must also express my endless gratitude and appreciation to my indomitable fierce tribe of friends, with special thanks to Dana Buchman and Maddy Reeves for their marketing

## Acknowledgments by Victoria Moore

prowess and expertise in helping shape the name of the program *Tap for All*. Their limitless love, support, and, for some of the above mentioned, copious amounts of proofreading kept this book train on its tracks, where otherwise it might just have been an unfinished dream, collecting dust on my bookshelf.

# Preface

The journey of going from tapping with my feet professionally for forty years to tapping with my hands has been wonderful, long, and difficult at times, but an incredibly inspiring and uplifting adventure to be sure. Keeping the artistry of tap not only alive but thriving is essential for the continuation and survival of the dance form. This is the deep-rooted belief my mother and I have long held as sacrosanct. This ideology became the core of our mission statement early on, from the very beginning of our teaching careers. But never in our wildest dreams could we have envisioned that our long-standing proclamation would entail us changing the perception of tap, by turning the once exclusive stand-up dance form into something inclusive and diverse. Whether disabled, mobility impaired or nondisabled, everyone deserves the opportunity to feel the jubilance and joy that tap has to offer. As Mom always said, "I have never met anyone who was unhappy while they were tap dancing." The number of people in the disabled and mobility-impaired community is enormous. This population has been left out of the tap dance equation for far too long, and it is high time to now not only add them in but to welcome them in with open arms.

The subject of this book came about from a simple conversation over dinner one night. That honest exchange became one of those rare illuminating light-bulb moments that make you think, "Why have I never thought about this before?" That transformational meal was with a bright and beautiful young woman who is an exquisite integrated dancer that has cerebral palsy. As we spoke, she commented on how wonderful it must have been to have danced in Broadway shows and teach tap to so many aspiring young dancers. As she finished her thought, it occurred to me that tap was not an accessible dance form for her. And as I drove home, I could not stop thinking about how exclusive

### Preface

tap really was for those with disabilities, and even more importantly, how that exclusivity needed to change. So what, exactly, was stopping her from enjoying tap like anyone else? Sure, she was unable to stand unassisted, but what if she did not need to stand? What if she was able to create the same rhythms with her hands just like stand-up dancers did with their feet? Tap dancers are percussionists, just like a drummer in a band, so it made perfect sense to me to take the taps off the shoes and put them onto a pair of gloves or mittens to no longer make standing a requirement to tap dance.

My sister-in-law is a brilliant pediatric physical therapist who has decades of experience working with children that have been stricken with a variety of conditions and diseases. I knew I was onto something special when her eyes lit up with excitement at the explanation of my proposed new tap program. She felt the project design had many highly advantageous applications for both young and old alike. This conversation led me down my next intriguing path, researching the benefits dance has on various aspects of a person's health. This was my Oprah Winfrey "ah-ha" moment and the point at which the light bulbs in my brain were lighting up like the Christmas tree in New York City's Rockefeller Center. Article after article cited not only the benefits of dance but also had the clinical proof to back up their conclusions. Tap dance was specifically mentioned to have many beneficial cognitive advantages for the elderly. It quickly became apparent to me just how important a class like this could be. It was also abundantly clear that this information needed to be passed on to the next generation of up-and-coming dance instructors, so introducing this concept at the college level was the perfect way to ensure the broadest reach of this material. However, college students are not the sole focus for the vital and valuable content of this book. Nondisabled teachers and studio owners also deserve to be educated on how to broaden their student base and increase not only their revenue, but also their reputation as diverse dance studios. Inclusivity should not be just a trendy buzzword but a call to action, and as defined by the dictionary it means "the practice or policy of providing equal access to opportunities and resources for people who might otherwise be excluded or marginalized, such as those having physical or mental disabilities or belonging to other minority groups."* This book is my

---

* Google.com, Google's English Dictionary (Oxford Languages).

## Preface

call to action for every one of you to be the seed of change, to understand that by thinking outside of the box, and maybe stepping outside your personal comfort zone, an entire population of our society will have the opportunity to experience and reap the benefits from this phenomenal dance form.

Nowhere could I find any book comparable to what Mom and I were about to undertake, but I was confident that with our combined teaching and choreographic knowledge, and combined expertise that spans more than 75 years, that we had the solid foundation we needed to make this book happen. We knew that inclusivity and diversity was the path forward in all things, and that included the world of dance. For our book to be truly comprehensive, though, it needed to cover a wide range of topics. From my extensive experience as a master tap instructor for dance conventions from coast to coast, I know that tap teachers are always looking for exciting new combinations to share with their classes. But this book had to be more than a publication chock full of challenging, fun combos, which it does have in abundance, it also had to impart our gold standard teaching methodology, applicable whether teaching stand-up nondisabled students or disabled and other mobility-impaired people. In addition, it had to include all the ways to get the most out of this program by laying out all the amazing benefits that scientific studies have proven, plus include a comprehensive breakdown of the diseases, conditions, and illness that an instructor will most likely encounter. It also needed to feature an easily digestible understanding of how disabled and mobility-impaired people can benefit not only from musicality but also from knowing the differences between rhythmic and Broadway tap and choreography versus improvisation. A brief peek into tap history, plus insight into how to approach teaching different age groups, whether disabled or nondisabled, gives the dance instructor and studio owner a well-rounded way to approach expanding their clientele. As a bonus I have interviewed four incredible professional integrated dancers to help assist you in understanding how to teach and communicate with disabled and mobility-impaired students. They have graciously shared their journeys, struggles, and triumphs with all of us in order that we may better comprehend their world, and to help other mobility-impaired dancers understand that even though they may be limited by their inability to stand, walk, see, or hear, there is no limit to what they can accomplish in dance and in life. I know for myself the knowledge, information, and messages each

## Preface

one of these outstanding women shared will remain with me for a lifetime. We all have it in us to do better and evolve into ever-improving human beings, and we can start by making a concerted effort at trying to gain a greater understanding of what it is like to stand (or sit) in someone else's shoes (or wheelchair).

# Introduction

If you are a nondisabled person, "the world is your oyster," as the saying goes. Your drive and determination are the only limiting factors when you are ready to reach for the stars and follow your dreams. For disabled people, however, roadblocks and limitations are everywhere, and grabbing the brass ring is most often an elusive endeavor. Disabled people have had to fight tooth and nail for even the most basic accommodations that nondisabled people take for granted.

Another often forgotten population is seniors. Some might say they have had their shot at the brass ring, but the truth is they still have a great deal of life left to live. The quality of their life has a direct correlation to the level of engagement and cognitive stimulation they receive. Without that, seniors have the potential to rapidly deteriorate, with feelings of isolation and loneliness a possible byproduct, not to mention the development of such conditions and diseases as dementia and Alzheimer's.

What if there was a way to alter a typically nondisabled activity, one that has shown tremendous beneficial potential, so disabled and senior populations could reap the benefits as well? The mission behind this book is to show dance instructors and dance studio owners how to shift their perspective of dance from one that is exclusive to one that is inclusive.

The writing of this book began as a collaboration in 2016 with my mother, Joan Gerrard. Sadly, my mom suddenly passed away April 29, 2018, leaving me shattered, heartbroken, and unable to focus on the project we were both so passionate about. When COVID hit and the world was shut down, I decided it was time to dust the book off and get to work, knowing my mother would want me to finish what we started. As you progress through this book, please understand I am speaking from my perspective while sharing the wisdom and expertise of my immensely talented mother along the way.

I first became intrigued with this idea after seeing my mother

## Introduction

deteriorate and become increasingly isolated in her final years. This was especially difficult to bear witness to since she had been a master tap instructor for more than 35 years. Since I too am a master tap instructor, with a professional career spanning 40 years now, I desperately wanted to find a way to keep her mind active and creative. A conversation with a disabled integrated dancer one afternoon gave me the inspiration I had been searching for. Once I began peeling back layer after layer of research and interviewed several professional integrated dancers, my eyes, heart, and mind all told me that I had the answer, not only for Mom, but also for countless other disabled and mobility-impaired people. The *Tap for All* program is applicable not only for tap but can also be the blueprint for any dance form. The reception to this way of teaching has been tremendous, from nondisabled people, disabled people, and seniors alike.

In the first chapter you will be introduced to the program, how it works, and what you will need to execute the classes. In Chapter 2, you will dive into all the many benefits of implementing this kind of program. Next, in Chapter 3, you will move on to comprehension of the various diseases and conditions you may encounter and how to approach teaching students affected by them. This chapter also covers the varying age groups you will see and additionally how to group your classes. Chapters 4, 5, and 6 contain valuable information on music, the two variations of tap styles and choreography and improvisation. Chapters 7 through 12 provide you with the progression and methodology that both my mother and I use when teaching. These chapters range from beginning to advanced levels, with one chapter dedicated solely to time steps and their breaks. Plenty of extra combinations have been given so that you will have endless ways to create your own pieces of choreography. In Chapter 13 you will be introduced to four outstanding professional female integrated dancers. They have generously shared their world with us so that we can better understand what it is like to live in their shoes. Chapter 14 presents a brief history of tap's rich and colorful past and present. The appendix gives you detailed directions on how to create your own tap gloves and tap board carrying bag, should you choose to make them for yourself.

Now that you know what lies ahead, I hope you are excited to see how *Tap for All* can turn your current and future classes and studio into one that welcomes everyone, not just those fortunate enough to have been graced with a fully functioning physique. *Tap for All* ... and all for tap!

# 1

# Tap
*Exclusive to Inclusive*

### OBJECTIVES

- Understanding how to take tap from exclusive to inclusive.
- Comprehension of a mobility impaired dance class and its variety of options.
- Knowledge of the *Tap for All* tap program and the reason behind its name.
- Awareness of the types of locations appropriate for this program.

Welcome to a whole new way of approaching the art of teaching tap. Within this book you will discover and learn how to take tap from exclusive to inclusive. Tap dance, the only dance form that is truly American based, has been enjoyed around the world for many decades by young and old alike. But there is one enormous segment of the population that has been relegated to merely enjoying this art form from the sidelines: disabled and mobility-impaired people. Whether reliant on a wheelchair, crutches, or a cane, or simply unsteady while standing, this community has falsely believed that creating rhythms and enjoying tap dancing was beyond their grasp. But now, not only will they have the opportunity to be included in this fun and amazing dance discipline, they will also have the possibility of reaping tremendous cognitive benefits as well.

As you progress through this book you will soon see that by opening your heart, mind, and most importantly your tap classes to disabled and mobility-impaired students, you will quickly become known locally as an inclusive dance teacher and / or studio. Additionally, you

## Tap Dance for All

can increase your client base, revenue, and types of tap classes available in your weekly schedule to serve your community better than ever before. The program *Tap for All* was created to give tap instructors more opportunities, more inclusivity, and more income possibilities plus more teaching diversity. The name *Tap for All* represents tap no longer solely belonging to individuals blessed with full access to every aspect of their physical bodies, but to everyone, irrespective of their physical and mental accessibility.

How is this new and inclusive class accomplished, and what types of students are we specifically talking about? As mentioned earlier, tap dancers are percussionists just like drummers, using their feet to create the unlimited out-of-this-world rhythms that we have seen from such tap legends as Gregory Hines, Savion Glover, Sarah Reich, and Ayodel Casel. Until now, for those in a wheelchair, unable to stand without assistance, and those who are visually or hearing impaired, this type of dancing has not been physically possible. But by bringing the percussive rhythm-making back up to the hands, that problem has been creatively solved. Hand and chair tap dancing allows anyone unable to bear weight in their legs and feet the ability to create the exact same rhythms as any stand-up tap dancer. At first when I was writing this, I thought there might be a couple of limitations a mobility-impaired dancer would have that a stand-up dancer would not—traveling and turning. But after my talks with Ginger Lane and Mary Verdi-Fletcher, two of the professional integrated dancers that I interviewed for this book, I came to understand that those two limitations were not really limitations at all. They enlightened me to the fact that wheelchair dancers would indeed be able to turn and travel while tapping. Hopefully at some point down the line, Mary and I will work together to bring tap into her professional company's choreography repertoire. I have goose bumps and am extremely excited and honored just thinking about that possibility. It would be an unprecedented triumph, and I look forward to the day we break that glass ceiling together. One other important piece of information for you to consider that I received from Mary is that a stand-up dancer can also be a disabled dancer. This type of disabled dancer may be either visually or hearing impaired but can still be considered a stand-up dancer. A blind dancer still has their sense of hearing, and a deaf dancer can still feel the beat of the music through the floor. Both are deserving of the one-of-a-kind magical experience of tap dancing.

Imagine for a moment the incomparable hoofer Sarah Reich, and

## 1. Tap

then add to her tap brilliance a hand tapper who is mobility impaired, both going head to head, or rather foot to hand, in a tap duet performance. This kind of powerful pairing could show the entire world that disabled and mobility-impaired dancers truly are limitless. The pursuit of inclusion, and the blending of a wide variety of abilities, has the potential to chip away at the stereotyping and labeling typically seen in the disabled and mobility-impaired population. This diverse program takes one small step in the direction of a much more welcoming and accepting world. As more instructors also commit to taking this step, our inclusive global footprint will grow bigger and more expansive with the addition of each new inclusive teacher. With the endless creativity that I know is out there reading this book right now, I am confident that this will merely be the jumping off point to even more innovative ways to bring together disabled and nondisabled people.

Let us talk for a moment about one other type of tap dancer: the chair tap dancer. This second type of sit-down dancer is also mobility impaired, even though he or she can stand. They have fully functioning lower extremities but are not stable enough to perform the balance and weight changes required to be a stand-up tap dancer. *Tap for All* classes can accommodate this style of tap-dancing aficionado as well. If you think that a sit-down chair tap dancer does not enjoy making rhythms like a regular stand-up tapper, just check out the Gene Kelly and Donald O'Connor dance medley from 1959 on YouTube, starting at the two minute and fifty second mark,* although I highly recommend viewing the entire video, as Gene Kelly's dancing is always worthwhile to watch, learn from, and enjoy.

Now that we have covered all three types of tap-dancing modalities, I want to share with you the possible class options that will be available to instructors of this curriculum. Besides the typical stand-up tap classes that are traditionally taught, including all the various ages and difficulty levels, the studio / teacher will also have the option to offer any or all the following classes in conjunction with their regular tap program:

1. Hand Tap (mobility-impaired dancers)
2. Hand Tap + Stand-Up Tap (mobility-impaired dancers + stand-up dancers)

---

* Vladmir Zworkin, "Gene Kelly & Donald O'Connor Dance Medley 1959," January 15, 2012, www.youtube.com/watch?v=9xkKhUj3C9M&t=175s.

# Tap Dance for All

3. Chair Tap (mobility-impaired dancers with use of their legs and feet)
4. Chair Tap + Hand Tap (mobility-impaired dancers with and without lower extremity use)
5. Chair Tap + Stand-Up Tap (mobility-impaired dancers + stand-up dancers)
6. Chair Tap + Hand Tap + Stand-Up Tap (all three types of dancers together in one class)

Combined with a studio's regular stand-up tap classes, there are six different pairings possible. Add to that all the different age groups and ability levels (beginning through advanced) and you can quickly see how easy it would be for a studio to fill an entire week's schedule with just these all-embracing, all-welcoming types of tap classes alone. Will a dance studio begin with all these options right away? Not likely, as it will take a little time to become known as an inclusive studio. Once a dance studio invites and welcomes their local disabled and mobility-impaired population into their facility, the word will spread throughout the community, and the classes will most certainly grow and expand. Dance studios and teachers should also take advantage of spreading the word about being diverse and inclusive through all the available social media outlets they have at their disposal. Using photos, videos, stories, and #hashtags all get the word out quickly, efficiently, and economically.

Over the summer of 2021 I was invited to teach this type of program at Parker Dance Academy in Parker, Colorado. I had the opportunity to try out all three modalities in a single class setting on students aged eight to 18. After each of the classes, we had a candid discussion where the students freely shared their likes and / or dislikes of this type of class. Thanks to the interviews of the professional integrated dancers that you will read in Chapter 13, I was able to educate these open and eager students on the importance of language, representation, and using our nondisabled privilege to be advocates for the disabled community. The feedback I received was outstanding, helpful, and unanimously positive. Across the board, all ages loved the class. They were completely interested and receptive to learning about people with disabilities, and they began to understand how disabled people simply want to be seen as real people who just so happen to also be in a wheelchair. In fact, they had so much fun in each class they experimented with improvisation while wearing the tap gloves while I changed out the music. Both

## 1. Tap

the dancers who were seated on the floor with tap boards and the dancers sitting in a chair executing chair tap soon realized that even though some access to their body was denied, they still had plenty of accessibility to the rest of their frame to create dynamics, levels, and expression in the choreography they were given. Each group learned to fully use, adapt, and incorporate whatever parts of their body were still available to them. The joy, fun, and creativity that resulted was beyond my wildest expectations. They all concluded that making rhythms with your hands was quite different from making rhythms with your feet, yet adapted in no time at all. I have to say that I received rave reviews on my tap mittens. Students thought they were very clever and tons of fun to work with. For an amateur tailor I did give myself a pat on the back for that little victory.

The second studio I introduced this class to was as equally successful as the first. I taught regular stand-up classes, of course, but like the first studio I also introduced them to tap for the mobility impaired and disabled. I again sectioned the class into three groups: stand-up, hand, and chair tap. First, I taught the choreography to all groups together standing up. The dancers then split up into the three different modalities. When the music played the students were amazed that even though they were performing the steps in separate ways, they were all able to execute the same choreography. The studio owner and instructors were equally astounded. Next, I gave each modality a different four-bar piece of choreography, creating a question / answer piece that highlighted how well and how creative this type of class can be if only studios would welcome and invite disabled people and seniors into their businesses. As I did with Parker Dance Academy, I shared the wisdom that I gained from the professional integrated dancers I interviewed regarding the ways in which they could make their studio more accessible and accommodating for disabled people. The overwhelming feedback and response from these two workshops prove that we really *can* make the dance world more inclusive, one instructor and one dance studio at a time.

Before you dive into teaching this type of class you need to understand the sort of students you will be instructing. Those that are disabled and mobility impaired encompass a wide variety of people and a wide variety of conditions. You may find yourself teaching everything from younger children that are in wheelchairs and have cerebral palsy, to seniors that are unsteady standing and have Parkinson's. As mentioned earlier, stand-up dancers can also be disabled: those who have a visual impairment or are blind, or those who have a hearing impairment or are deaf. There are many different diseases, disorders, and conditions that disabled and mobility-impaired people deal with daily. There are also many varying degrees of those diseases, disorders, and conditions. Some of the most common ones that you are likely to encounter are Parkinson's, dementia, Alzheimer's, cerebral palsy, and arthritis. You will also see people recovering from strokes and, again, people with visual or hearing disabilities. I go into further detail and explanation of all of these in Chapter 3. Another factor to keep in mind is that the age of the student afflicted with these issues will need to be considered when approaching the class. Cerebral palsy, for example, can affect a person's ability to communicate verbally, be mobile, eat, and take care of themselves, or be as mild as being fully functional, save the ability and use of their lower extremities. Gauging the functionality of the student joining the class is important, because placing a higher functioning student into a lower functioning class will end up being a frustrating mismatch for both types of students as well as the teacher. Even when teaching a regular stand-up tap class, whether disabled or nondisabled, the instructor should match the developmental capacity and age appropriately to have a cohesive, smooth-running class. The combination of all these factors may seem daunting at first, but once you understand these various conditions you will be able to easily design a fun, exciting, and extremely worthwhile and beneficial program. This book is meant to assist you along this much needed, important journey.

What equipment / tools are needed to teach this type of specialized tap class? To teach *Tap for All* classes the only items required beyond music are tap gloves and a tap board. There are a couple of options for the gloves depending on the location and situation of the class. The first consideration is, will you need to be able to remove the taps for cleaning purposes due to students reusing the gloves? A senior assisted living facility would be such an example of this need. In this situation, since it is highly likely that the seniors would either lose or misplace the gloves, collecting them after class and laundering them is the best solution. So in this case the answer is *yes*, and the tap gloves will require Velcro to adhere the taps to the gloves or mittens to (1) not rust the metal taps during cleaning and (2) not destroy your washer and dryer by having large pieces of metal banging around inside the machines. When I say tap "glove" please note that a mitten or glove can be used. If using Velcro, you will need the self-adhesive type for the back of the metal taps

## 1. Tap

and the sew-on kind for the two areas of the palm of the hand where the taps will be affixed to the gloves. Should your target program not require sanitizing the gloves between classes, you can simply sew the taps directly onto the gloves through the four pre-drilled holes on the taps. A set of toe taps will need to be attached towards the top of the four fingers on the palm side of the glove, and another set of taps will need to be secured to the "heel" of your hand, also on the palm side of the glove. Any glove or mitten fabric will work if you are simply sewing the taps directly onto the gloves, but if you are wishing to make them, I recommend using a material such as Lycra for its breathability and stretch-ability. If you are interested in sewing the gloves, I have provided detailed sewing instructions in the appendix.

The tap boards can be as simple as a large (12" × 16") wooden kitchen cutting board. If you would like to construct the tap boards yourself, it's slightly more labor intensive. You can cut the perfect size tap boards out of 2' × 4' board panels that you can purchase from any local big box hardware store. Some stores will even cut them for you. If you use a 2' × 4' board, look for a board that is no more than ¼" thick. I travel around to my various classes with 18 tap boards, cut from three 2' × 4' pieces of wood, and they weigh 21 pounds. That weight, along with 18 sets of front and back taps, plus an iPad and portable speaker, makes for a very hefty bag for me to lift in and out of my car or at the airport baggage drop-off. Since I have two cages in my back to stabilize my spine, I needed to lighten the load by removing the boards before lifting the rest of the bag. For that reason, I made a faux leather fabric case with a handle just for the boards to accomplish this. I am adding this information in case lifting heavy objects is or becomes an issue for anyone else. You will find the directions for how I made the board bag also in the appendix, where the mitten instructions are. The board bag has worked out extremely well and is saving my back from undue strain. Now, back to making the tap boards…

One panel will yield six tap boards by first cutting the board in half, and then cutting each 1' × 4' board into three 1' pieces. Once you have your boards cut, all that is left to do is lightly sandpaper smooth any edges that are rough, and if you desire a different final look, simply apply a stain in the finish of your choice. *Please note*: When applying stain be sure to follow all manufacturer's instructions on the product and use in a well-ventilated area. If you find the board slips when used on top of a table, adhesive backed non-slip strips can be applied to the bottom side of the board. You can also apply the non-slip strips to the kitchen cutting boards as well if that is your board of choice.

Let us now discuss the elements of a mobility-impaired class versus a traditional nondisabled stand-up class. The content and progressions to follow later in this book are the keys to the success of a student's learning process and to ensure a smooth class structure and through line. Just as in any stand-up class, a warm up is necessary, but the variation in a mobility-impaired class is that you will be warming up different parts of the body depending on which type of tap modality you are teaching. Warming up before any kind of workout is critical for preventing injury and prepping your body for movement. According to the American Heart Association, "A good warm up before a workout dilates your blood vessels, ensuring that your muscles are well supplied with oxygen. It also raises your muscles' temperature for optimal flexibility and efficiency."* If you are teaching regular stand-up or sit-down chair tap classes, the lower extremities (feet, ankles, and legs) will need the focus of the warm up. Hand tap classes will require all the upper extremities to be fully warm. This latter warm up is vital when teaching seniors and those with arthritis. For hand tap it is important that the range of motion of the fingers, wrists, elbows, and shoulder joints are thoroughly warm. In the first five minutes of class start with a small range of motion, working through flexion, extension, and rotation of all the above-mentioned joints, and then gently and gradually increase that range of motion as tolerated without pain. This will prime and lubricate the joints safely and effectively. If any of the warm up exercises cause your students pain, either decrease the range of motion or swap out the exercise with another until the student can perform the warm up pain-free.

Whether teaching stand-up disabled or nondisabled tap, sit-down hand tap, or chair tap, once the warm up is complete the main class begins. Here is where repetition is the secret to success, counting cannot be stressed enough, and, as the saying goes, "patience is a virtue." Seniors, especially those dealing with Alzheimer's, dementia, or stroke, will need a slower progression. Since remembering is no longer their strong suit, giving them a narrow range of tap steps in any one class is the instructor's best plan of attack. Repetition is vitally important for

---

* American Heart Association Editorial Staff, "Fitness—Warm Up, Cool Down," September 1, 2014, www.heart.org/en/healthy-living/fitness-basics/warm-up-cool-down.

# 1. Tap

these groups. I experienced the importance of this firsthand in the third week of class at an assisted living facility. One of my students came into the room just as class was about to begin, not remembering that she had been coming to class the previous two weeks. She looked around the room and asked, "What are we doing here today?" I surveyed the faces of the other students who knew her well, and they all compassionately smiled a knowing smile at me that said yes, in her mind she had no recollection that she had taken the class twice before.

The wide variety of tap steps, combinations, and time steps in this book have been selected for their capacity to cover the broadest scope of tap instruction and provide a succession of level progressions. The entire tap spectrum is vast, so having the opportunity to gain more knowledge from multiple resources is invaluable. Every dancer is a byproduct of the instructors under whom they have studied. With each additional teacher comes an additional layer of expertise that when combined creates a dancer that is singularly unique. Tap is all about mixing up the basic steps in creative, crazy ways. By varying the rhythms, adding pauses, breaks, and even pulling steps apart to reinvent them, tap dancers of all genres have endless possibilities at their fingertips or toe tips.

The body of the class should begin with simple short steps or combinations that can be built upon week after week. Laying a solid foundation with the basic steps in tap is crucial. Without the basics the student cannot build combinations and will find it extremely difficult when it comes to mastering an entire routine. It would be like trying to take an algebra class before understanding what addition, subtraction, multiplication, and division are. Whenever I have brand new nondisabled students, I let them know that right now they have an empty toolbox. But by the end of class, they will have added, at the very least, Forward Brushes, Backward Brushes, Crossing Brushes, Ball Heels, Toebacks, Shuffles, Slaps, Heel Digs, Ball Changes, and Basic Cramp Rolls. And with just these ten basic steps in their toolbox they will be able to start creating some cool combinations. However, teaching seniors dealing with Alzheimer's, dementia, or stroke, the pace will be much slower, and the content amount will be far less to be sure they have more time to assimilate the information. Breaking down seemingly difficult combinations, like a Stomp Time Step, into their most basic components (A: Stomp - Hop, B: Step - Flap - Step) can take away the fear and intimidation students often internalize when tackling such a combination. Once students realize that they already know everything they need to execute the combination, they can then focus on the correct step order, rhythm, tap separation, and finally work up the speed of the combination and begin adding shading and dynamics. Making sure early on that your students know that there is nothing they cannot do with enough practice is vital to instill confidence in them, and trust in you as their teacher. The following Michael Jordan quotes have come in handy in my classes from time to time: "Anything you do 1,000 times you will get good at" and "If you put in the work the results will come." He was not wrong. After having made 120 individual tap mittens, something that I had never attempted before in my life, I can definitively attest to those two statements being accurate. Students need to feel secure that you are progressing them at the perfect pace, not too easy to impede their progress, but not so difficult as to frustrate and deflate them emotionally. The latter point is especially important when working with seniors that have cognitive issues. It is a fine line to tread at times, but with experience, an inclusive teacher will understand the cues their students are giving them and adjust their content accordingly.

I now want to briefly touch on tap vocabulary and the written steps that are in this book. More so than any other form of dance, the names of steps and combinations tend to vary the greatest in tap. One of the best examples of this is the Paradiddle. The term paradiddle in the dictionary means "one of the basic patterns (rudiments) of drumming, consisting of four even strokes."[*] While many instructors call this step a Paradiddle, many more refer to this short combination as a Paddle and Roll. Neither name is incorrect but tap dancers and instructors should know both names for speed and ease of digesting choreography. When teaching a student that has learned different terminology from their previous instructor, you will have the opportunity as their new teacher to expand their tap vocabulary and knowledge. Please note not all combinations in tap have names associated with them, and when the step does have an official name I have provided it for you in **<u>underlined bold</u>** type.

Every choreographer has their own unique way of writing down choreography. This too can be as varied as the choreographers themselves. My style of writing has been created for maximum effortlessness while allowing for quick learning and retaining of steps. Following the outline below, in the order given, is the simplest and easiest way to

---

[*] Google.com, Google's English Dictionary (Oxford Languages).

## 1. Tap

understand my system of writing out choreography. If a count is underlined, such as the number 1 below, it means that the count is accented when executing.

1. Look at the counts first, counting them aloud to get the feel of the rhythm.
   Ex. 1&a2, 3-4, 5&a6, 7-8
2. Look at the written steps in the combination. Say them aloud in the rhythm of the counts. For this example, do not forget to accent the first count.
   Ex. Shuffle Ball Change, Step - Dig, Shuffle - Ball Change, Step - Step
3. Execute the combination while saying the steps of the combination in the rhythm of the counts.
4. The **BOLD / CAPS** type: this is your quick reference guide should you need it during a class to refresh your memory of what to do next in your combination.
   Ex. **(SHUFFLE - BALL CHANGE, STEP - DIG, SHUFFLE - BALL CHANGE, STEP - STEP)**

The core of a traditional stand-up tap class continues from here with tap work (a) at the bar, which helps students learn steps without the additional difficulty of needing balance and stability; (b) across the floor work, which focuses on traveling tap steps and turns; and finally (c) center floor work, where time steps, combinations, and routines are put together and practiced. How does the body of a class for disabled and mobility-impaired people differ from this? Here are where the main differences between these two types of classes are seen, the traveling and turning components, with the exception being dancers in wheelchairs that are proficient enough to add navigating their wheelchair while performing the choreography. Although, the best and easiest way to teach a tap turn is to show the combination without turning first. Here is where both types of dancers are on equal footing. Once the combination is understood by all students, the nondisabled tappers can then begin implementing the turn across the floor or in the center, and the hand and / or chair tappers can perform the combination seated in place.

When it comes to choreographing a performance piece for hand and chair tap dancers, let your creativity soar by reimagining your tap choreography. Think of all the innovative possibilities that are open to you now that you have more than one type of tapper in your class.

## Tap Dance for All

Imagine choreographing a multi ambulatory tap piece for a dance competition. How incredible would it be for disabled and mobility-impaired dance students to have the door to the dance competition world opened for them? You as their teacher can create a whole new type of competition piece, one that includes *all* dancers. As someone who has been a dance competition judge from coast to coast for many years, I would have loved to have seen such a spectacular piece of choreography. Why not bring out the talent of wheelchair dancers between the ages of five to 18? Earning a Gold, High Gold, or Platinum score for a nondisabled stand-up dancer is an esteem builder, a teaching moment, and validation for all the many hours of studying, hard work, and practice that they have put in. The same holds true for the disabled and mobility-impaired dancer. They work just as hard as any nondisabled stand-up dancer when it comes to honing their craft. I encourage and challenge you to stretch the boundaries of how tap is viewed and see the limitlessness of the mobility impaired and disabled.

Now that you have a sense of what the class is all about, let us talk about the wide variety of places an inclusive tap teacher can teach. Besides the typical dance studios, this program is a perfect fit for assisted living centers, adult day care centers, children's centers, physical therapy facilities, rehabilitation facilities, YMCAs, and park districts and recreation centers as well as private in-home classes. Start by looking at what is within a ten- to 15-mile radius of where you live. Make a list of possible locations and then make calls to their activity directors to set up meetings to propose implementing the program at their facility. Sell yourself as an inclusive dance instructor that believes dance should be for everyone, not just for those lucky enough to have full use of their limbs. Use the research that you are about to learn here to validate the importance of dance for someone with Parkinson's, Alzheimer's, cerebral palsy and arthritis and even for someone who has suffered a stroke.

As I have been introducing *Tap for All* classes in the senior community throughout Los Angeles, inevitably there is at least one student that comes up to me every class exuding excitement and joy, telling me how they took tap when they were little and never thought at this stage of their life they would ever be able to experience tap again. When this exact scenario happened straight out of the gate, in the very first class I taught, I knew this program was a winner, not only for me personally, but for all disabled and mobility-impaired people everywhere.

## 1. Tap

Left to right: Phyllis Boos, Sachi Kubota, and Pamela Rinaldi from Atria Simi Hills Retirement having fun and learning the basics in a *Tap for All* hand tap class (photograph by the author).

In today's competitive world, anything that can set you apart, help you stand out from the pack, and shines a spotlight on your knowledge and expertise is not only a good thing, but a necessity. This course is about to take you on a journey, not only into the unparalleled world of tap dancing, but also into a better understanding of the unique, and often misunderstood, world of disabled and mobility challenged people.

QUOTABLE QUOTE

> "Never doubt that a small group of thoughtful, committed citizens can change the world; indeed, it's the only thing that ever has."
> —Margaret Mead

## CHAPTER 1 REVIEW QUESTIONS

1. What are the advantages to offering inclusivity and diversity to disabled and mobility-impaired people?

## Tap Dance for All

2. What are all the possible class options / combinations available to an instructor?
3. What does the name *Tap for All* represent?
4. What factors need to be considered when building a disabled / mobility-impaired class?
5. What items / equipment are needed for teaching this program?
6. What similarities / differences are there in a *Tap for All* tap class versus a traditional nondisabled stand-up tap class?
7. What should the structure of a *Tap for All* class consist of?
8. What types of locations could this program benefit and be offered at?

## ⇒ 2 ⇐

# Dance
*Mind, Body, and Soul Benefits*

#### OBJECTIVES

- Understanding the benefits associated with exercise and dance.
- Comprehension of how dance affects neurological issues.
- Knowledge of what diseases, illnesses, and conditions can benefit from this program.
- Understanding the decline in motor function with the aging process.
- Awareness of the improvements possible with the initiation of a dance program.

Dancers are athletes, with bodies that move through space with grace, control, strength, and flexibility. They can spin, leap, balance, and often accomplish all three of those things at the same time. Tap dancers have the unique added skill set of playing an instrument while still being able to accomplish all the above. So if dance is so beneficial to a person's cardiovascular and musculoskeletal systems, could it also be advantageous for one's brain? Could dance help stave off degenerative neurological disorders and diseases? As you are about to discover, the answer is a resounding *yes*!

Regular types of exercise like biking, hiking, strength work, and so on are all excellent for your heart, muscles, and bones, and they play a role in healthy brain function by aiding the creation and maintenance of neurons and increasing cerebral blood flow. To create new neural pathways in the brain, though, the above exercises completely miss the mark. The repetitive motion of the above exercises will not

## Tap Dance for All

lay a foundation for those much-needed new neural channels. Dance, however, requires mental concentration to execute new movement patterns, which in turn requires greater mental focus and can create new neural pathways in the brain. To be more resistant to a cognitive decline later in life, having a more complex and varied neurological network builds a sturdy foundation that can help stave off such a decline.

The link between dance and cognition has been scientifically studied since the early 2000s. In 2003, the *New England Journal of Medicine* published an article on a study done by researchers at Syracuse University and Albert Einstein College that sought to find out if physical exercise and regular participation in cognitive activities could influence mental aptitude. The study measured the rates of dementia, including Alzheimer's, in 469 individuals 75 years old and older over a 21-year span. The researchers looked at how regular participation in six different cognitive activities such as reading, crossword puzzles, and playing an instrument as well as 11 different physical activities like bicycling, golf, walking, and dance affected those rates. The results showed that only one form of physical activity had a measurable impact on dementia—dance. Only four of the 17 leisure activities—reading, playing board games, playing a musical instrument, and, again, dancing—were found to have a quantitative impact on preventing dementia.\*

Another study done by the *New England Journal of Medicine* compared 500 senior citizens over a five-year span, looking at physical and cognitive activities as well as their likelihood of developing dementia. The seniors who used dancing frequently as their physical activity had a 76 percent reduction in risk of developing dementia. That is not an insignificant number! Each time a person dances they are activating and incorporating the areas of the brain involved with movement, music, and rhythm. Coordination and memory brain functions improve when a person is required to think about a physical response to music with dance. Research has proven that the brain stimulation from dancing engages the same areas of the brain that are also required for basic sensory motor activities, like vision, hearing,

---

\* Joe Verghase, Richard B. Lipton, Mindy J. Katz, Charles B. Hall, Carol A. Derby, Gail Kuslansky, Anne F. Ambrose, Martin Sliwinski, and Herman Buschke. "Leisure Activities and the Risk of Dementia in the Elderly," *The New England Journal of Medicine*, 2003, www.nejm.org/doi/full/10.1056/nejmoa022252.

## 2. Dance

and touch. The parietal lobe in the brain controls movement and recognition. The frontal lobe of the brain controls reasoning and decision making. Both areas of the brain are exercised each time a dancer goes through a choreographed dance routine or puts together a sequence of dance moves. When a dancer engages these parts of the brain, they are promoting neuroplasticity, the brain's ability to reorganize itself by forming new neural connections. Through dance, the brain is exercised just like every other muscle in the body, becoming stronger and healthier.*

Is it possible to not only slow the progression of degenerative memory loss but prevent it before it begins? Aga Burzynska, assistant professor of human development at Colorado State University, set out to find the answer. Her findings were published in 2017 in *Frontiers in Aging Neuroscience*. The researchers looked at adults ranging in age from 60 into their 80s. The participants had baseline brain scans performed and were then assigned to one of the three activity groups: brisk walking, stretching and balance training, or dance classes. Those in the dance classes learned country dance choreography three times a week. The goal was to find out which activity protected the brain the most from aging. Would increasing aerobic exercise, increasing aerobic activities, or introducing activities such as dance generate the greatest results? When the study was complete, brain scans were performed again on all participants. When the before scans were compared to the after scans, the dancers fared better and had less deterioration in their brains than the other two groups. The memory involvement required from the dance group involved a great deal of learning, unlike straight aerobic exercise and stretching workouts.†

Dance also has a positive effect on a person's mood. Not unlike a "runner's high," rhythmic movement has been shown to trigger the release of endorphins, a mood booster. In a study done by the American Medical Association, adolescent females who participated in a regular recreational dance class reported improved feelings regarding their overall health, had more confidence, and had more positive thoughts

---

\* Hannah Eckstein, "Just Dance: The Physical and Mental Benefits of Dancing," HC at Notre Dame, April 11, 2014, www.hercampus.com/school/notre-dame/just-dance-physical-and-mental-benefits-dancing/.
† Robert Jimison, "5 Reasons Why Dancing Is Good for Your Health," CNN Health, October 19, 2017, www.cnn.com/2017/06/08/health/health-benefits-of-dancing/index.html.

after dancing. Focusing on enjoying movement rather than perfection and performance provided them that mental shift.*

We all know movement is good for everyone. Dance is the all-in-one activity that integrates the mind, body, and soul relationship that a healthy lifestyle requires. Everyone can do something, even if that something is tapping a foot or tapping a hand. Dancing, whether from a standing or seated position, puts the participant in touch with their body and can be the first step to physical fitness for those that are inactive. Dance therapy movement was developed decades ago, so using dance as a curative exercise is not a new concept. In the 1940s Marian Chace introduced dance to psychiatric patients at St. Elizabeth's Hospital in Washington, D.C. Offering a way for World War II vets to communicate their feelings, Chace taught a class called "Dance for Communication." This class was especially beneficial for psychologically traumatized patients. In 1966 Chace helped found the American Dance Therapy Association. Its dance / movement therapy classes focus on dancing's psychological benefits and its ability to encourage emotional connections. With the many disorders being dealt with today, from autism, to depression, to eating disorders, dance provides hope to not only those that are suffering but also to their families and loved ones.†

Our hands are important as a means of nonverbal communication, a creative set of tools, and an extension of intellect. Of all the various parts of the upper extremity, the hand is the most active and important part. As we age, our hands undergo many physiological and anatomical changes. A decline as much as 20 to 25 percent in hand-grip strength can occur after the age of 60. Bone density of the hand decreases 0.72 percent per year after the age of 50. Seniors over the age of 70 can experience a 12 percent decline in wrist flexion, a 41 percent decline in wrist extension, and a 22 percent decline in ulnar deviation. These declines can double in the following decade. By the time a senior is in their 90s, range of motion of their wrist is expected to be only 60 percent of that of a 30-year-old. These reductions can put seniors at a greater risk for

---

\* Anna Duberg, Lars Hagberg, Helena Sunvison, and Margareta Möller. "Influencing Self-Rated Health Among Adolescent Girls with Dance Intervention," JAMA Network (January 2013), www.jamanetwork.com/journals/jamapediatrics/fullarticle/1390784.

† Christina Lanzito, "The Healing Powers of Dance," *AARP The Magazine*, March 2011, www.aarp.org/health/fitness/info-03-2011/dance-for-health.html.

## 2. Dance

developing cumulative trauma disorders.* Fine motor skills can also become impaired due to injury, illness, stroke, congenital deformities, cerebral palsy, or other developmental disabilities. Problems with the brain, spinal cord, peripheral nerves, muscles, or joints can also influence fine motor skills and can decrease control. Conditions such as arthritis, lupus, Parkinson's, and multiple sclerosis can all contribute to a much faster degeneration of fine motor skills simply because of the nature of the diseases. For seniors, when neurons can no longer communicate successfully to send messages to other parts of the brain and the body, they can begin to lose physical capabilities like fine motor skills. The very ability to dress and feed oneself, as well as to perform basic everyday functions such as turning a door knob, holding a pen to write, buttoning a shirt, and even picking something up off a counter, relies on the coordination and movement of small tendons and muscles in the hand.† Having those

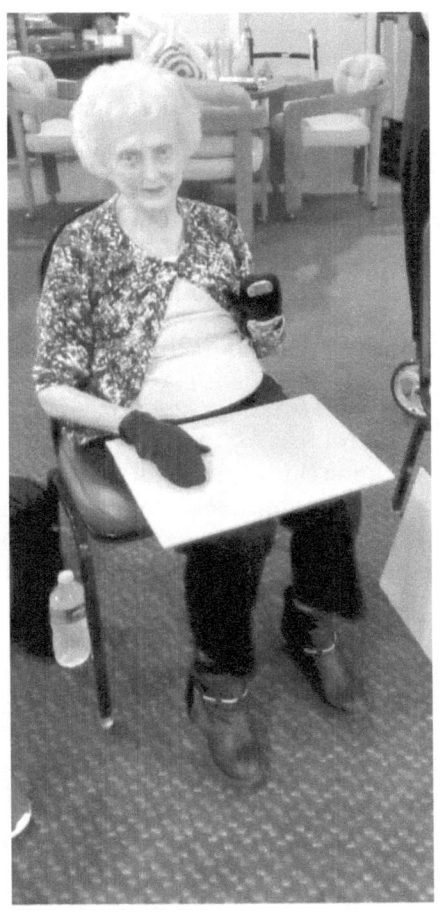

Bette Compton from Atria Simi Hills Retirement is all smiles learning how to tap in a *Tap for All* hand tap class (photograph by the author).

---

\* Eli Carmeli, Hagar Patish, and Raymond Coleman. "The Aging Hand," *The Journals of Gerontology*, Volume 58, Issue 2 (February 1, 2003), pp. M146–M152, www.academic.oup.com/biomedgerontology/article/58/2/M146/593573?login=true.
† Yoo Young Hoogandam, Fedde vander Lijn, Meike W. Vernooij, Albert Hofman, Wiro J. Niessen, Aad van der Lugt, M. Arfan Ikram, and Jos N. van der Geest. "Older Age Relates to Worsening of Fine Motor Skills: A Population-Based Study of Middle-Aged and Elderly Persons," *Frontiers in Aging Neuroscience*, September 25, 2014, www.ncbi.nih.gov/pmc/articles/PMC4174769/.

fine motor skills can mean the difference between living independently and requiring extra care as you age. By using gentle warm ups and exercises, seniors can achieve a greater range of movement and flexibility, plus possibly retard functional aging changes. Using hands to tap is a fun way to work on those fine motor skills without it feeling like actual work. Even small gains can mean the world to someone who has lost the ability to accomplish tasks that used to be elementary.

The following is a list of six improvements and benefits that can happen when beginning a tap program, especially for seniors.

1. **Spatial-Relations Training:** Most people are better at performing tasks on their dominant side. Tap requires the student to execute the steps on both the right and left sides. This is great training for the brain. Hearing and seeing the combinations is one thing, but physically accomplishing the steps on a student's non-dominant side is usually not so easy. Even the nondisabled students I taught in Denver commented about tapping with their hands versus tapping with their feet and the difficulty they found with their non-dominant sides in both modalities. More work will be needed to bring the weaker side up to the level of the stronger side and in turn makes for a great workout for the brain. This discipline aligns with how I teach my young tappers. When I ask them what the three Ps of tap are, they know to respond with "Practice, Practice, Practice!" This principle holds true whether for the seniors or the littles.

2. **Rhythm:** In tap, the fun is in the ability to change up the rhythms, which in turn provides a cognitive challenge for all types of students. Beginning classes should keep to basic, simple tempos and rhythms. But to keep the student's mind and body progressing, introducing slightly more complex rhythm patterns and tempos are essential for continued growth. Adding holds (no tap sounds) also encourages the brain to stop and think. Training the brain to think ahead about the next upcoming four counts while executing the current four counts is a skillset that a student's brain will only achieve by implementing the three Ps mentioned in the previous paragraph. Students may find it difficult to do at first, but with positive reinforcement from the teacher, and arduous practice applied by the student, their brain can be trained to learn this extremely helpful and necessary technique.

## 2. Dance

3. **Physicality:** Whether standing or sitting, tap is physically demanding. The theory for Specificity of Training states that the adaptation of the body or change in physical fitness is specific to the type of training undertaken. The more you train your muscles in a specific pattern, motion, or movement, the more they will adapt and strengthen. This principle holds true in tap whether you are standing (training muscles to learn how to make the sounds, balance, and body weight shifts) or sitting (training the muscles in the hands, wrists, forearms, and upper arms).
4. **Memory:** Like making a sentence out of words, or a story out of paragraphs, tap requires remembering steps and putting them into a sequence. Repeating the sequence requires focus, attention, and much practice repeated over time.
5. **Complexity:** Rhythms are created to add interest and intricacy to a sequence. Throwing a break into a combination is just one way to change up the rhythm, creating a surprise for the viewer / listener.
6. **Emotional Release:** Tap is most often thought of as the "happy" dance form. Emotion in tap is not solely communicated through the shoe taps. What an artist feels from the music and wishes to express to the audience should initiate from inside the dancer's emotional core. Only then can the physicality of the performer's movement translate into an authentic representation of the emotion behind the story of the choreography. An audience can tell if a dancer is truly connected or not. If a dancer is not dancing from an authentic place, the audience will experience a disconnect and may not even understand why. They may express that the performance did not make them "feel" anything or that they found their minds wandering off, thinking about other things. What is missing is the dancers' connection to their emotions and the story. This holds true for every dance form, including tap. The audience wants to be taken on the journey with the performer. In that same vein, if a dancer continually looks down while performing, they are cutting the audience off, denying them access to the dancer's passion, expression, and interpretation of the piece. That kind of dancer selfishly dances solely for themself, which is the opposite of what should be transpiring on stage. So, while it is important to execute the tap sequences correctly, it is just as important to express the

choreography's emotions and story. Perfect technical taps without an authentic emotional connection are only half of a dancer's artistic equation.*

QUOTABLE QUOTE

*"To everything there is a season and a time to every purpose under the heaven ... a time to weep, and a time to laugh: a time to move, and a time to dance..."—Ecclesiastes*

## CHAPTER 2 REVIEW QUESTIONS

1. How does exercise benefit the body?
2. How does dance do a better job at staving off degenerative neurological issues than regular repetitive types of exercise?
3. What types of illnesses, conditions, and diseases can this program benefit?
4. How long has the positive effects of dance been scientifically studied?
5. What other positive results can dance have beyond the cognitive?
6. How quick is the decline in hand-grip strength in someone 60 years old?
7. What percentage in range of motion does a 90-year-old have compared to a 30-year-old?
8. Why are fine motor skills so important to maintain as one ages?
9. What kinds of improvements are possible when someone starts a dance program?

---

* Francine Toder. "6 Reasons Why The Brain Loves Dancers Over 60," HuffPost, August 22, 2013, www.huffpost.com/entry/tap-dancingt_b_3749600.

# 3

# Diseases, Conditions, and Age Groups

## Objectives

- Understanding the basics of Parkinson's, Alzheimer's, cerebral palsy, arthritis, and stroke.
- Knowledge of what areas of the body can be affected by the above diseases / conditions.
- Comprehension of how tap can play a positive part in a rehabilitation program.
- Considerations of teaching the visually impaired and hearing impaired.

There are many types of cognitive diseases and conditions that can affect the human body. We will cover Parkinson's and Alzheimer's first since these two diseases are likely to be the most common ones an instructor will encounter when working with seniors. Later in this chapter we will cover cerebral palsy, arthritis, and stroke. With Parkinson's, Alzheimer's, and all other dementias, learning, memory, and perception are factors someone with these diseases may be dealing with in varying degrees of severity. Extra patience and compassion will be necessary when instructing these types of students. Thanks to tap's ability to create new neural pathways, even the smallest improvement in memory can become a monumental accomplishment—one that can potentially translate in the student remembering things more regularly in their everyday life. Since coordination, balance, and walking can be exceedingly difficult or even impossible for those with the above diseases, hand tap and / or chair tap can provide them the opportunity to improve or even slow down the worsening of their condition. By providing them a way to work on building their cognitive functionality with an activity that does not require them to stand, you are offering them access to an enjoyable way to stay active, both physically and mentally.

## *Parkinson's*

Parkinson's disease is a brain disorder that usually begins gradually, progressively worsens over time, and is highly variable from person to person. Although both men and women can develop Parkinson's, men are 50 percent more likely to be afflicted by the disease. Even though the average age of a person initially affected is around 60, early onset of the disease can affect people by the age of 50. Starting a program that stimulates new neural pathways in that early stage is one important way to slow down the progression. Movement problems occur in Parkinson's patients when the important brain chemical called dopamine is not being produced because nerve cells (neurons) around the area of the brain that controls movement become weakened and / or die. Why this occurs in the brain is still a mystery to scientists.

There are five stages in the progression of Parkinson's. They are being listed here so that you can better understand where a student falls in the advancement of the disease so you can instruct them appropriately. The initial stage of Parkinson's is relatively mild, with changes in facial expression, posture, and walking occurring, as well as tremors and movement symptoms beginning on one side of the body. In the second stage all the symptoms worsen, with rigidity beginning and both sides of the body becoming affected. Stage three is where the loss of balance begins, movements slow, and falls are more common. In the fourth stage the symptoms are severe and limiting. It is at this point the person can no longer live alone due to the inability to cope with daily activities unassisted. Stage five is the most advanced and debilitating. The person may require a wheelchair or may be bedridden due to stiffness in their legs, making it impossible to stand or walk. Full-time care is now required at this point. In each stage the non-motor symptoms of the disease increases along with the motor symptoms.

The following are the four main manifestations that will be present with someone with Parkinson's disease...

- impaired balance and coordination
- trembling (tremor) in hands, arms, head, jaw, or legs

## 3. Diseases, Conditions, and Age Groups

- slowness of movement
- stiffness in the trunk or limbs

Since, in most cases, there are no definitive diagnostic tests to identify the disease, it is difficult to accurately pinpoint, and many times the early signs can be subtle and often dismissed as simply the normal effects of aging. The symptoms may present on only one side of the body initially, but over time as the disease progresses both sides can be affected, although one side may be affected more than the other. Currently there is no cure for Parkinson's. Drug therapies that help increase the level of dopamine in the brain, as well as positively affect other brain chemicals and assist in helping with the non-motor symptoms of tremors, rigidity, and speech in conjunction with physical and occupational therapies, have the possibility of producing a positive effect in slowing the decline of mental function while strengthening muscles, coordination, and balance.* This is where a program such as *Tap for All* comes in. By helping to slow down the progression of the disease through the utilization of this program, you will be giving them the gift of more days of feeling normal, a sense of accomplishment, and an inclusive fun class that they do not have to feel like an outsider taking. Bringing joy, fun, and a welcome distraction with them focusing on what they can do for one hour, as opposed to what they can no longer do for is pure gold. Put yourself in the shoes of someone with Parkinson's for a moment. Imagine what it must be like to lose the ability to perform many of the daily functions that you used to take for granted. If you can do that, you can clearly see and understand how valuable and important a program like *Tap for All* could be to someone in the preliminary stages of Parkinson's.

Teaching someone with Parkinson's disease can have its challenges on a physical level, depending what stage of the disease they are in. Hand tap or chair tap may be an option, again depending on their disease progression, and patience will be the key to working with them. The focus should not be on how perfectly they execute the steps, but on helping to create those new neural pathways by giving them simple yet stimulating and appropriately challenging combinations. Using fun, era-appropriate music they can connect with will help them dive into the class with fearlessness. Including the students in the selection

---

*Parkinson's Foundation. "What is Parkinson's," Parkinson's Foundation, 2021, www.parkinson.org/understanding-parkinsons/what-is-parkinsons.

of the musical artists for the next upcoming class can give them something fun to look forward to and help make sure they come back the following class. Anything you can do to help them feel like their instructor cares and is invested in creating a class that is geared toward inclusiveness, compassion, and an understanding of what they live with daily, is sure to be a win-win for all.

## *Alzheimer's*

As a type of dementia, Alzheimer's accounts for 60 to 80 percent of dementia cases. Alzheimer's can affect memory, thinking, and behavior. Because the disease typically begins by affecting the part of the brain that learns and retains new things, a person in the early stage of Alzheimer's will have difficulty retaining newly learned information. Taking tap, learning short combinations, and continually working on retention of those combinations is a fantastic way to help strengthen those neural connections and help to slow the progression of the disease. According to the Alzheimer's Association, "A number of studies indicate that maintaining strong social connections and keeping mentally active as we age might lower the risk of cognitive decline and Alzheimer's."* Dancing, unlike regular activities such as walking, biking, and other repetitive forms of exercise, has the unique characteristic of integrating several brain functions all at the same time: musical, emotional, rational, and kinesthetic. Any activity that requires a person to think quickly, such as learning and remembering dance combinations, will be beneficial in preserving and improving a person's mental acuity.

Even though aging is a main risk factor, Alzheimer's is not a normal part of aging. While there is no known cure currently, slowing the progression is the main objective once the disease has begun. As a person's brain cells begin to fail, so does their memory. Brain cells need to be able to communicate with other cells to function properly and keep the various parts of the brain running smoothly. When one area in the brain begins to have a problem, it can cause a breakdown in another area. As the damage spreads, the cells lose their ability to function correctly, and can cause irreversible damage to the brain due to the cell dying. By offering a class such as *Tap for All* to those heading down

---

*Alzheimer's Association. "Can Alzheimer's Disease Be Prevented?" Alzheimer's Association, 2021, www.alz.org/alzheimers-dementia/research_progress/prevention.

this life-robbing path, you are helping to delay and even slow down that journey for as long as possible. The key to decelerating the speed of the progression is to not only perform a brain challenging activity, but do it often. In the *New England Journal of Medicine* study mentioned in the last chapter, seniors that did crossword puzzles four days a week had a measurably lower risk of dementia compared to those who only did crossword puzzles one day a week. Offering both hand and chair tap classes a couple times a week accomplishes that four-day-a-week benchmark. Not only will their brains get the neurological stimulation needed to assist in delaying the disease, they will benefit in a big way emotionally, physically, and socially. Until a cure is found for this insidious disease, giving those afflicted the opportunity to feel included and a part of something special, plus letting them know that life can still be fun, creative, and worth participating in, is an invaluable gift you will not only be giving them, but yourself as well.

Teaching those with any type of dementia will require immense patience, just like Parkinson's. Repetition will be the key to helping them with their memory retention. Using one step at a time and slowly building a combination is the best way to progress with this type of student. Using music to help them connect the step to the lyrics in the song can also assist them in memory retention.

## Cerebral Palsy

What is cerebral palsy, or CP? Is it a disease? No, it is a disorder, and that is one of the biggest misconceptions about cerebral palsy. Unlike the first two diseases, the cause for CP is brain damage that leads to motor and movement disabilities. It is the most common disability in children. According to Cerebral Palsy Guidance, "As an umbrella term, cerebral palsy refers to a group of symptoms and disabilities. They are all related, but each will have a unique and individual experience of cerebral palsy." Also interestingly, "One in approximately 345 kids has CP."[*]

There are four types of cerebral palsy:

1. **Spastic Cerebral Palsy**—Muscles can be stiff and spastic, and movement can be abnormal, inhibited, and difficult to control.

---

[*] Gina Jansheki. "Cerebral Palsy," Cerebral Palsy Guidance, June 11, 2020, www.cerebralpalsyguidance.com/cerebral-palsy/.

Movement development milestones can be delayed as well. This type of CP encompasses 75 percent of the cerebral palsy cases.
**Spastic Quadriplegia**—This is the most severe type of the spastic cerebral palsy in that it means "loss of use of the whole body." It involves muscle tremors, tightness, spasticity, and rapid contract and release. Language disorders, seizures, and cognitive disabilities are also seen in these types of cases.
**Spastic Diplegia**—Many of these children can walk with the aid of walkers or crutches to assist them with their mobility impairments.
**Spastic Hemiplegia**—Most of these children can walk, as this type of CP only affects one side of the body, usually the arm more so than the leg.
2. **Dyskinetic Cerebral Palsy**—This is the second most usual form of CP. These children's movements can be dystonia (repetitive and twisting), athetosis (writhing), choreo (unpredictable), and painful. Their posture is usually poor, and they have difficulty talking and swallowing.
3. **Ataxic Cerebral Palsy**—This is the least common type of CP, characterized with limited coordination, tremors, poor balance, difficulty in motor control, and jittery movements.
4. **Mixed Cerebral Palsy**—This one is characterized by combining two or three of the above.

There is no cure, but various therapies, including occupational and physical therapy in addition to music, can prove to be not only beneficial but can "…reduce impairment and lessen the risk of developing other associated conditions."*

What are the most common types of motor and movement limitations an instructor might encounter with students that have CP? Someone with cerebral palsy may be as mobile as being able to walk with the assistance of crutches (more than half of the children diagnosed with CP can walk independently) or may be as restricted as needing the aid of a wheelchair. The instructor may also see speech and learning difficulties, joint issues, spinal deformities, hearing or vision loss, and cognitive impairment. Some affected with cerebral palsy may also have sensitivities to certain sounds and / or volume levels. Should you find

---

* Gina Jansheki. "Cerebral Palsy," Cerebral Palsy Guidance, June 11, 2020, www.cerebralpalsyguidance.com/cerebral-palsy/.

### 3. Diseases, Conditions, and Age Groups

yourself with a class that is adversely affected by the sounds of the taps, one option is to remove the taps and simply perform the class without them. It is important to make sure that your students feel understood, and not made to feel weird or less than because of their condition. When you accomplish this, you accomplish inclusion, turning their <u>dis</u>ability into their <u>a</u>bility.

So, what does this mean when it comes to teaching a class of CP students? This is where the instructor needs to understand the severity of their students beforehand. Like any regular nondisabled stand-up dance class, it is important to have students that are not widely far apart in their ability to comprehend and learn. Of course, not all students learn at the same pace, but having some that learn and catch on quickly in the same class as others that need much more time and patience to grasp the information will only prove to be frustrating for all, including you as a teacher. If you have a group that is affected mildly to moderately by the disorder you will have an evenly balanced class. On the other hand, if you find yourself with a mixture of mild and severe students, splitting them into two separate classes will support each group for the best possible outcome: a fun, appropriately challenging class situation. If you have a class where some of your students can walk via crutches and others are wheelchair users, consider using the combination of chair tap and hand tap. If the chair tappers do not have tap shoes, they can use any hard-soled pair of shoes as an alternative.

What if you have a combination of all three conditions—Parkinson's, Alzheimer's, and cerebral palsy—in one class? My suggestion would be to begin with hand tap to feel out where the students are at, both mentally and physically. If from there you find that some would benefit from chair tap you can look at adding and introducing that tap form in subsequent classes. After teaching even just a few classes you will find yourself being able to quickly discern the capabilities of your students, and which tap modality or modalities will best serve them.

## Arthritis

Osteoarthritis and rheumatoid arthritis are the two most common forms of arthritis, and the most prevalent types encountered when teaching this program. The disease is characterized by swelling and tenderness in one or more joints in the body. The symptoms of pain and stiffness typically worsen with age. The main difference between these two types of arthritis is that with osteoarthritis, a breakdown of the joint cartilage (the tissue that covers the ends of the bones) occurs, and with rheumatoid arthritis the breakdown begins with the lining of the joints, plus the immune system attacks the affected joints.

Since symptoms such as pain, swelling, stiffness, and a decreased range of motion are typical in both kinds of the above-mentioned arthritis, when teaching these types of students it is important for the instructor to understand that their symptoms can vary daily. They may come in for your class with a decent range of motion and some mild pain one day, and then have extraordinarily little pain-free range of motion and acutely increased pain the next. Communication at the beginning of each class and staying aware during the class are the keys to ensuring a safe and effective session each time. Modifications may need to be made in the warm up if the students are experiencing flare ups and their joints are particularly angry that day. I have rheumatoid arthritis myself, and on my "bad" days I know to show my body the kindness it needs and be gentle with my irritated, inflamed joints. The important message to convey to all your students, no matter what disease or disorder they are dealing with, is to work with how they are feeling that day. Help them to understand that good days and bad days are to be expected, and that you have more than enough tools in your toolbox to make any adjustments needed from one class to another.

If any students communicate that their hands are particularly painful at the onset of class, offering the option of a modified upper body warm up and chair tap may be what is called for that day. Stick to smaller range of motions. Exercise can reduce joint pain, increase strength and flexibility, and reduce fatigue. Lack of exercise for someone with arthritis can make joints more stiff and painful. Any movement is better than no movement, but if your arthritic students notice joint swelling or redness, pain that is stronger than usual, or sharp pain, they should stop, take a break, and switch to chair tap.

In many parts of the United States the Arthritis Foundation offers exercise programs for those with arthritis. If you have a local branch in your area, this would be another suitable place to reach out to and inquire about teaching opportunities.

## 3. Diseases, Conditions, and Age Groups

## *Stroke*

According to the American Stroke Association, "Stroke is the number five cause of death and a leading cause of disability in the United States."*

Most strokes (87 percent) are ischemic strokes. These types of strokes are caused by an artery blockage of oxygen-rich blood flow to the brain. The cause of these blockages is usually due to a blood clot. The second type of stroke is a hemorrhagic stroke. This stroke is due to brain cell damage caused by an artery in the brain leaking or rupturing blood, putting an inordinate amount of pressure on the brain cells, and thus causing damage. The last type of stroke is a transient ischemic attack, or TIA. This stroke is often referred to as a "mini stroke," because the blood flow to the brain is blocked for usually five minutes or less. Having a TIA is often a warning sign of a larger future stroke. Blood clots, like with ischemic strokes, are the main cause of TIAs.

The area of the brain that was deprived of blood will determine what functions of the body will be affected. How much brain tissue is damaged depends on the obstruction and location of the blockage. For example, if a blockage occurs in the back of the brain, it is likely that a visual disability will be experienced. Each side of the brain controls the opposite side of the body. In the case of the stroke occurring at the brain stem, both sides of the body can be affected. Depending on the severity of this stroke location the person may experience a "locked-in" state, where they are unable to speak or accomplish movement from the neck down.†

Stimulating neuroplasticity—the system the brain uses to heal and rewire itself after receiving an injury—is vital in recovering arm, leg, and speech skills. Progress, in most cases, takes time and can feel slow, but the more neuroplasticity is engaged, the more mobility will improve. For new neural connections to strengthen and rebuild, the brain needs constant stimulation. A stroke victim that works their rehabilitation program every day will progress much better and faster than someone who only engages one time per week.

Consistency is a key factor in recovering from a stroke, and taking

---

* American Stroke Association. "About Stroke," American Stroke Association, 2022, www.stroke.org/en/about-stroke.

† American Stroke Association. "Types of Stroke and Treatment," American Stroke Association, 2022, www.stroke.org/en/about-stroke/types-of-stroke.

a *Tap for All* class fits perfectly into a rehabilitation program. Making sure a well-rounded, thorough five-to-ten-minute warm up begins every class, is again vitally important to gently warm up all joints and muscles so that they will be able to perform class with the least amount of discomfort and chance of injury. Your students that have endured a stroke will most likely have greater mobility on one side of their body than the other. The side of the body that was affected to a greater degree needs the most work. Encouragement is key for these students, as they may experience immense frustration that what they once were able to easily accomplish is difficult or next to impossible now. Understanding what has happened to them is important to help them move forward and progress. If one week executing a shuffle was futile, but the next week they are moving their fingers much closer to the actual mechanics of a shuffle, make sure to take note and point out their progress with much praise for their improvement. Who among us does not love having breakthrough moments? The thrill is real, and encouragement to continue in that positive direction by the instructor is essential, plus the emotional lift they will feel thanks to your optimism is immeasurable.

Tap can be an immense help in the rehabilitation process for a stroke victim. Counting out rhythms and repeating names of steps can help those whose speech was affected. Hand tap can assist those whose upper limbs were impaired, and chair tap can benefit those with debilitated lower limbs.

## *Hearing and Visually Impaired Students*

What if you were told that something that looked so incredibly fun to try was off limits to you because you had a physical issue that really had nothing to do with whether you could, or should try it? The main factor depriving the deaf and blind from the opportunity of experiencing tap and all other dance forms is the word "can't." Some instructors are of the belief that if a student cannot see or hear, they cannot and should not dance. Nothing could be further from the truth. This type of belief system harms disabled people. As educators it is up to us to communicate and foster an atmosphere of "Yes, you *can* dance," rather than "No, you can't dance." The bottom line is that the hearing and visually impaired absolutely and resolutely can and should dance, and nothing and no one has the right to tell them otherwise.

### 3. Diseases, Conditions, and Age Groups

For the hearing impaired, with even a limited vocabulary in sign language, coupled with gestures, points, and touch, any instructor can welcome these students into their studio. The hearing-impaired student learns best with a very visual approach, using hand gestures whenever possible and writing on index cards or a whiteboard to assist in learning dance terminology. When giving corrections or instructions it is better to maintain eye contact, rather than moving around the dance room like in a typical nondisabled class. Techniques that dance instructors are already currently using for their hearing students can easily be modified and adjusted for non-hearing students. Although, one thing to avoid when instructing a hearing-impaired student is exaggerating when speaking to them, as it makes it more difficult for the deaf student to speech read. Simply speaking in your normal voice, using your regular speech pattern, is the best way to verbally communicate with a hearing-impaired person. Use of hands and arms are great ways to demonstrate the movements you want them to execute. Therefore, hand tap is a wonderful vehicle for the hearing impaired to learn how to tap. Instructors need to remember that all students perform to the expectation level of the teacher, and that you should never hold a disabled dancer to a lower standard than you would a nondisabled dancer. It is our job as educators to find the best and most appropriate ways in which to bring out the excellence in every one of our students, not just the most technically talented.

Most of us who can hear are under the impression that the deaf and hearing impaired can feel the vibrations of music through the floor to "hear" the rhythm of a song. If the dance floor is constructed of a suspended type of flooring, or if the music has a very heavy bass, the hearing impaired will in fact be able to feel the vibrations. But take music that is typically used in ballet. This genre of dance usually consists of music played at a high frequency, and that high frequency range of hearing is where most deaf students have lost their ability. To assist the hearing impaired in following such music, using a drum or bass beat can give the rhythm to the student where the high frequency music cannot. Beating a drum and visually counting with your fingers can help the deaf student visualize and "hear" the rhythm much easier. The visual focus that deaf dancers innately have gives them a powerful tool that hearing dancers often lack. The focused use of their eyes makes the hearing-impaired dancer an expert communicator with their fellow dancers, and they also have

## Tap Dance for All

the unique ability to share language through dance. When the deaf communicate, they not only communicate with their hands but also with their facial expressions. Those facial expressions convey ideas that they want to express, which gives them a distinct advantage when it comes to telling the story behind any piece of choreography. Dance companies that utilize the hearing impaired, understanding that they are just as capable as their nondisabled performers and treating them as they would any nondisabled dancer, show their audiences that disabled people are indeed not only capable, but can do everything and anything if only given the chance. To ascend to company level in ability, the hearing-impaired dancer needs to be given the opportunity to learn and hone their craft just as any other hearing dancer. The dance instructors that welcome the hearing impaired into their classes by making slight adjustments to how they teach will soon discover what a joy it is to dance with these special individuals. The artistry of the hearing-impaired dancer is just waiting for the right instructor to give them the freedom to learn, grow, and soar to heights previously denied to them.

How do you teach dance to students who cannot see what you as an instructor are executing? How do you communicate your passion for dance when your students cannot see your body and how it is moving through space? Should the visually impaired simply not be allowed to experience the delight dance brings to one's mind, body, and soul, just because one aspect of their physicality is not functioning fully? Of course not, so this then becomes another outside-of-the-box challenge for the dance instructor.

How does communication need to be adjusted to better convey the information accurately? The use of descriptive language is much more helpful than simple, general words. Instead of saying, "Step-Together-Step," try, "Open the door, close the door, then open again." One can also label each pattern of steps as they learn them, such as A, B, C, D and so forth. For a simple time step with a break the teacher could say, "Do move A three times, followed by move B once."

I recently gained my first visually-impaired senior as a hand tap student in my *Tap for All* park district class. Utilizing the above techniques worked brilliantly with this student. She was perfectly able to understand and keep pace with the rest of the class. She was an absolute joy to teach, and I highly recommend welcoming both the visually and hearing impaired into your classes.

## 3. Diseases, Conditions, and Age Groups

Another physical aspect for the dance teacher to consider is the posture of the visually impaired dancer. Standing tall with shoulders back and down, chin up, should be postural goals to strive for, not only for nondisabled dancers but the visually-impaired as well. The visually impaired dancer typically needs an improved awareness of their bodies as slumping shoulders and much tension in their necks and upper backs are common. Including head isolation work in the warm up is immensely helpful for the visually impaired to loosen up and gain mobility in their usually tight neck muscles. Walking taller and moving more comfortably is beneficial for everyone, especially for those who cannot see how they move, but can feel the difference and confidence proper posture can bring.

Another helpful tip is having visually impaired stand-up dancers dance in pairs, especially when traveling across the floor in a stand-up tap class or any other type of dance class. Helping your visually-impaired students become familiar with the layout of the studio they will be dancing in, will help them be able to judge where the bars and other difficulties lie. Knowing where the sound system is, where the edges of the floors are, and where any other obstacles are located within the studio space, plus how to avoid them, can give the student more confidence that they can circumvent impediments. By understanding their dance space, the visually-impaired student can more fully focus on the choreography and their artistry.

Sometimes a visually impaired stand-up dancer can have a slight weakness in one side of their body. Tap may make this condition more obvious because of taps technical use of one foot while requiring stabilization with the other foot. If you as a teacher observe this in your visually-impaired students, understand that the weakness is involuntary, so shining a spotlight on their condition and situation during class is never helpful.

It is common for younger visually-impaired students to have difficulty in tying their tap shoes. The best option in this situation is suggesting elastic ties, or sneaker style jazz shoes. If balance is an issue, avoiding higher heeled tap shoes is preferable. When the visually-impaired dancer's balance becomes too much, switching them to seated hand tap is a fantastic alternative. Instead of risking a fall, or giving up tap altogether, having such a fun, creative option can reenergize their enthusiasm for dance, and show them that nothing is impossible.

## Age Groups

The last consideration we will discuss here are the different age groups. How you teach tap to a five-year-old is vastly different from how you teach tap to a 15- or 50-year-old, whether the student is stand-up or mobility impaired. Developmentally, each requires a different approach and a different understanding. Throw into the equation a condition such as cerebral palsy or a disease such as Alzheimer's, and the need for the instructor to have a strong understanding of how all the pieces of the puzzle need to fit together cohesively to create a class situation that benefits everyone is vital.

There are different schools of thought when it comes to the best way to group classes. Some instructors lean towards organizing classes according to age, while others assign students to a class based on their skill level and proficiency. Is one way better than another? This subject has many differing opinions.

Let us look at both sides of the coin for a moment. For young students, ages four to nine, an instructor is likely to find a considerable disparity with respect to mental development and attention span. A teacher may find that the youngest students in this age group do not yet have the physical capability to accomplish steps and combinations that their older students can. The teacher's dilemma becomes apparent when the four- to six-year-olds cannot keep pace with the seven- to nine-year-olds, who then become frustrated and begin to ask, "When is class over?" On the other hand, if the class is too easy for the older students, they will become bored and start asking that same question. Dance conventions, in general, prescribe to the class structure of age over ability level. Throughout my years teaching master tap classes for dance conventions, I have found that teaching absolute beginners, i.e., never tapped before, in conjunction with advanced students of the same age group, is a challenging balancing act. I believe that no other dance form has quite the difficulty with this issue the way tap does, because without at least the technical basics of tap, you have next to nothing with which to build on. Stand-up adult and teen classes are a bit easier to work around since they are more equally developed mentally than younger children, and when in a studio setting, they can be divided into distinct levels more easily.

On the other side of the coin is a class based by level, rather than age. Here you may very well see nine-year-old children keeping pace

*3. Diseases, Conditions, and Age Groups*

with teenagers or even adults. The instructor may however find the older students are less than thrilled having "babies" in their class. This was the situation in my youth. I was too advanced for the kids' classes, but too young for the older classes. Lou Conte, of Hubbard Street Dance in Chicago, put me in his advanced level tap class, irrespective of my youthful age. Yes, I did experience some animosity from the older students, especially with the looks I received from them when Lou had me demonstrate pullbacks and grab offs solo across the floor. The stares intensified when he referred to my speed and precision as "like a machine gun." Lou knew the advanced class was the right place for me to be challenged and to help me grow into the mature dancer I was to become.

For me, it is more important to have the mental and physical levels of a class be on an even keel than it is to have a class with students that are all the same age. If students are not having fun, not being challenged, and not growing in their tap ability, they will not continue coming to class. Striving to group classes that have both similar ages and similar abilities is the ideal scenario. When it comes to hand and chair tap, it is even more important to teach classes based on level. The priority for teaching a mobility-impaired class should be one of an appropriate mental and physical level for all the students, regardless of age. If you find yourself with a high number of students with memory difficulties, you might consider grouping them into their own class for a more evenly balanced situation. This is where your understanding and expertise of the students' challenges will be of great benefit and an asset at whatever facility you are teaching.

The following **Master Tap Tips** are not only appropriate for children, but also greatly beneficial for those dealing with Parkinson's, Alzheimer's, recovering from a stroke, and cerebral palsy.

- **Rhythm Train** (All Count Out Loud)
  1. Straight 8 Train: (1-8)
  2. The "And" Train: (&1&2&3&4&5&6&7&8)
  3. The "E&A" Train: (1e&a, 2e&a, 3e&a, 4e&a, 5e&a, 6e&a, 7e&a, 8e&a)
  4. The Syncopated Train: (1&2&3&4&5&6&7&8&)
     *Accent the Underlined Number or the And Count*
- **Clap and Count** (both #1 & #2 above)
- **March and Count** (Straight 8 Train: hand and / or chair, and stand-up tap)

# Tap Dance for All

- **Mix It Up Game**
  1. Ask everyone to raise and shake their right hand. Repeat with the left hand.
  2. Mix up which hand you ask to raise and shake.
  3. Mix it up faster and faster until students start laughing because it's too fast.
- **Three R's and Three "Its" - Tap Questions**
  1. QUESTION (TEACHER): Do you know what the three **R**'s stand for in tap?
     ANSWER (STUDENTS): **R**epetition / **R**epetition / **R**epetition
  2. QUESTION (TEACHER): Do you know what the important 3 **Its** are in tap?
     ANSWER (STUDENTS): Count **It** / Say **It** / Do **It**
- **T-A-P Puzzle**
  1. QUESTION (TEACHER): Besides the dance form, what else do the letters **T-A-P** stand for?
     ANSWER (STUDENTS): **T**appers **A**lways **P**ractice
- **Mix and Match Tap Game**
  1. TEACHER: Name any three tap steps?
     STUDENTS: Students choose any three steps (Ex. Flap, Shuffle, Heel Dig), and put them in any random order.
     ACTIONS
     a. Ask a student to list the three steps in any order to create a combination.
     b. Have a student demonstrate the combination.
     c. All students then Count **It**, Say **It**, and Do **It**.
     d. See how many other combinations can be made using the same three steps.
     e. Have other students take turns doing the same thing.
- **Stump the Teacher Game** (Mix and Match Tap Game, with roles reversed)
  1. STUDENTS: Call out any three or four steps to the teacher.
     TEACHER: Do as many combinations as possible using the three or four steps called out.
     STUDENTS & TEACHER: Hum the different rhythms (combinations will have different rhythm patterns).

## 3. Diseases, Conditions, and Age Groups

- **Connect Names of Steps to the Steps** (beneficial for memory and retention)
  *For Full Explanation of Steps Below, Please See Chapters 7 and 8*
  1. Teacher should demonstrate each step they say. Example of steps...
      a. Irish: Shuffle - Hop - Step
      b. Swing and Sway: Step - Back Flap (cross behind) - Step (front)
      c. Gum Off the Shoe: Drawback with an added Shuffle - Heel
      d. Tack Annie: Brush - Dig - Step 3×, Brush - Step - Ball Change
      e. Train: Cross - Step - Step
      f. Shim Sham: Shuffle - Step 2×, Shuffle - Ball Change - Shuffle - Step
      g. Essence: Front and Back
      h. Scissors: Slow and Fast
      i. Grapevine: Step - Cross (front / back)
      j. Maxie Ford: Shuffle - Jump - Toe Back
      k. Susie Q: Cross - Step - Cross - Kick
      l. Buffalo: Jump - Shuffle - Jump
      m. Lindy: Flap - Ball Change, Cross - Step
      n. Froggy: Stamp - Toe - Toe 4×, Stamp - Toe - Step

The benefits to be gained by incorporating hand and chair tap for any of the conditions / diseases listed in this chapter should now be obvious. By having a clear understanding of what causes these issues and what limitations could be present in students, you will be able to teach with compassion, empathy, and dignity. For those who have developed Parkinson's and Alzheimer's, or have suffered a stroke, what happened to them has likely left them with feelings of exclusion and isolation. Helping them to feel included and a part of something again is the best gift you could ever give them, and one that they will treasure and come back for repeatedly.

Quotable Quote

*"We dance for laughter, we dance for tears, we dance for madness, we dance for fears, we dance for hopes, we dance for screams, we are the dancers, we create the dreams."—Albert Einstein*

# Chapter 3 Review Questions

1. What causes Parkinson's, and which gender is most affected by it?
2. What are the five stages of progression for Parkinson's?
3. What are the four main symptoms that may be present in someone suffering from Parkinson's?
4. What is Alzheimer's, and how does it present in people affected with it?
5. How does tap benefit someone with early developing Alzheimer's?
6. Is cerebral palsy a disease, and what causes it?
7. What are the four distinct types of cerebral palsy?
8. What needs to be considered when teaching someone with cerebral palsy?
9. What types of physical difficulties could someone with cerebral palsy have?
10. What is the best strategy in managing a new class that has a mixture of diseases / conditions?
11. What are the two main types of arthritis and how do they present differently / similarly?
12. How should you handle a student that is having sharp pain when executing an exercise?
13. Explain the three diverse types of strokes, and which one is the most common?
14. How can this program assist the rehabilitation process for a stroke victim?
15. Discuss how to adjust a typical nondisabled dance class to accommodate both visually and hearing-impaired students.
16. What are the three **R**'s and three **It**'s of Tap?
17. Describe some teacher / student tap games and how they can help students remember and retain class information.

# ≋ 4 ≊

# The Power of Music

### OBJECTIVES

- Understanding how music can help those suffering with memory loss from Alzheimer's and dementia.
- Knowing the benefits of music for stroke survivors.
- Knowledge of musical artists that seniors will connect with to use in your classes.

Music is the one thing more than anything else that connects us to both our past and present. Whether you are disabled, nondisabled, a wheelchair user, have Alzheimer's, dementia, or are a stroke survivor, music has the power to bring people together from all walks of life. Music can instantly change moods: at times inspiring us to jump up and dance, and at other moments connecting us to joyful or sorrowful memories from our past. Music does not care about the listener's background or ability. It cuts across generations of people. Lyrics can reach down deep into a listener's soul, make one pause to contemplate the intended message, and sometimes just make us sing along in silliness.

Music can even bring communities of differing views together, creating common bonds where there were none before. John Lennon's beautiful and meaningful song *Imagine* is the perfect example of such a song. The part of the brain that responds to music being played has been studied by scientists using advanced imaging, and they are discovering that there are many health benefits to listening and singing to our favorite tunes.

During the COVID-19 pandemic in 2020, people all around the world felt more alone and isolated than any other time in recent history. Think back to the uplifting scenes we all saw on the news of people

## Tap Dance for All

standing on the balconies of their apartments singing in unison at the same time every day in New York City and also Italy. Why did they do that? For at least a brief time each day people were able to see and connect with other human beings through music, even though they did not know each other, were quarantined, and living in total isolation. It brought a tiny slice of solace and joy during a very frightening time when thousands of people a day were dying and the fear of an unknown silent killer was roaming the earth. We all sought any outlet we could to de-stress and fight off the feelings of isolation and fear. Music offered relief then, and still does today. The desire for live music, shows, and other large events has never been stronger. Coming together, whether it is a live music concert, a Broadway show, or a sporting event, provides the connection with other people we crave, and is a vital basic human trait. We are not meant or built to be detached and devoid of human contact. The isolation that seniors feel, even without a pandemic thrown into the mix, does not make for a healthy, positive mental state. I guess you could say that not only have we had to deal with a health pandemic, but we have also been struggling with a loneliness epidemic—especially in the case of seniors. As dance instructors who will someday also become seniors, we owe it to that population to create ways to help prevent them from feeling like they have been discarded and are just biding their time until they pass.

By giving their brain the challenge of anticipating musical patterns and connecting song segments to dance steps, you are providing their brain with not only a mood lifting fun experience, but also an excellent brain workout. The aging process is challenging for most people but is something we all must face sooner or later, preferably later. By consistently engaging the brain, it can make a person more capable of handling those impending changes. Speech and music function reside in different areas of the brain. So, if someone with Alzheimer's disease or dementia has trouble recollecting people or memories, playing music from their past can help spark that connection. Think about a particular song from your own past. What emotion does that song bring up? What people or events does that make you think of? Or were you alone when you heard the song? What pictures flash in your memory? The memories that a song can trigger can be like suddenly discovering a buried treasure. How many times have you heard a song from your past and was suddenly taken back to that time, those people, and all the feelings you felt back then, and then say to yourself, "Wow! I haven't thought

## 4. The Power of Music

about that in forever." Music is immensely beneficial for helping those suffering from cognitive memory loss, and even helping to prevent cognitive memory loss in the first place.

Even the simple act of listening to music during physical therapy sessions can be of great benefit to those who have suffered a stroke. According to the American Heart Association, improvements in strength and balance are magnified when music is playing during physical therapy and occupational therapy. Music may help a stroke survivor access the parts of their brain that are involved in movement and coordination, plus lessen their depression, anxiety, and stress level.*

The music you choose should be compatible and appropriate with the age of your students. Whatever music you use, make sure it is a clean version of the song. Inappropriate language never goes over well and should be avoided. Parents of young students, as well as seniors, will not appreciate being exposed to foul language in songs during class. The following is a list to help you jump start your selection of appropriate music for students that you may have that are more mature in age.

### 60+ year olds

*Search top hits from the 1930s, 1940s, 1950s, 1960s*

| | |
|---|---|
| Aretha Franklin | The Beatles |
| Frankie Valli | The Four Seasons |
| The Rolling Stones | The Beach Boys |
| James Brown | The Supremes |
| Sam Cooke | Ray Charles |
| Otis Redding | The Temptations |
| Smokey Robinson | Wilson Pickett |
| Stevie Wonder | The Shirelles |
| The Drifters | The Four Tops |
| Martha and the Vandellas | Jackie Wilson |
| Chubby Checker | Tina Turner |
| The Jackson Five | Gladys Knight and the Pips |
| Van Morrison | Barry Manilow |
| Duke Ellington | Ella Fitzgerald |

---

* American Heart Association. "Healing From Stroke," American Heart Association, 2021, https://www.heart.org/en/about-stroke/effects-of-stroke/physical-effects-of-stroke/healing.

## Tap Dance for All

| | |
|---|---|
| Louis Armstrong | Frank Sinatra |
| Dean Martin | Fred Astaire |
| Gene Kelly | Judy Garland |
| Elvis Presley | Sammy Davis, Jr. |
| Tony Bennett | Nat "King" Cole |
| Bobby Rydell | Glenn Miller and His Orchestra |
| Benny Goodman | The Andrews Sisters |
| Tony Evans and His Orchestra | Kenny Burrell |
| Bobby Darin | Edyie Gorme and Steve Lawrence |
| John Coltrane | Miles Davie |
| Charlie Parker | |

Michael Bublé and Harry Connick, Jr., have nicely re-imagined some of the classic songs from earlier decades. The full orchestrations they use are a big hit with senior students. Tony Bennett has also recreated many songs with a slew of current popular singers like Lady Gaga, Aretha Franklin, Faith Hill, Sheryl Crow, Mariah Carey, Carrie Underwood, Josh Groban, Michael Bublé, Queen Latifah, Natalie Cole, Norah Jones, and many more.

To quote the incomparable soul singer Ray Charles, "Music is powerful. As people listen to it, they can be affected. They respond." As the prolific and legendary music composer Leonard Bernstein expressed once, "Music can name the unnamable, and communicate the unknowable." When you see the faces of your senior students light up with recognition of a time, place, and memory, all because of a song you chose, you will know they appreciate that you cared enough to take the time to understand the era they grew up in. Their bodies may be betraying them and breaking down, but because of your ingenuity and conscientiousness, their spirit will be lifted and more positive than before they came into your class. Music is a gift always, a lifeline sometimes, and meaningless never. When you give the gift of music and rhythm to seniors through your classes, you will not only be enhancing their lives and bringing them fun and joy, but you will also be reminding them that there is still much left to enjoy in life.

### Quotable Quote

*"Music, once admitted to the soul, becomes a sort of spirit, and never dies."—Edward Bulwer-Lytton*

*4. The Power of Music*

## CHAPTER 4 REVIEW QUESTIONS

1. What benefits does music provide?
2. How can music help someone with Alzheimer's or dementia?
3. How can music help in the rehabilitation process of a stroke survivor?

CHALLENGE

1. Name a song from your past and explain how it makes you feel mentally, physically, and emotionally when you hear it.
2. Pick a song from before you were born, one you have never heard before, and create a short piece of choreography to it.
3. Watch a movie musical from the 1940s or 1950s and write a summary about that era, music, and story, and how you might incorporate the essence of that film into your choreography and class.

# 5

# Tap Styles
*Rhythmic vs. Broadway*

## OBJECTIVES

- Understanding the differences between Broadway and rhythmic tap.
- Learning how teaching both styles benefits disabled and mobility-impaired people.
- Comprehension of the connection between seniors and the music and movie musicals of the era they grew up in.

Broadway tap and rhythmic tap—how can knowing their similarities and differences be beneficial when teaching a mobility-impaired dance class? Once we dive into each style the answer will become clear.

Because rhythmic tap superseded Broadway tap in history, it is only right to start there. Whenever I instruct a new group of students I invariably ask at the top of class, "Can anyone tell me the difference between Broadway and rhythmic tap?" Nine times out of ten I will hear, "Rhythmic is fast, and Broadway is slow and much easier." Do you think that is correct? I know many teachers feel that this *is* the correct answer. But, if you have ever rehearsed for and performed in a tap-based Broadway show, you would know that is a false statement, and you would vehemently disagree. Speed is not the differentiating factor between these two styles. Their physicality and approach on the other hand is. Rhythmic tap can entail incredible, lightning-fast footwork for sure, but it is the focus on the rhythm of the feet rather than the upper body, plus being more grounded into the floor that sets rhythmic tap apart from Broadway tap.

## 5. Tap Styles

A more accurate description of Broadway tap would include adjectives such as light, effortless, and elegant. Broadway tap is usually choreographed from head to toe, whereas rhythmic tap has a more free-flowing upper body, more like what the body naturally does in response to movement such as walking; naturally swinging your arms in opposition to your lower limbs. In Broadway tap, the choreographer has usually given the dancers specific placements for every part of their body.

For comparison purposes, look at footage of Eleanor Powell, with her nerve tap turns that had her spinning at the speed of sound, and Ayodele Casel, with footwork so fast that one would not be surprised if she ignited sparks from the wood floor she taps on. Both women are incredible and exciting, but both are also completely different in their physicality, style, and overall feel and approach to tap. The same could be said for Gene Kelly and Savion Glover. If you have never seen these four dancers, I highly suggest you treat yourself to these kings and queens of tap by pulling up videos of their tap prowess from YouTube.

Teaching both styles to your senior and disabled students can not only expand their minds, but also challenge them to try a different style than they may have ever previously experienced. Simply teaching the steps to students is not what any good dance instructor should be striving for. If you genuinely want to make an impact with this career path you need to go beyond the steps.

Seniors are our living history books. Their minds are full of memories and life experiences that we can only imagine. Unfortunately, many times aging is accompanied by the loss of those precious memories. Sometimes it is a slow decline, and other times it is rapid. We, as instructors of this class, have the unique opportunity to offer a way to try to help stave off and slow down that deterioration. By weaving a little tap and music history into your classes you will give seniors the opportunity to open their memory bank and make neural connections that had previously been inaccessible. Establishing and re-establishing those cognitive pathways are the way to living a long fully functional life.

The songs and musical artists listed in the previous chapter is an excellent way to not only connect to your senior students, but also stimulate that area of the brain where their memories reside. Before I play a song for a combination, I will usually see how many of the senior students remember the song and artist, and then ask if anyone cares to share a memory or story that was inspired by that song choice. Having

## Tap Dance for All

the ability to recall important, special, once-in-a-lifetime moments is precious and something that should never be taken for granted.

Just as music and musical artists can hold the key to unlocking memories, the same holds true for famous tap dancers of the past. World War II lasted from 1939 to 1945, and the movie musical exploded during these years—mostly to lift the spirits of the United States via song and dance during that challenging time. It is quite possible you will have some seniors in your class that served in World War II or had loved ones that served. Please, always remember to thank them for their service to our country.

The cream of the crop dancers from the movie musicals of this era were ...

| | | |
|---|---|---|
| Fred Astaire | Ginger Rogers | Gene Kelly |
| Donald O'Connor | Eleanor Powell | Rita Hayworth |
| Ann Miller | Mickey Rooney | Paul Draper |
| Vera Ellen | Betty Grable | |

Movie Musicals of the 1940s ...

| | | |
|---|---|---|
| *Anchors Aweigh* | *Babes on Broadway* | *Broadway Melody* |
| *Cover Girl* | *DuBarry Was a Lady* | *For Me and My Gal* |
| *Holiday Inn* | *Lady Be Good* | *Living in a Big Way* |
| *Me and My Gal* | *On the Town* | *Stormy Weather* |
| *Strike Up the Band* | *The Pirate* | *Thousands Cheer* |
| *Ziegfeld Follies* | | |

Do some research, not only on the music in these movie musicals but also the choreography and dance style of those who starred in the movies. Considering that going to the movie theater was the main form of entertainment in the 1940s, it is a safe bet that the seniors you will teach saw most of the movies listed above. If you are an instructor in your twenties, you are sure to receive surprise followed by much gratitude from your senior students for caring enough to familiarize yourself with the music and dancers of their generation. The added bonus for them is that you are helping keep their minds and memories sharp and intact. Seniors will love having the opportunity to tap like their favorite movie musical idols.

For younger students in a regular dance studio class setting, the music choice will be more current, but you should still research the

### 5. Tap Styles

wonderful songs that Broadway musicals offer. Many times, I have used music from Broadway hits such as *Hamilton, Dear Evan Hansen, The Prom, Once Upon This Island, Bring in Da Noise Bring in Da Funk, Smokey Joe's Café, Bandstand, Aladdin, Newsies, 13 The Musical, Catch Me If You Can,* and *Hairspray.* Even though I do use more contemporary music to get my younger students to connect and engage during class, I will also look and search for more contemporary versions of older classics. I do this in hopes of opening their minds to other eras and genres of music. Classic Broadway-style combinations and routines set to more current music from both Broadway and pop can set the stage for a fun, creative class.

Introducing rhythmic tap and how the styles differ gives students the ability to add layers and depth to their dancing. Switching between styles within a combination is a great tool to teach students when to be up on the balls of the feet and have a light, effortless feel to their dancing, and when to embody a more down-into-the-ground and free-flowing upper body expression of their artistry.

#### Quotable Quote

*"When you dance to your own rhythm, life taps its toes to your beat."—Terri Guillemets*

## Chapter 5 Review Questions

1. Explain the core differences / similarities between rhythmic and Broadway tap?
2. How can you as a teacher utilize the two styles to benefit both your senior and younger students?
3. What are three popular movie musicals from the 1940s?

#### Challenge

1. Create a short piece of choreography to a song from a Broadway show, mixing up the choreography between rhythmic and Broadway styles. Be prepared to dissect the choreography and explain which parts belong to rhythmic tap, and which belong to Broadway tap.

# 6

# Choreography vs. Improvisation

### OBJECTIVES

- Understanding the differences between choreography and improvisation.
- Comprehension of how the three different modalities of tap can benefit from both choreography and improvisation.
- Learning how to simplify and take the fear out of learning improv for those new to the concept.

Whether teaching a stand-up, hand, or chair tap dancer, exploring both improvisation and choreography is helpful, beneficial, and very applicable for the disabled and physically unsteady student. Each brings tremendous potential for growth—not only mentally and emotionally, but physically as well. In this chapter we will explore the ways in which you as an instructor can utilize both improvisation and choreography to challenge, inspire, and expand your disabled and mobility-impaired student's view of tap dance, all through creativity and fun.

## *Choreography*

Choreography is where most dancers begin their tap journey. Starting with Chapter 7, you will be given not only a tried-and-true progressive syllabus for teaching tap, but also countless steps and combinations to combine and choreograph to your heart's content. Teaching choreography prior to teaching improvisation is important so that students have a solid foundation of the basic steps used in tap. Were they to only know

## 6. Choreography vs. Improvisation

two or three steps, they would be extremely limited in their improvisational options. Could students still work on their improv chops? Sure, but with such a limited tap vocabulary they would only be able to go so far. Learning and retaining simple steps, progressing to longer combinations, then eventually advancing to fully choreographed routines is highly beneficial for disabled and mobility-challenged students on many levels.

When I teach seniors that have taken tap when they were younger, I always take the time to let them know that tap is like riding a bike; even if you have not ridden that bike for decades, once you hop on it your muscle memory will start to kick in and your body will begin to remember how to peddle, balance, and brake. Tap is no different than that bike. Once their hands or feet start to make those rhythms again, little by little those steps will slowly start to come back to them. They may be rusty at first and slow to remember, but it is possible for them to draw upon their muscle memory and pick tap back up, no matter their age.

Using choreography with both seniors and disabled students helps to build confidence, improve cognitive functionality, and instills a positive affirmation that they have not lost the ability to learn and have fun. When they reach the point where the tap steps you are teaching them start to "click" and their brain and body begins to "get it," they will not only want more, but will undoubtedly experience a wonderful sense of accomplishment and pride in themselves.

## *Improvisation*

Inevitably, the moment I walk into a dance convention and announce that we will be honing the dancer's improvisational chops, those that have never taken classes from me before instantly look like a deer caught in the headlights of an oncoming car. The panic and fear from those new to improvisation is palpable every time. Recognizing that look and knowing that you need a game plan for when it happens is vital to the success of your class, or you will risk losing them straight out of the gate. I can absolutely empathize with those that are fearful as I too used to stand in those terrified tap shoes. I grew up without learning how to express my tap voice through improvisation. My early initial tap training was picking up someone else's choreography as fast as humanly possible, and then layering my own physical artistry

## Tap Dance for All

on top of that. As with most things in life, nothing stays the same and trying something new can oftentimes be met with much apprehension. This can be especially true when it comes to a tap dancer that has only known and trained in choreography their entire dance life and is now being presented with something completely novel and foreign—improvisation. The dancer has two choices: resist change and remain stagnant in ability and possibility or embrace trying something new and different and in turn create real opportunity for growth, not only as a dancer, but also as a performer and artist.

When desiring to learn something new and unfamiliar, I absorb all I can from those who are expertly skilled in that field. Improv masters such as Leon Collins, Dianne Walker, Brenda Bufalino, and Barbara Duffy are the best of the best when it comes to tap improvisation and are great improv geniuses to learn from. Through Barbara Duffy's book, *Tap into Improv*[*] I discovered that Barbara also started out like I did, learning choreographed routines at the beginning of her tap journey, and initially approaching improvisation as something to be cringed at. Determined to overcome and conquer my fear, I started slow, and as Barbara suggested, I allowed myself to fail to improve. After a ton of arduous work and endless trial with much error, it was not long before I was passing on what worked exceptionally well to others. Ms. Duffy has created a wonderful set of improvisation exercises that assist all levels of tappers, beginning through advanced. Barbara has graciously given me permission to share her wealth of improv knowledge here with all of you. We will only be covering the more basic exercises in this section, as they will be the most appropriate and beneficial for the scope of our subject matter. However, I highly encourage you to obtain a copy of her book to continue honing your skills from this true improvisation tap master. The following exercises from Barbara's book are applicable to any type of tap student, be it stand-up, hand, or chair.

Barbara encourages teachers to begin by creating a safe, nurturing, supportive environment. A setting that gives your students the freedom to explore and experiment without judgment is the key to opening their tap improvisation potential.

The first step in creating that safe space is to deal with any fears surrounding improvisation. Right off the bat, simply ask your students

---

[*] Barbara Duffy. Tap into Improv, 2017, https://www.amazon.com/Tap-Into-Improv-Guide-Improvisation/dp/1977783066/ref=sr_1_1?dchild=1&keywords=tap+into+improv&qid=1630357780&sr=8-1.

## 6. Choreography vs. Improvisation

if there is anyone that is nervous or scared about trying improvisation. I usually kick off the hand raising because I was once sitting where they are now. When they see other students raise their hands it can help them from feeling like they are the only one who is scared. Once that big sigh of relief is over, ask them why they are anxious about trying it. Verbalizing and opening a dialogue about their fears can help take the scariness out of the issue. This type of tap can be particularly intimidating to many dancers, whether disabled or nondisabled. You can begin to break down those walls of fear your students have built by making sure they understand that they are in a safe space, and that everyone is there to learn how to find their own unique tap voice through trial and error. An open mind, free of self judgment and criticism, is necessary for growth. Mistakes are expected along the way and are a necessary element in the process of improving. Perfection is not only an unnecessary goal, it can also hold a dancer back. Such an enormous weight on a dancer's shoulders has the possibility of not only resulting in being a disservice to the dancer, but also creating a disintegration in their love of tap. This holds true for all types of dance classes, and even more so with disabled and mobility impaired dance classes. The unrealistic expectations dancers from every dance genre often place on themselves, whether it stems from their technical ability or body image, can only result in becoming counterproductive to their evolution as an artist.

Comparisons to other dancers are also unproductive as it turns into an unending cycle of self chastisement. Disabled people can vary in their physical accessibility—the functionality they have available to them to dance with. Just as every snowflake is distinctive, so too are disabled students. Each disabled student's access to their physical body and cognitive mind will be unique. Praising your students for stepping out of their comfort zone by trying something new and challenging will help encourage them to not only give themselves a pat on the back, but also praise and support each other. This will build the special class bond and the supportive, nurturing, inclusive environment you are looking to establish. By doing so your students will feel free to explore and experiment without experiencing the anxiety of being judged.

Now that everyone is feeling more relaxed and confident that they have got this, Barbara suggests starting your students with their voice before their feet. If you have ever heard a singer who is great at scatting, like Ella Fitzgerald, Louis Armstrong, or Sarah Vaughan, you have heard great vocal improvisation. By singing the rhythm first, you can

## Tap Dance for All

get specific with what you want to create rhythmically, plus it removes the pressure of having to think about what your feet should be doing in this early stage of learning. Beginning with any simple two-bar musical phrase (1-2-3-4, 1-2-3-4), have the dancers vocally scat an easy phrase. Example: "He's the boogie woogie bugle boy from company B," or "Shave and a haircut, two bits." Use an uncomplicated phrase from a popular song your students will be familiar with, as this will make learning how to scat or sing rhythms easier for them. Once they have gotten comfortable with that, you can begin adding tap sounds that match the rhythms being sung. Encourage them not to forget that they can use Stamps, Hops, Chugs, Holds, Shuffles, Flaps, Ball Changes, Heel and Toe Drops, Claps, etc. Continue repeating the initial rhythm, having them switch out the steps they are using little by little with other steps, while still maintaining that original scat rhythm.

Another way Barbara offers to mitigate class anxiety is to give students that first rhythm and have everyone tap it out together without music. By doing this early in the class structure it can reduce the fear and worry about dancing solo. Practice the rhythm you have just given them all together in unison. This will become the "question" rhythm. Once that has been absorbed, have each student create their own rhythm. This is the "answer" to that first unison "question" rhythm. When all of those are locked down it is time to put these two pieces together in what may sound a bit nutty, but it will, again, deescalate that fear of performing alone. From here have everyone tap out that first "question" rhythm you gave them and have one dancer at a time execute the "answer" rhythm they have created. Continue the question / answer back and forth until each student has had a chance to answer. If they make a mistake with their rhythm, simply let them try it again. As I mentioned earlier, mistakes are a part of the learning process in tap improvisation. This exercise is a fun and simple improvisation ice breaker and stress reducer. For seniors with cognitive issues, it is a terrific way to help them retain small pieces of information at a time all while feeling creative and having fun. With your disabled and senior students this may very well be as far as you will want to go so as not to make improv too overwhelming for them. New question / answer phrases can continually be created class after class though.

To progress your students beyond the above exercises, the next step would be to create a new first rhythm after the initial question / answer

## 6. Choreography vs. Improvisation

rhythms. In this way you have eliminated the repetition by beginning to build two-bar phrases, and once they are comfortable you can practice this exercise by adding a medium-tempo song. As your student's confidence grows you can continue to add on two-bar phrases as deemed appropriate.

Another way to strengthen a student's confidence is to give them exercises that will help them overcome their apprehensions and expand beyond the steps they frequently fall back on and repeat. This next exercise of Barbara's is another good option for senior students that have cognitive issues. By giving your students certain specific steps, such as only using heels and steps in any combination without using Shuffles, Flaps, Brushes, etc., you limit the steps they must remember and allow them to focus more on the rhythm. When they have the hang of that drill, you can then flip the exercise by using only Brushes, Shuffles, and Steps, eliminating all other basics.

One more exercise of Barbara's that is slightly more advanced is to pick only one main step, like only Riffs, Cramp Rolls, Paradiddles, or Pullbacks. This time in their improvisation have them try using as many as they can of that single step.

The last one I will offer here is one that my mother was an expert at: taking a step and reinventing it by fitting it into as many different rhythm patterns as you can. You will see evidence of this in later chapters, which is why it is vitally important to initially sing or scat the rhythm and then fit the step to that rhythm. Take the example of a Cramp Roll; there are numerous ways in which to execute that step based on the rhythm it is given.

> One typical rhythm might be: e&a1, e&a2, e&a3, e&a4.
> Other possibilities are:
> 1&2&, 3&4&
> Hold: 1, 2&a3, Hold: 4, 5&a6
> 1, Hold: 2, &a3, 4, Hold: 5, &a6
> 1-2, Hold: 3, &4
> e&a1, Hold: 2, e&a3, Hold: 4
> *All underlined counts are accented counts*

As you can see there are many options available to use just from this one simple step. Have your students choose the rhythm they want the step to have, sing or scat it, and then put the step to the rhythm. By doing this exercise you will again be training your students to focus on the rhythm rather than their feet. If using a piece of music, sing or scat the rhythms first, then add the steps that fit that rhythm.

Keeping the number of the steps small while using a piece of music will allow students to focus on the individual rhythms in the song. Help your students find the downbeat, or the 1 count, because the downbeat will cement you in the music immediately. To assist students in hearing how the rhythm of the steps meld with the rhythm of the music, Barbara suggests having half the class sing the 1 and 3 counts, and clap on the 2 and 4 counts. At the same time have the other half of the class execute the tap combination. This exercise is immensely helpful in making those new neural pathways seniors so greatly need.

For the more advanced improvisation students, combining rhythms in four-bar phrases gives them the chance to experiment with straight, swing, triplet, double time, and syncopated rhythms. Once you have introduced your students to each of those types of rhythms you can start combining a couple of them together for your students to play with. One of the many exercise options Barbara Duffy offers is to place the students in a circle and have each student dance four bars of their choice while the other students hold the tempo. Continue around the circle until each student has had a chance to dance their rhythm.

For a couple of reasons, time steps are also particularly useful as an exercise in improvisation. The first reason is that it strengthens their retention of time steps, and the second is that it gives students the exercise of creating breaks with different rhythms. After dancing a six-bar phrase of any time step, the students can try adding a break by singing or scatting it first and then dancing out swing, triplet, or double time rhythms, thus creating a two bar break. Give each student a chance at producing their own break rhythms. Once they are feeling confident with all the above, expand the number of bars to eight, 16, and a full 32-bar chorus in the same fashion. They will now be creating full-length rhythmical sentences that have a beginning, middle, and end. You have the option of having them dance all together, split them into groups, or have them individually dance.

By focusing your hearing on individual instruments in any given song, you will find many different rhythm patterns emerging from the bass, percussion, horns, guitar, saxophone, piano etc. Each instrument lends the opportunity to experiment with a dancer's improv skills. Begin this process by mimicking the melody of the song exactly by singing it

## 6. Choreography vs. Improvisation

first, followed by dancing it with your feet. From there have your students focus on one instrument in the song, again vocally imitating the rhythms then physically imitating those same rhythms by tapping them out. Choosing a solo in the song would then be the next step. You can even have one student take on the solo while the rest of the class holds the melody.

So far, the music has been the dancer's partner in all of this and has been immensely helpful in getting the student comfortable with and courageous in improvisation. It is at this point Barbara suggests that it is time to take away their partner, the music. This is where the student has no rules to follow, where they get to create a story with a beginning, middle, and ending of their choosing. They have complete control of things like tempo, accents, melody, solos, and breaks. They can add emotion, builds, and any other parts that add richness and creativity to the story they want to tell.

The options available to you as an instructor of improvisation are limited only by your imagination and creativity. Using improvisation with disabled students, unstable elderly, or those recovering from a stroke, or have early onset Parkinson's or Alzheimer's, can help them continue to improve both cognitively and physically. The areas of the brain required for this kind of work have most likely rarely, if ever, been used in this challenging way before. Whether disabled, nondisabled, or mobility impaired, making new neurological connections in the brain should be the ever-present predominant goal to remain physically and mentally functional for as long as humanly possible.

Thank you again to Barbara Duffy for her generosity in sharing her expertise with all of us.

### QUOTABLE QUOTES

"Choreography is writing with your feet."—*Bob Fosse*

"Improvisation is the ability to talk to oneself."—*Cecil Taylor*

## CHAPTER 6 REVIEW QUESTIONS

1. Explain the key differences between choreography and improvisation.

## Tap Dance for All

2. How can both choreography and improvisation-based teaching be beneficial to the disabled and mobility-impaired student?
3. Explain how best to alleviate the fear of improvisation in a class setting.

CHALLENGE

1. Lead a class in a beginning-level improvisation "Question / Answer" exercise.
2. Take any simple tap step and reinvent it by changing its rhythm.

# 7

# Beginning and Beginning II Levels

1. Forward Brush / Back Brush
   **(BRUSH - BRUSH)**
   <u>Counts</u>: 1-2, 3-4, 5-6, 7-8
2. <u>**Crossing Brushes**</u> (Out - Cross Over - Uncross - Back)
   **(BRUSH: OUT - CROSS - UNCROSS - BACK)**
   <u>Counts</u>: 1-2-3-4, 5-6-7-8
3. Heel Dig (front) - Step 4× Alternating
   **(HEEL DIG - STEP 4× ALT)**
   <u>Counts</u>: 1-2, 3-4, 5-6, 7-8
4. Ball - Heel R (in place), Reverse, Repeat R Side, Heel Dig (front) L, Hold
   **(BALL - HEEL 3× ALT, HEEL DIG, HOLD)**
   <u>Counts</u>: 1-2, 3-4, 5-6, 7, Hold: 8
5. Heel Dig (front) R, Brush (back) R, Step R, Hold, Reverse All
   **(HEEL DIG, BRUSH - STEP, HOLD, REVERSE ALL)**
   <u>Counts</u>: 1-2-3, Hold: 4, 5-6-7, Hold: 8
6. <u>**Paradiddle / Paddle & Roll**</u>
   Heel Dig (front), R, Brush (back) R, Ball - Heel (in place) R, Reverse All and Repeat All
   **(HEEL DIG, BRUSH, BALL - HEEL 4× ALT)**
   <u>Counts</u>: 1&2&, 3&4&, 5&6&, 7&8&
7. <u>**Paradiddle / Paddle & Roll Combination**</u>
   Same as #6 doing Paradiddle 3× (R-L-R), ending with a Heel Dig (front) L, Hold, Reverse All
   **(HEEL DIG, BRUSH, BALL - HEEL 3× ALT, HEEL DIG, HOLD, REVERSE ALL)**

## Tap Dance for All

   Counts: 1&2&, 3&4&, 5&6&, 7, Hold: 8
   1&2&, 3&4&, 5&6&, 7, Hold: 8

8. Toe Back - Step 3× R-L-R, Step - Step L-R
   **(TOE - STEP 3× ALT, STEP - STEP)**
   Counts: 1-2, 3-4, 5-6, 7-8

9. Shuffle (2 Brushes: Forward - Back), Hold, Repeat 3×
   **(SHUFFLE, HOLD, REPEAT 3×)**
   Counts: &1, Hold: 2, &3, Hold: 4, &5, Hold: 6, &7, Hold: 8

10. Shuffle 8×
    **(SHUFFLE 8×)**
    Counts: &1, &2, &3, &4, &5, &6, &7, &8

11. Shuffle R - Hop L 3×, Step - Step R-L
    **(SHUFFLE - HOP 3×, STEP - STEP)**
    Counts: &1-2, &3-4, &5-6, 7-8

12. Shuffle R - Hop L - Toe Back R 3×, Step - Step R-L
    **(SHUFFLE - HOP - TOE BACK 3×, STEP - STEP)**
    Counts: &1&2, &3&4, &5&6, 7-8

13. Shuffle - Ball Change R 3×, Step - Step R-L
    **(SHUFFLE - BALL CHANGE 3×, STEP - STEP)**
    Counts: &1&2, &3&4, &5&6, 7-8

14. Shuffle R 2×, Ball Change R 2×, Repeat All 3× (4 sets total)
    **(SHUFFLE 2×, BALL CHANGE 2×, REPEAT ALL 3×)**
    Counts: &1&2, &3&4, &5&6, &7&8
    &1&2, &3&4, &5&6, &7&8

15. **Maxie Ford** (Broadway Step = Heels Up)
    Shuffle R - Jump R - Toe Back L, Step L, Hold, Repeat All 3× (4 sets total)
    **(SHUFFLE - JUMP - TOE BACK - STEP, HOLD, REPEAT ALL 3×)**
    Counts: &1&2-3, Hold: 4, &5&6-7, Hold: 8
    &1&2-3, Hold: 4, &5&6-7, Hold: 8

16. Shuffle R - Jump R - Toe Back L, Hold, Reverse All, Ball Change - Step R
    **(SHUFFLE - JUMP - TOE BACK, HOLD, SHUFFLE - JUMP - TOE BACK, HOLD, BALL CHANGE - STEP)**
    Counts: &1&2, Hold: 3, &4&5, Hold: 6, &7-8

## 7. Beginning and Beginning II Levels

17. Maxie Ford (Shuffle - Jump - Toe Back) 3× R-L-R, Step - Step L-R
    **(MAXIE FORD 3× ALT, STEP - STEP)**
    Counts: &1&2, &3&4, &5&6, 7-8

18. **Slap**
    Brush (front), Toe (tap front) - Lift (back to start position, do not scrape foot along the way), Repeat 3×
    **(BRUSH - TOE - LIFT, REPEAT 3×)**
    Counts: &1-2, &3-4, &5-6, &7-8

19. **Slap Progression I**
    (A) Slap R - Heel (drop) R
    **(SLAP - HEEL)**
    Counts: &1-2
    (B) Slap R - Heel (drop) L
    **(SLAP - HEEL)**
    Counts: &1-2
    (C) Slap R, Heel - Heel R-L
    **(SLAP - HEEL - HEEL)**
    Counts: &1&2
    (D) Slap R, Heel - Heel L-R
    **(SLAP - HEEL - HEEL)**
    Counts: &1&2

20. Hop L 3×, Jump R, Reverse All
    **(HOP 3× - JUMP, REVERSE ALL)**
    Counts: 1-2-3-4, 5-6-7-8

21. Heel Dig (front) R - Ball Change R, Repeat All 2×, Step R, Clap
    **(HEEL DIG - BALL CHANGE, REPEAT ALL 2×, STEP - CLAP)**
    Counts: 1&2, 3&4, 5&6, 7-8

22. Shuffle - Ball Change R 3×, Ball Change - Step R
    **(SHUFFLE - BALL CHANGE 3×, BALL CHANGE - STEP)**
    Counts: &1&2, &3&4, &5&6, &7&8

23. Hop L - Shuffle R - Hop L 3×, Step - Step R-L
    **(HOP - SHUFFLE – HOP 3×, STEP - STEP)**
    Counts: 1&a2, 3&a4, 5&a6, 7-8

24. **Irish** (Broadway Step = Heels Up)
    Shuffle R - Hop L - Step R (ball: heel tap lifted), Reverse & Repeat All

## Tap Dance for All

(SHUFFLE - HOP - STEP, REVERSE & REPEAT ALL)
Counts: &1&2, &3&4, &5&6, &7&8

25. Step R, Shuffle - Ball Change L, Step L, Repeat All 2×, Step R, Hold, Step L, Hold
    **(STEP - SHUFFLE - BALL CHANGE – STEP 3×, STEP - HOLD - STEP - HOLD)**
    Counts: 1&2&3-4, 5&6&7-8,
           1&2&3-4, Step: 5, Hold: 6, Step: 7, Hold: 8

26. **Cramp Roll (basic)**
    Ball R, Ball L, Heel Drop R, Heel Drop L, Repeat 2×, Step R - Hold, Reverse All (jump into the Cramp Roll, and execute in place)
    **(CRAMP ROLL 3×, STEP - HOLD, REVERSE ALL)**
    Counts: 1&a2, 3&a4, 5&a6, Step: 7, Hold: 8

27. **Slap Progression II**
    **(A)** Slap R - Hold 3× (front - side - back), Step - Step R-L
    **(SLAP - HOLD 3×, STEP - STEP)**
    Counts: &1, Hold: 2, &3, Hold: 4, &5, Hold: 6, Steps: 7-8
    **(B)** Slap (front) R, Heel (drop) R, Repeat 2× (side / back), Step - Step R-L
    **(SLAP - HEEL 3×, STEP - STEP)**
    Counts: &1-2, &3-4, &5-6, 7-8
    **(C)** Slap (front) R, Heel (drop) L, Repeat 2× (side / back), Step - Step R-L
    **(SLAP - HEEL 3×, STEP - STEP)**
    Counts: &1-2, &3-4, &5-6, 7-8
    **(D)** Slap (front) R, Heel - Heel (drops) R-L, Repeat 2× (side / back), Step - Step R-L
    **(SLAP, HEEL - HEEL 3×, STEP - STEP)**
    Counts: &1&2, &3&4, &5&6, 7-8
    **(E)** Slap (front) R, Heel - Heel (drops) L-R, Repeat 2× (side / back), Step - Step R-L
    **(SLAP, HEEL - HEEL 3×, STEP - STEP)**
    Counts: &1&2, &3&4, &5&6, 7-8

28. **Straight Front & Back Brush – Heels**
    Brush R - Heel (bounce) L 6×, Step R - Hold, Reverse All
    **(BRUSH - HEEL 6×, STEP - HOLD, REVERSE ALL)**
    Counts: &1&2&3&4&5&6, Step: 7, Hold: 8
           &1&2&3&4&5&6, Step: 7, Hold: 8

## 7. Beginning and Beginning II Levels

29. **Crossing Brush - Heels**
    Front - Cross (over L) - Uncross - Back - Front - Cross, Step R (over L), Hold
    **(CROSSING BRUSH-HEEL 6×, STEP - HOLD)**
    Counts: &1&2&3&4&5&6, Step: 7, Hold: 8

30. Stamp R, Clap, Reverse, Stamp - Stamp R-L, Clap - Clap
    **(STAMP - CLAP 2× ALT, STAMP - STAMP, CLAP - CLAP)**
    Counts: 1-2-3-4-5-6-7-8

31. Dig (ball of foot) - Step R, Shuffle - Ball Change L, Reverse All
    **(DIG - STEP, SHUFFLE - BALL CHANGE, REVERSE ALL)**
    Counts: 1-2, &3&4, 5-6, &7&8

32. **2 Count Riff**
    Toe Back (inside edge, front tap) R - Heel Scuff R (strike board by flexing wrist) 4×
    **(TOE BACK - HEEL SCUFF 4×)**
    Counts: 1-2, 3-4, 5-6, 7-8

33. **3 Count Riff**
    Toe Back (inside edge, front tap) R - Heel Scuff R - Heel (bounce) L
    **(TOE BACK - HEEL SCUFF - HEEL)**
    Counts: 1-2-3 or &a1 or 1&2

34. **Scuffles**
    Heel Dig - Brush (back) R 3×, Stamp R - Hold, Reverse All
    **(SCUFFLE 3×, STAMP - HOLD, REVERSE ALL)**
    Counts: &1, &2, &3, &, Hold: 4, &5, &6, &7, &, Hold: 8

35. Scuffle - Step R - Hold, Reverse All
    **(SCUFFLE - STEP - HOLD, REVERSE ALL)**
    Counts: 1-2-3, Hold: 4, 5-6-7, Hold: 8

36. Shuffle - Ball Change, Step R - Hold, Reverse All, Shuffle - Ball Change R 3×, Step R - Hold
    **(SHUFFLE - BALL CHANGE, STEP - HOLD, REVERSE ALL, SHUFFLE - BALL CHANGE 3×, STEP - HOLD)**
    Counts: &1&2-3, Hold: 4, &5&6, 7, Hold: 8,
    &1&2, &3&4, &5&6, 7, Hold: 8

37. Hop L - Shuffle - Step R, Shuffle - Ball Change L, Reverse All
    **(HOP - SHUFFLE - STEP, SHUFFLE - BALL CHANGE, REVERSE ALL)**
    Counts: 1&a2, &3&4, 5&a6, &7&8

## Tap Dance for All

38. Shuffle - Ball - Heel R (use front and / or side shuffle) 4× R-L-R-L
    **(SHUFFLE - BALL - HEEL 4× ALT)**
    Counts: 1&2&, 3&4&, 5&6&, 7&8&

39. Shuffle R - Hop L - Shuffle - Ball Change R 3×, Step R - Drag (back) L
    **(SHUFFLE - HOP - SHUFFLE - BALL CHANGE 3×, STEP - DRAG)**
    Counts: &a1e&a2, &a3e&a4, &a5e&a6, 7-8

40. Toe Back - Ball Change R 3×, Step - Step R-L
    **(TOE BACK - BALL CHANGE 3×, STEP - STEP)**
    Counts: 1&2, 3&4, 5&6, 7-8

41. Flap 3× R-L-R, Heel (drop) R, Reverse All, Flap 8× R-L-R-L-R-L-R-L
    **(FLAP 3× ALT, HEEL, REVERSE ALL, FLAP 8× ALT)**
    Counts: &1, &2, &3-4, &5, &6, &7-8,
    &1, &2, &3, &4, &5, &6, &7, &8

42. Flap - Heel R, Toe Back L - Heel (bounce) R, Reverse, Flap - Heel (drop) 2× R-L, Flap - Heel R, Toe Back L - Heel (bounce) R
    **(FLAP - HEEL, TOE BACK - HEEL, REVERSE ALL, FLAP - HEEL 2× ALT, FLAP - HEEL, TOE BACK - HEEL)**
    Counts: a1&2&, a3&4&, a5&, a6&, a7&8&

43. Slap R - Heel (bounce) L (lift R to R corner), Brush (back) - Ball - Heel R, Reverse All
    **(SLAP - HEEL, BRUSH - BALL - HEEL, REVERSE ALL)**
    Counts: &1-2, &3-4, &5-6, &7-8

44. Flap (front) R - Step L 3×, Ball - Heel R
    **(FLAP - STEP 3×, BALL - HEEL)**
    Counts: &1-2, &3-4, &5-6, 7-8

45. Tap R (to R) - Heel (bounce) L, Ball - Heel R, Reverse All, Tap R (to R) - Heel (bounce) L, Ball R, Heel (drops) 4× L-R-L-R
    **(TAP - HEEL, BALL - HEEL, REVERSE ALL, TAP - HEEL, BALL, HEEL 4× ALT)**
    Counts: 1&2&, 3&4&, 5&6, &7&8

46. **(A)** Step - Step R-L, Shuffle - Ball Change R, Step R - Dig L, Step L - Dig R
    **(STEP - STEP, SHUFFLE - BALL CHANGE, STEP - DIG 2× ALT)**
    Counts: 1-2, &3&4, 5-6, 7-8

## 7. Beginning and Beginning II Levels

(B) Step - Step R-L, Shuffle - Ball Change R, Step R - Dig L, Step - Step L-R
**(STEP - STEP, SHUFFLE - BALL CHANGE, STEP - DIG, STEP - STEP)**
<u>Counts</u>: 1-2, &3&4, 5-6, 7-8

47. Step R (front) - Dig (back) L, Step (back) L - Dig (front) R, Step R (front) - Dig (back) L, Step - Step L-R
**(STEP - DIG 3× ALT: FRONT - BACK - FRONT, STEP - STEP)**
<u>Counts</u>: 1-2, 3-4, 5-6, 7-8

48. Heel (bounce) L - Heel Dig R - Heel (bounce) L - Step (Ball) R, Reverse All, Heel (bounce) L, Ball - Heel 3× R-L-R, Step L
**(HEEL - HEEL DIG - HEEL - STEP, REVERSE ALL, HEEL, BALL - HEEL 3× ALT, STEP)**
<u>Counts</u>: &<u>1</u>&2, &<u>3</u>&4, &, <u>5</u>&<u>6</u>&<u>7</u>&<u>8</u>

49. 3 Count Riff - Ball Change R 3×, Ball Change R 2×
**(3 COUNT RIFF - BALL CHANGE 3×, BALL CHANGE 2×)**
<u>Counts</u>: &a<u>1</u>, &2, &a<u>3</u>, &4, &a<u>5</u>, &6, &7, &8

50. Flap Cramp Roll R, Back Flap - Heel 2× R-L, Repeat All 2×, Flap - Heel (drop) R - Heel Dig L, Step L, Hold
**(FLAP CRAMP ROLL, BACK FLAP - HEEL 2× ALT, REPEAT ALL 2×, FLAP - HEEL - HEEL DIG, STEP, HOLD)**
<u>Counts</u>: &1&a2, &a3&a4, &5&a6, &a7&a8,
&1&a2, &a3&a4, &5&6-7, Hold: 8

51. **<u>Grapevine (regular)</u>**
Step 4× (side - cross back - side - cross front), Repeat All
**(SIDE - CROSS BACK - SIDE - CROSS FRONT REPEAT ALL)**
<u>Counts</u>: 1-2-3-4, 5-6-7-8

52. **<u>Grapevine Combination</u>**
Step - Step R-L (side - cross back), Jump R - Cross (front) L, Step R (to R), Reverse All
**(SIDE - CROSS, JUMP - CROSS, STEP, REVERSE ALL)**
<u>Counts</u>: 1-2&<u>3</u>-4, 5-6&<u>7</u>-8

53. **<u>Buffalo</u>** (Broadway Step = Heels Up)
Jump (ball) R (to R) - Shuffle L - Jump L (behind R, Coupé R), Repeat All 3×
**(JUMP - SHUFFLE - JUMP 4×)**
<u>Counts</u>: <u>1</u>&a2, <u>3</u>&a4, <u>5</u>&a6, <u>7</u>&a8

54. Flap - Heel R (to R), Back Flap - Heel L, Flap - Heel R (to R), Dig (toe) L, Hold
    **(FLAP - HEEL, BACK FLAP - HEEL, FLAP - HEEL, TOE DIG, HOLD)**
    Counts: &1-2, &3-4, &5-6, Dig: 7, Hold: 8

55. Brush (front) - Step 2× R-L, Flap - Ball Change 2× R-L
    **(BRUSH - STEP 2× ALT, FLAP - BALL CHANGE 2× ALT)**
    Counts: 1-2, 3-4, &5&6, &7&8

56. Flap 4× R-L-R-L, Flap - Heel (drop) R - Dig (toe) L, Reverse (Flap - Heel - Dig)
    **(FLAP 4× ALT, FLAP - HEEL - TOE DIG 2× ALT)**
    Counts: &1, &2, &3, &4, &5&6, &7&8

57. Flap - Ball Change R, Step - Step L-R, Reverse All, Back Flap 6× R-L-R-L-R-L, Step - Step R-L
    **(FLAP - BALL CHANGE, STEP - STEP, REVERSE ALL, BACK FLAP 6× ALT, STEP - STEP)**
    Counts: &1&2, 3-4, &5&6, 7-8,
    &1&2&3&4&5&6, 7-8

58. Flap - Heel R (to R), Back Flap - Heel L, Repeat All, Flap - Heel R - Shuffle L (over R) - Hop R - Step L (over R) 2×
    **(FLAP - HEEL, BACK FLAP - HEEL, REPEAT ALL, FLAP - HEEL - SHUFFLE - HOP - STEP 2×)**
    Counts: &1-2, &3-4, &5-6, &7-8
    &1-2&3&4, &5-6, &7&8

59. Heel (dig) - Toe (drop) R, Step - Step L-R, Reverse All, Heel (dig) - Toe (drop) R - Dig (ball) L, Hold, Reverse
    **(HEEL - TOE, STEP - STEP, REVERSE ALL, HEEL - TOE - DIG - HOLD 2× ALT)**
    Counts: 1&2&, 3&4&, 5&6, Hold: &, 7&8, Hold: &

60. Brush (front) R - Hop L - Step R, Reverse, Flap - Ball Change R, Flap 2× L-R
    **(BRUSH - HOP - STEP 2× ALT, FLAP - BALL CHANGE, FLAP 2× ALT)**
    Counts: &1-2, &3-4, &5&6, &7&8

61. Flap 2× R-L, Flap - Ball Change R, Reverse All
    **(FLAP 2× ALT, FLAP - BALL CHANGE, REVERSE ALL)**
    Counts: &1&2, &3&4, &5&6, &7&8

## 7. Beginning and Beginning II Levels

62. Back Flap - Heel 4×, R-L-R-L, Flap R - Heel - Heel L-R 4× Alternating
    **(BACK FLAP - HEEL 4× ALT, FLAP - HEEL - HEEL 4× ALT)**
    Counts: &1-2, &3-4, &5-6, &7-8,
    &1&2, &3&4, &5&6, &7&8

63. Scuff R - Hop L - Step R 4× Alternating,
    Syncopated: Scuff R - Hop L - Step R - Scuff L - Hop R - Step L - Ball Change R 2×
    **(SCUFF - HOP - STEP 4× ALT,
    SYNCOPATED: SCUFF - HOP - STEP - SCUFF - HOP - STEP - BALL CHANGE 2×)**
    Counts: &1-2, &3-4, &5-6, &7-8,
    Syncopated: &1&2&3&4, &5&6&7&8

64. **Buffalo Combination**
    Buffalo R 3×, Shuffle - Ball Change R
    **(BUFFALO 3×, SHUFFLE - BALL CHANGE)**
    Counts: 1&a2, 3&a4, 5&a6, &7&8

65. Flap 3× R-L-R, Heel (drop) R - Heel Dig L, Reverse All
    **(FLAP 3× ALT, HEEL - HEEL DIG, REVERSE ALL)**
    Counts: &1, &2, &3, &4, &5, &6, &7, &8

66. Shuffle R - Heel L, Flap - Heel 3× R-L-R, Reverse All
    **(SHUFFLE - HEEL, FLAP - HEEL 3× ALT, REVERSE ALL)**
    Counts: &a1, &a2, &a3, &a4, &a5, &a6, &a7, &a8

67. Flap - Ball Change 2× R-L, Brush (front) R - Hop L - Step R, Brush (front) L - Hop R - Step L
    **(FLAP - BALL CHANGE 2× ALT, BRUSH - HOP - STEP 2× ALT)**
    Counts: &1&2, &3&4, &5-6, &7-8

68. **Shag**
    Flap 3× R-L-R - Single Chug R (L knee raises, hands to shoulders, palms face front), Reverse All
    **(SHAG: FLAP 3× ALT, SINGLE CHUG, REVERSE ALL)**
    Counts: &1&2&3-4, &5&6&7-8

69. Back Flap R, Heel - Heel L-R, Reverse & Repeat All
    **(BACK FLAP - HEEL - HEEL 4× ALT)**
    Counts: &1&2, &3&4, &5&6, &7&8

70. Flap - Ball Change R, Shuffle L - Hop R - Step L, Flap 3× R-L-R, Ball Change L

**(FLAP - BALL CHANGE, SHUFFLE - HOP - STEP, FLAP 3× ALT, BALL CHANGE)**
Counts: &1&2, &3&4, &5, &6, &7, &8

71. Shuffle - Step (ball) 3× R-L-R, Heel - Heel (drop) L-R
    **(SHUFFLE - STEP 3× ALT, HEEL - HEEL)**
    Counts: 1&2, 3&4, 5&6, 7-8

72. Step 3× R-L-R (side-together-side) - Dig (toe) L, Reverse All, Step - Dig (toe) 4× Alt. R-L-R-L
    **(SIDE - TOGETHER - SIDE - DIG, REVERSE ALL, STEP - TOE DIG 4× ALT)**
    Counts: 1-2-3-4, 5-6-7-8,
    1-2, 3-4, 5-6, 7-8

73. **Jazz Square**
    Step R (to R), Step L (cross over R), Step R (to back), Step L (together), Repeat
    **(STEP - CROSS - STEP - STEP, REPEAT)**
    Counts: 1-2-3-4, 5-6-7-8

74. Jazz Square R, Jump R - Dig (ball) L, <u>Quick</u>: Jump - Dig (toe) 2× L-R
    **(JAZZ SQUARE, JUMP - TOE DIG, <u>QUICK</u>: JUMP - DIG 2× ALT)**
    Counts: 1-2-3-4, 5-6, &7&8

75. **Lindy**
    Flap - Ball Change R (to R), Step - Step L-R (cross back, step front), Reverse All
    **(FLAP - BALL CHANGE, STEP - STEP, REVERSE ALL)**
    Counts: &1&2, 3-4, &5&6, 7-8

76. Heel - Heel (weighted), Step - Step (balls), Repeat All, Step R - Toe Back L, Step L - Toe Back R
    **(HEEL - HEEL, STEP - STEP, REPEAT ALL, STEP - TOE BACK 2× ALT)**
    Counts: &1, &2, &3, &4, 5-6, 7-8

77. **Buck Time Step** (Single / Broadway Step = No Heels)
    Shuffle R - Hop L - Step R - Flap (forward) L - Step R, Reverse All
    **(SHUFFLE - HOP - STEP - FLAP - STEP, REVERSE ALL)**
    Counts: 8&1-2&3&, 4&5-6&7&

## 7. Beginning and Beginning II Levels

78. **Waltz Clog Time Step** (Single / Broadway Step = No Heels)
    Jump R (to R) – Shuffle - Ball Change L, Reverse, Step R - Scuff L - Hop L, Reverse
    **(JUMP – SHUFFLE - BALL CHANGE 2× ALT, STEP – SCUFF - HOP 2× ALT)**
    Counts: 1&2&3, 4&5&6,
           1-2-3, 4-5-6

79. **Scissors (Slow)**
    Step R (to R) - Cross L (over R) - Step R (to R) - Heel Dig L, Reverse All
    **(STEP - CROSS - STEP - HEEL DIG, REVERSE ALL)**
    Counts: 1-2-3-4, 5-6-7-8

80. **Scissors (fast)**
    Jump R (to R) - Cross L (over R) - Jump R (to R) - Heel Dig L, Reverse All & Repeat All
    **(JUMP - CROSS – JUMP - HEEL DIG, REVERSE ALL & REPEAT ALL)**
    Counts: &1&2, &3&4, &5&6, &7&8

81. **Shim Sham**
    Shuffle - Step 2× R-L, Shuffle - Ball Change R, Shuffle - Step R, Reverse All
    **(SHUFFLE - STEP 2× ALT, SHUFFLE - BALL CHANGE, SHUFFLE - STEP, REVERSE ALL)**
    Counts: &a1, &a2, &a3e&a4, &a5, &a6, &a7e&a8

82. Heel (weighted) R, Cross L (behind R), Jump R - Cross L (over R), Repeat All, Step R - Dig (toe, inside edge)
    **(HEEL - CROSS - JUMP - CROSS 2×, STEP - TOE DIG)**
    Counts: 1-2&3, 4-5&6, 7-8

83. **Riffs**
    (A) **4 Count Riff** (accents on counts 2-6)
    Toe (inside edge) - Scuff (heel) - Heel Dig - Toe (drop), Reverse
    **(TOE - SCUFF - HEEL DIG - TOE, REVERSE)**
    Counts: 1-2, 3-4, 5-6, 7-8
    (B) **5 Count Riff** (1 foot / accents on counts 1-3-5-7)
    Toe (inside edge) - Scuff (heel) - Heel Dig - Toe (drop) - Heel (bounce) R, Reverse All and Repeat All

## Tap Dance for All

   (TOE - SCUFF - HEEL DIG - TOE - HEEL, REVERSE ALL AND REPEAT ALL)
   Counts: &a1&2, &a3&4, &a5&6, &a7&8
(C) **5 Count Riff** (Two feet / accents on counts 1-3-5-7)
   Toe (inside edge) - Scuff (heel) R, Heel (bounce) L, Heel Dig, Toe (drop) R, Reverse All and Repeat All
   **(TOE - SCUFF - HEEL - HEEL DIG - TOE, REVERSE ALL AND REPEAT ALL)**
   Counts: &a1&2, &a3&4, &a5&6, &a7&8
(D) **6 Count Riff** (accents on counts 1-3-5-7)
   Toe (inside edge) - Scuff (heel) R, Heel (bounce) L, Heel Dig - Toe (drop) - Heel (bounce) R, Reverse All and Repeat All
   **(TOE - SCUFF - HEEL - HEEL DIG - TOE - HEEL, REVERSE ALL AND REPEAT ALL)**
   Counts: &a1&a2, &a3&a4, &a5&a6, &a7&a8
(E) **7 Count Riff** (accents on counts 1-2-3-4-5-6-7-8)
   Toe (inside edge) - Scuff (heel) R, Heel (bounce) L - Heel Dig - Toe (drop) R - Heel - Heel L-R, Reverse All and Repeat All
   **(TOE - SCUFF - HEEL, HEEL DIG - TOE - HEEL - HEEL, REVERSE ALL AND REPEAT ALL)**
   Counts: &a1e&a2, &a3e&a4, &a5e&a6, &a7e&a8

QUOTABLE QUOTES

*"The dancer ought to be light as a flame."—author unknown*

# 8

# Extra Combinations
## *(Beginning / Beginning II Levels)*

### *Beginning Level*

1. **(A)** Shuffle R 6×, Ball Change R 2×, Repeat All
    **(SHUFFLE 6×, BALL CHANGE 2×, REPEAT ALL)**
    <u>Counts</u>: &1&2&3&4&5&6, &7&8
    &1&2&3&4&5&6, &7&8
    **(B)** Shuffle R 2×, Ball Change R 2×, Repeat All
    **(SHUFFLE 2×, BALL CHANGE 2×, REPEAT ALL)**
    <u>Counts</u>: &1&2, &3&4, &5&6, &7&8
    **(C)** Shuffle - Ball - Heel (drop) 4× R-L-R-L
    **(SHUFFLE - BALL - HEEL 4× ALT)**
    <u>Counts</u>: &1&2, &3&4, &5&6, &7&8
    **(D)** Reverse All
    **(SHUFFLE 6×, BALL CHANGE 2×, REPEAT ALL ||
    SHUFFLE 2×, BALL CHANGE 2×, REPEAT ALL ||
    SHUFFLE - BALL - HEEL 4× ALT)**
2. **(A)** Shuffle R 4×, Toe Back - Ball Change R, Toe Back - Step R, Reverse All
    **(SHUFFLE 4×, TOE BACK - BALL CHANGE, TOE BACK - STEP, REVERSE ALL)**
    <u>Counts</u>: &1&2&3&4, 5&6, 7-8
    &1&2&3&4, 5&6, 7-8
    **(B)** Shuffle R 2×, Ball Change - Step R, Reverse All
    **(SHUFFLE 2×, BALL CHANGE - STEP, REVERSE ALL)**
    <u>Counts</u>: &1&2, &3-4, &5&6, &7-8
    **(C)** Toe Back - Step 4× R-L-R-L
    **(TOE BACK - STEP 4× ALT)**
    <u>Counts</u>: 1-2, 3-4, 5-6, 7-8

## Tap Dance for All

3. **(A)** Shuffle 3× R, Ball Change R, Step R - Hit L (inside of R front tap), Step L - Hit (inside of L front tap), Repeat All
   **(SHUFFLE 3×, BALL CHANGE, STEP - HIT 2× ALT, REPEAT ALL)**
   Counts: &1&2&3, &4, 5-6, 7-8
   &1&2&3, &4, 5-6, 7-8
   **(B)** Shuffle 6×, Ball Change - Step R, Reverse All
   **(SHUFFLE 6×, BALL CHANGE - STEP, REVERSE ALL)**
   Counts: &1&2&3&4&5&6, &7-8
   &1&2&3&4&5&6, &7-8

4. **(A)** Shuffle R - Hop, Step - Step R-L, Shuffle R - Hop L - Ball Change R - Step R, Hold, Reverse All
   **(SHUFFLE - HOP, STEP - STEP, SHUFFLE - HOP - BALL CHANGE - STEP, HOLD, REVERSE ALL)**
   Counts: &a1, 2-3, 4&5&6-7, Hold: 8
   &a1, 2-3, 4&5&6-7, Hold: 8
   **(B)** Shuffle - Ball Change 7×, Step R, Hold
   **(SHUFFLE - BALL CHANGE 7×, STEP, HOLD)**
   Counts: &1&2, &3&4, &5&6, &7&8
   &1&2, &3&4, &5&6-7, Hold: 8
   **(C)** Reverse All
   **(SHUFFLE - HOP, STEP - STEP, SHUFFLE - HOP - BALL CHANGE - STEP, HOLD, REVERSE ALL ||
   SHUFFLE - BALL CHANGE 7×, STEP, HOLD)**

5. **(A)** Step R - Shuffle - Ball Change L - Step L, Toe Back - Step 2× R-L, Repeat All
   **(STEP - SHUFFLE - BALL CHANGE - STEP, TOE BACK - STEP 2×, REPEAT ALL)**
   Counts: 1&2&3-4, 5-6, 7-8
   1&2&3-4, 5-6, 7-8
   **(B)** Step R - Shuffle - Ball Change L - Step L, Repeat All
   **(STEP - SHUFFLE - BALL CHANGE - STEP, REPEAT ALL)**
   Counts: 1&2&3-4, 5&6&7-8
   **(C)** Toe Back - Step 4× R-L-R-L
   **(TOE BACK - STEP 4× ALT)**
   Counts: 1-2, 3-4, 5-6, 7-8

## 8. *Extra Combinations*

6. **Crossing Brush Combination**
   Brush R: Out - Cross (over L) - Out - Back, Step R - Toe Back L, Ball Change - Toe Back L, Reverse All
   **(CROSS BRUSH: OUT - CROSS - OUT - BACK, STEP - TOE BACK, BALL CHANGE - TOE BACK, REVERSE ALL)**
   Counts: 1-2-3-4, 5-6, &7-8
   1-2-3-4, 5-6, &7-8

7. **Paradiddle / Paddle & Roll Combination**
   (Heel Dig - Back Flap - Heel Drop) 3× R-L-R, Heel Dig L, Hold, Reverse All
   **(PARADIDDLE / PADDLE & ROLL 3×, HEEL DIG, HOLD, REVERSE ALL)**
   Counts: 1&2&, 3&4&, 5&6&, 7, Hold: 8
   1&2&, 3&4&, 5&6&, 7, Hold: 8

8. **Maxie Ford Combination**
   (A) Maxie Ford (Shuffle - Jump - Toe Back) R, Step - Step L-R, Reverse All
   **(MAXIE FORD, STEP - STEP, REVERSE ALL)**
   Counts: &1&2, 3-4, &5&6, 7-8
   (B) Maxie Ford 3× R-L-R, Step - Step L-R
   **(MAXIE FORD 3× ALT, STEP - STEP)**
   Counts: &1&2, &3&4, &5&6, 7-8

9. Same as #8, Adding a Heel Drop to the Maxie Ford
   (Shuffle - Jump - Heel Drop - Toe Back)
   **(MAXIE FORD WITH HEEL DROP, STEP - STEP, REVERSE ALL ||
   MAXIE FORD WITH HEEL DROP 3×, STEP - STEP)**
   Counts: &1&a2, 3-4, &5&a6, 7-8
   &1&a2, &3&a4, &5&a6, 7-8

10. **Tack Annie** (Rhythmic Tap Step = Tap Weight Into Floor)
    (A) Brush (back) - Dig (ball) - Step R, Reverse All & Repeat R, Back Flap L - Ball Change (feet apart) R, Repeat All
    **(BRUSH - DIG - STEP 3× ALT, BACK FLAP - BALL CHANGE, REPEAT ALL)**
    Counts: &1-2, &3-4, &5-6, &7&8
    &1-2, &3-4, &5-6, &7&8
    (B) <u>Break</u>: Brush (back) - Dig (ball) - Step R, Back Flap L - Ball Change (feet apart) R, Repeat All

(**BREAK**: BRUSH - DIG - STEP, BACK FLAP - BALL CHANGE, REPEAT ALL)
Counts: &1-2, &3&4, &5-6, &7&8

(**C**) Break Cont.: Brush (back) - Dig (ball) - Step 2× R-L, Dbl Chug R-L 4×
(**BRUSH - DIG - STEP 2×, DBL CHUG 4×**)
Counts: &1-2, &3-4, &5, &6, &7, &8

11. **Irish Combination** (Broadway Step = Heels Up)
(**A**) (Travel Back): Shuffle R - Hop L - Step R, Reverse All & Repeat R, Step - Step L-R, Reverse All (Travel Front)
(**SHUFFLE - HOP - STEP 3× ALT, STEP - STEP, REVERSE ALL**)
Counts &1&2, &3&4, &5&6, 7-8
&1&2, &3&4, &5&6, 7-8

(**B**) Break: (In Place) Shuffle R - Hop L - Step R, Step - Step L-R, Reverse All
(**BREAK**: SHUFFLE - HOP - STEP, STEP - STEP, REVERSE ALL)
Counts: &1&2, 3-4, &5&6, 7-8

(**C**) Break Cont.: (Travel Back) Shuffle R - Hop L - Step R, Reverse All & Repeat R, Step - Step L-R
(**BREAK CONT**: SHUFFLE - HOP - STEP 3× ALT, STEP - STEP)
Counts: &1&2, &3&4, &5&6, 7-8

12. (**A**) Slap (front) R - Heel (bounce) L, Repeat 2× (side, back), Ball Change - Step R, Reverse All
(**SLAP - HEEL 3×: FRONT - SIDE - BACK, BALL CHANGE - STEP, REVERSE ALL**)
Counts: &1-2, &3-4, &5-6, &7-8
&1-2, &3-4, &5-6, &7-8

(**B**) Slap (front) R, Heel - Heel (drops) R-L, Repeat 2× (side, back), Ball Change - Step R, Reverse All
(**SLAP - HEEL - HEEL 3×: FRONT - SIDE - BACK, BALL CHANGE - STEP, REVERSE ALL**)
Counts: &1&2, &3&4, &5&6, &7-8
&1&2, &3&4, &5&6, &7-8

(**C**) Same as (**B**), use L-R Heel - Heel
(**SLAP - HEEL - HEEL 3×: FRONT - SIDE - BACK, BALL CHANGE - STEP, REVERSE ALL**)

## 8. *Extra Combinations*

Counts: &1&2, &3&4, &5&6, &7-8
&1&2, &3&4, &5&6, &7-8

13. **Single Front Essence** (Broadway Step = Heels Up)
    Jump R - Ball Change L (cross over R), Reverse All
    Break: Jump R, Ball Change L 3× (front - back - front)
    **(JUMP - BALL CHANGE, REVERSE All**
    **BREAK: JUMP, BALL CHANGE 3×: FRONT -**
    **BACK - FRONT)**
    Counts: 1&2, 3&4, 5&6&7&8

14. **Double Front Essence** (Broadway Step = Heels Up)
    Flap R, Brush (front) - Ball Change L (cross over R), Reverse All
    Break: Flap R, Brush - Ball Change L 3× (front - back - front)
    **(FLAP - BRUSH - BALL CHANGE, REVERSE ALL**
    **BREAK: FLAP, BRUSH - BALL CHANGE 3×: FRONT -**
    **BACK - FRONT)**
    Counts: &1&a2, &3&a4, &5&a6&a7&a8

15. Flap 2× R-L, Flap - Ball Change R, Reverse All, Brush (front) R -
    Hop L - Step (ball) R 4× R-L-R-L
    **(FLAP 2×, FLAP - BALL CHANGE, REVERSE ALL, BRUSH -**
    **HOP - STEP 4× ALT)**
    Counts: &1&2, &3&4, &5&6, &7&8
    &1-2, &3-4, &5-6, &7-8

16. **3 Count Riff Combination**
    Ball Change - 3 Count Riff, Repeat 2×, Ball Change R 2×
    **(BALL CHANGE - 3 COUNT RIFF 3×, BALL CHANGE 2×)**
    Counts: &1, &a2, &3, &a4, &5, &a6, &7&8

17. **4 Count Riff Combination**
    4 Count Riff 3× R-L-R, Step - Step L-R, Reverse All
    **(4 COUNT RIFF 3×, STEP - STEP, REVERSE ALL)**
    Counts: &<u>1</u>&2, &<u>3</u>&4, &<u>5</u>&6, 7-8
    &<u>1</u>&2, &<u>3</u>&4, &<u>5</u>&6, 7-8

18. Heel Dig - Heel Dig (weighted) R-L, Step - Step (balls) R-L,
    Repeat All, Ball Change R - Hold 4× (Apart - Together - Apart - Together)
    **(HEEL DIG - HEEL DIG, STEP - STEP, REPEAT ALL,**
    **BALL CHANGE - HOLD 4×)**
    Counts: 1-2-3-4, 5-6-7-8
    &1, Hold: 2, &3, Hold: 4, &5, Hold: 6, &7, Hold: 8

## Tap Dance for All

19. Ball Change - Step R, Dig (toe) - Step 2× L-R, Ball Change 2× L, Reverse All
    **(BALL CHANGE - STEP, DIG - STEP 2×, BALL CHANGE 2×, REVERSE ALL)**
    <u>Counts</u>: &1-2, 3-4, 5-6, &7&8
    &1-2, 3-4, 5-6, &7&8

20. **(A)** Shuffle 2× R, Ball Change - Step R, Heel Dig - Step 2× L-R, Reverse All
    **(SHUFFLE 2×, BALL CHANGE - STEP, HEEL DIG - STEP 2×, REVERSE ALL)**
    <u>Counts</u>: &1&2, &3-4, 5-6, 7-8
    &1&2, &3-4, 5-6, 7-8

    **(B)** Shuffle - Ball Change - Step R, Hold, Reverse All, Heel Dig - Step 4× R-L-R-L
    **(SHUFFLE - BALL CHANGE - STEP, HOLD, REVERSE ALL, HEEL DIG - STEP 4× ALT)**
    <u>Counts</u>: &1&2-3, Hold: 4, &5&6-7, Hold: 8
    1-2, 3-4, 5-6, 7-8

21. **(A)** Shuffle (to side) - Ball - Heel 3× R-L-R, Heel Drop 4× L-R-L-R, Reverse All
    **(SHUFFLE - BALL - HEEL 3× ALT, HEEL DROP 4×, REVERSE ALL)**
    <u>Counts</u>: &1&2, &3&4, &5&6, &7&8
    &1&2, &3&4, &5&6, &7&8

    **(B)** Shuffle (to side) - Ball - Heel R, Heel Drop 2× L-R, Reverse All
    **(SHUFFLE - BALL - HEEL, HEEL DROP 2×, REVERSE ALL)**
    <u>Counts</u>: &1&2, 3-4, &5&6, 7-8

    **(C)** Shuffle (to side) - Ball - Heel 4× R-L-R-L
    **(SHUFFLE - BALL - HEEL 4× ALT)**
    <u>Counts</u>: &1&2, &3&4, &5&6, &7&8

22. **(A)** Shuffle R - Heel (bounce) L 4×, Ball Change - Step 2× R-L
    **(SHUFFLE - HEEL 4×, BALL CHANGE - STEP 2×)**
    <u>Counts</u>: &a1, &a2, &a3, &a4, &5-6, &7-8

    **(B)** Hop L - Shuffle R - Hop L, Hop L - Shuffle R - Jump L, Reverse All
    **(HOP - SHUFFLE - HOP, HOP - SHUFFLE - JUMP, REVERSE ALL)**
    <u>Counts</u>: 1&a2, 3&a4, 5&a6, 7&a8

## 8. *Extra Combinations*

    (C) Repeat (A)
        **(SHUFFLE - HEEL 4×, BALL CHANGE - STEP 2×)**
        Counts: &a1, &a2, &a3, &a4, &5-6, &7-8
    (D) Hop L - Shuffle - Jump R, Reverse All,
        Rolling Shuffle 4× R-L-R-L
        **(HOP - SHUFFLE - JUMP, REVERSE ALL,**
        **ROLLING SHUFFLE 4× ALT)**
        Counts: 1&a2, 3&a4, &a5&a6&a7&a8

23. (A) Brush R - Heel (bounce) L 6× (brushes: front - back - front - back - front - back), Ball Change R 2×, Repeat All
        **(BRUSH - HEEL 6×, BALL CHANGE 2×, REPEAT ALL)**
        Counts: &1&2&3&4&5&6, &7&8
        &1&2&3&4&5&6, &7&8
    (B) Brush R - Heel (bounce) L 2×, Ball Change R 2×, Repeat All, Clap - Jump (both hands) 4×
        **(BRUSH - HEEL 2×, BALL CHANGE 2×, REPEAT ALL,**
        **CLAP - JUMP 4×)**
        Counts: &1&2, &3&4, &5&6, &7&8
        1-2, 3-4, 5-6, 7-8

24. Hop L - Shuffle - Step R, Shuffle - Ball Change L, Heel Dig - Step 2× L-R, Reverse All
    **(HOP - SHUFFLE - STEP, SHUFFLE - BALL CHANGE,**
    **HEEL DIG - STEP 2×, REVERSE ALL)**
    Counts: 1&a2, &3&4, 5-6, 7-8
        1&a2, &3&4, 5-6, 7-8

25. (A) Heel Dig - Ball Change R, Heel Dig - Step R, Reverse All
        **(HEEL DIG - BALL CHANGE, HEEL DIG - STEP,**
        **REVERSE ALL)**
        Counts: 1&2, 3-4, 5&6, 7-8
    (B) Step - Dig (ball) 4× R-L-R-L
        **(STEP - DIG 4× ALT)**
        Counts: 1-2, 3-4, 5-6, 7-8

26. (A) Heel (bounce) L - Tap R 3× (taps: front - back - side), Heel (bounce) L - Step R, Reverse All
        **(HEEL - TAP 3×: FRONT - BACK - SIDE, HEEL - STEP,**
        **REVERSE ALL)**
        Counts: &1, &2, &3, &4, &5, &6, &7, &8
    (B) Heel (bounce) L - Tap R - Heel (bounce) L - Step R, Reverse & Repeat All

(HEEL - TAP - HEEL - STEP, 4× ALT)
Counts: &1&2, &3&4, &5&6, &7&8

27. **Maxie Ford Combination**
    (A) Maxie Ford (with heel drop) R, Heel (bounce) R - Step L, Repeat All
    **(MAXIE FORD WITH HEEL DROP, HEEL - STEP, REPEAT ALL)**
    Counts: &1&a2, 3-4, &5&a6, 7-8
    (B) Maxie Ford (with heel drop) 3× R-L-R, Step - Step L-R
    **(MAXIE FORD WITH HEEL DROP 3× ALT, STEP - STEP)**
    Counts: &1&a2, &3&a4, &5&a6, 7-8

28. **Swing & Sway**
    Step R (to R) - Brush (back) L, Step L (behind R) - Step R, Reverse & Repeat All
    **(STEP - BRUSH - STEP - STEP 4× ALT)**
    Counts: 1&2&, 3&4&, 5&6&, 7&8&

29. **Shim Sham, With Break** (Simple & Regular)
    (A) Shuffle - Step 2× R-L, Shuffle - Ball Change R, Shuffle - Step R, Reverse All & Repeat R Side
    **(SHUFFLE - STEP 2×, SHUFFLE - BALL CHANGE - SHUFFLE - STEP, REVERSE ALL & REPEAT R SIDE)**
    Counts: &a1, &a2, &a3e&a4, &a5, &a6, &a7e&a8, &a1, &a2, &a3e&a4
    (B) **Break** (Simple)
    Step - Step L-R, Hop R - Step - Step - Step L-R-L
    **(STEP - STEP, HOP, STEP - STEP - STEP)**
    Counts: 5-6, &7&8
    (C) **Break** (Regular)
    Step L - Ball Change R, Hop L - Step R, Hop R, Step - Step - Step L-R-L
    **(STEP - BALL CHANGE, HOP - STEP, HOP, STEP - STEP - STEP)**
    Counts: 5e&, 6&, a7&8

30. **Irish** (with double ball change)
    (Travel Back) Shuffle R - Hop L - Step R, Reverse All & Repeat R Side, Ball Change 2× L, Reverse All (Travel Forward)
    **(SHUFFLE - HOP - STEP, REVERSE ALL & REPEAT R SIDE, BALL CHANGE 2×, REVERSE ALL)**

## 8. *Extra Combinations*

   Counts: &1&2, &3&4, &5&6, &7&8
   &1&2, &3&4, &5&6, &7&8

31. Slap R (to R) - Heel (bounce) L, Back Flap - Heel R, Reverse All & Repeat R Side, Flap - Heel 2× L-R
    **(SLAP - HEEL, BACK FLAP - HEEL, REVERSE ALL & REPEAT R SIDE, FLAP - HEEL 2×)**
    Counts: &1-2, &3-4, &5-6, &7-8
    &1-2, &3-4, &5-6, &7-8

32. **Back Flaps with Heel Drops**
    Back Flap - Heel (drop) 8× R-L-R-L-R-L-R-L
    **(BACK FLAP - HEEL 8× ALT)**
    Counts: &a1, &a2, &a3, &a4, &a5, &a6, &a7, &a8

33. Step (back) L - Brush (back) R - Heel (drop) L - Flap (front, raising back foot up) - Heel R, Repeat All 2×, Ball - Heel L, Step - Step R-L
    **(STEP - BRUSH - HEEL - FLAP - HEEL 3×, BALL - HEEL, STEP - STEP)**
    Counts: 1&2&3-4, 5&6&7-8
    1&2&3-4, 5-6, 7-8
    *Note: Good practice for Drawbacks

34. **Double Buffalo**
    Flap R - Shuffle L - Jump L (behind R, Coupé R), Repeat All 3×
    **(FLAP - SHUFFLE - JUMP, REPEAT ALL 3×)**
    Counts: &1&a2, &3&a4, &5&a6, &7&a8

35. Brush (front) R - Hop L - Step R, Brush (front) L - Hop R, Step L - Ball Change R, Repeat All 2×, Flap 4× R-L-R-L
    **(BRUSH - HOP - STEP, BRUSH - HOP - STEP - BALL CHANGE, REPEAT ALL 2×, FLAP 4× ALT)**
    Counts: &1-2, &a3&4, &5-6, &a7&8
    &1-2, &a3&4, &5, &6, &7, &8

36. Flap - Heel R - Step L, Flap - Heel R - Heel Dig L, Reverse All, Flap - Heel - Heel Dig 4× R-L-R-L
    **(FLAP - HEEL - STEP, FLAP - HEEL - HEEL DIG, REVERSE ALL, FLAP - HEEL - HEEL DIG 4× ALT)**
    Counts: &1&2&3&4, &5&6&7&8
    &1&2, &3&4, &5&6, &7&8

37. **(A)** Heel Dig - Ball Change R, Step R - Dig (toe) L, Reverse All
    **(HEEL DIG - BALL CHANGE, STEP - DIG, REVERSE ALL)**
    Counts: 1&2, 3-4, 5&6, 7-8
    **(B)** Heel Dig - Ball Change R 2×, Sugar (on balls twisting out on each step) 4× R-L-R-L
    **(HEEL DIG - BALL CHANGE 2×, SUGAR 4× ALT)**
    Counts: 1&2, 3&4, 5-6-7-8
38. Step R (to R), Shuffle - Ball Change - Ball Change L, Kick - Ball Change L 2×, Reverse All
    **(STEP, SHUFFLE - BALL CHANGE - BALL CHANGE, KICK - BALL CHANGE 2×, REVERSE ALL)**
    Counts: 1, &2&3&4, 5&6, 7&8
    1, &2&3&4, 5&6, 7&8
39. **Shag Combination**
    **(A)** Shag (Flap 3× R-L-R, Single Chug R) 2× R-L
    **(SHAG 2× ALT)**
    Counts: &1&2&3-4, &5&6&7-8
    **(B)** Step R, Hold, Heel Dig L, Ball Change L 2×, Hold, Sugar 2× L-R
    **(STEP, HOLD, HEEL DIG, BALL CHANGE 2×, HOLD, SUGAR 2× ALT)**
    Counts: 1, Hold: 2, 3&4&5, Hold: 6, 7-8
40. **(A)** Heel Dig - Toe (drop) R, Heel - Heel (bounce) R, Reverse All
    **(HEEL DIG - TOE, HEEL - HEEL, REVERSE ALL)**
    Counts: 1-2, 3-4, 5-6, 7-8
    **(B)** Heel - Heel (weighted) R-L, Step - Step R-L, Twist R: Toes - Heels - Toes, Chug (forward)
    **(HEEL - HEEL, STEP - STEP, TWIST R: TOES - HEELS - TOES, CHUG)**
    Counts: 1-2, 3-4, 5-6-7, 8

## *Beginning II Level*

1. **(A)** Slap R (to R) - Heel - Heel R-L, Back Flap R - Heel - Heel L-R, Reverse All
    **(SLAP - HEEL - HEEL, BACK FLAP - HEEL - HEEL, REVERSE ALL)**
    Counts: &1&2&3&4, &5&6&7&8

## 8. *Extra Combinations*

**(B)** Slap R (to R) - Heel - Heel R-L, Back Flap R - Heel - Heel L-R, Heel (bounce) R, Ball - Heel 3× L-R-L (Jazz Square), Step R
**(SLAP - HEEL - HEEL, BACK FLAP - HEEL - HEEL, HEEL, BALL - HEEL 3× ALT, STEP)**
Counts: &1&2, &3&4, &5, &6, &7-8

2. **Double Shuffle** (NOT The Rhythm of a Regular Shuffle)
Shuffle - Shuffle
**(SHUFFLE - SHUFFLE)**
Counts: 1&a2, 3&a4, 5&a6, 7&a8

3. **Double Shuffle Combination**
Double Shuffle - Dig (ball) R, Repeat 2×, Heel (drop) R - Toe Back L - Heel (bounce) R - Step L, Repeat All
**(DOUBLE SHUFFLE - DIG, REPEAT 2×, HEEL - TOE BACK - HEEL - STEP, REPEAT ALL)**
Counts: &1&a2, &3&a4, &5&a6, &7&8

4. **Paradiddle / Paddle & Roll Combination**
   **(A)** Paradiddle 3× R-L-R, Heel Dig L, Hold, Reverse All
   **(PARADIDDLE / PADDLE & ROLL 3× ALT, HEEL DIG, HOLD, REVERSE ALL)**
   Counts: 1&2&, 3&4&, 5&6&, 7, Hold: 8
   1&2&, 3&4&, 5&6&, 7, Hold: 8
   **(B)** Break: Paradiddle R, Heel Dig L, Hold, Reverse All, Paradiddle 3× R-L-R, Heel Dig L, Hold
   **(BREAK: PARADIDDLE - HEEL DIG, HOLD, REVERSE ALL, PARADIDDLE 3× ALT, HEEL DIG, HOLD)**
   Counts: 1&2&, 3, Hold: 4, 5&6&, 7, Hold: 8
   1&2&, 3&4&, 5&6&, 7, Hold: 8

5. **Traveling Flap - Heels**
   **(A) Single**
   Flap R (to R) - Heel R, Back Flap - Heel L, Repeat All
   **(SINGLE: FLAP - HEEL, BACK FLAP - HEEL, REPEAT ALL)**
   Counts: &1-2, &3-4, &5-6, &7-8
   **(B) Double**
   Flap R (to R) - Heel - Heel L-R, Back Flap L - Heel - Heel R-L, Repeat All

## Tap Dance for All

  (**DOUBLE: FLAP - HEEL - HEEL, BACK FLAP - HEEL - HEEL, REPEAT ALL**)
  Counts: &1&2, &3&4, &5&6, &7&8
 (**C**) <u>Triple</u>
  Flap R (to R) - Heel - Heel L-R, Back Flap L - Heel - Heel R-L, Heel Dig R, Repeat All
  (**TRIPLE: FLAP - HEEL - HEEL, BACK FLAP - HEEL - HEEL - HEEL DIG, REPEAT ALL**)
  Counts: &1&2, &3&a4, &5&6, &7&a8

6. **Flap & Back Flap Double Heels**
 (**A**) (Travel Forward) Flap R - Heel - Heel L-R, Reverse All & Repeat R, Step L, Hold
  (**FLAP - HEEL - HEEL 3× ALT, STEP, HOLD**)
  Counts: &1&2, &3&4, &5&6-7, Hold: 8
 (**B**) (Travel Back) Back Flap R - Heel - Heel L-R, Reverse All & Repeat R, Step L, Hold
  (**BACK FLAP - HEEL - HEEL 3× ALT, STEP, HOLD**)
  Counts: &1&2, &3&4, &5&6-7, Hold: 8

7. **Flap-Heel Grapevine**
 (Travel R) Flap - Heel R (to R), Back Flap - Heel L (behind R), Repeat All 3× (cross over R 2nd ×, behind R 3rd ×), Flap - Heel R (to R), Ball Change L
 (**FLAP - HEEL - BACK FLAP - HEEL 3×, FLAP - HEEL, BALL CHANGE**)
 Counts: &a1&a2, &a3&a4, &a5&a6, &a7, &8

8. **Drawbacks** (Start R Heel Down, R Toe Tap Up)
 Brush (back) R - Heel L - Step R 8× R-L-R-L-R-L-R-L
 (**BRUSH - HEEL - STEP 8× ALT**)
 Counts: &a1, &a2, &a3, &a4, &a5, &a6, &a7, &a8

9. **Military Cramp Roll**
 Ball R - Ball L, Heel - Heel (drops) R-L 8×
 (**BALL - BALL, HEEL - HEEL 8×**)
 Counts: e&a<u>1</u>, e&a<u>2</u>, e&a<u>3</u>, e&a<u>4</u>, e&a<u>5</u>, e&a<u>6</u>, e&a<u>7</u>, e&a<u>8</u>

10. **Military Cramp Roll Combination**
 Military Cramproll R 3×, Step - Step R-L, Repeat All 3×
 (**MILITARY CRAMP ROLL 3×, STEP - STEP, REPEAT ALL 3×**)
 Counts: e&a<u>1</u>, e&a<u>2</u>, e&a<u>3</u>, &4, e&a<u>5</u>, e&a<u>6</u>, e&a<u>7</u>, &8
  e&a<u>1</u>, e&a<u>2</u>, e&a<u>3</u>, &4, e&a<u>5</u>, e&a<u>6</u>, e&a<u>7</u>, &8

## 8. *Extra Combinations*

11. **(A)** Back Flap R, Shuffle, Ball Change L 2×, Reverse All
    **(BACK FLAP, SHUFFLE, BALL CHANGE 2×, REVERSE ALL)**
    Counts: &1, &2, &3&4, &5, &6, &7&8
    **(B)** Back Flap R, Shuffle, Ball Change L 2×, Dig (ball) - Step 2× L-R
    **(BACK FLAP, SHUFFLE, BALL CHANGE 2×, DIG - STEP 2×)**
    Counts: &1, &2, &3&4, 5-6, 7-8

12. Stamp - Stamp R-L, Brush (back) R - Heel (bounce) L, Repeat All, Stamp - Stamp R-L, Double Chug R 3×
    **(STAMP - STAMP, BRUSH - HEEL, REPEAT ALL, STAMP - STAMP, DBLE CHUG 3×)**
    Counts: &1, &2, &3, &4, &5, &6, &7, &8

13. Same as #12, but alternate feet by doing a Stamp - Stomp
    (Stomp = no weight)
    Stamp - Stomp R-L, Brush (back) L - Heel (bounce) R, Reverse All, Stamp - Stomp R-L, Double Chug L 3×
    **(STAMP - STOMP, BRUSH - HEEL, REVERSE ALL, STAMP - STOMP, DBLE CHUG 3×)**
    Counts: &1, &2, &3, &4, &5, &6, &7, &8

14. **Back Essence**
    Brush (back) R - Step R (cross behind L), Ball Change L, Reverse All & Repeat All
    **(BRUSH - CROSS - BALL CHANGE 4× ALT)**
    Counts: &1&2, &3&4, &5&6, &7&8

15. **Single Waltz Clog**
    **(A)** Step R - Shuffle - Ball Change L, Reverse All, Step R - Scuff L - Hop R 2× R-L
    **(STEP - SHUFFLE - BALL CHANGE 2× ALT, STEP - SCUFF - HOP 2× ALT)**
    Counts: 1&2&3, 4&5&6, 1-2-3, 4-5-6
    **(B)** Step R - Shuffle - Ball Change L, Reverse All, Step R - Scuff L - Hop R - Step L, Hold 2 counts
    **(STEP - SHUFFLE - BALL CHANGE, REVERSE ALL, STEP - SCUFF - HOP - STEP, HOLD 2 CTS)**
    Counts: 1&2&3, 4&5&6, 1-2-3-4, Hold: 5-6

16. **Double Waltz Clog**
    Same as #15, but start with a Flap instead of a Step

(A) Flap R - Shuffle - Ball Change L, Reverse All, Step R - Scuff L - Hop R 2× R-L
   **(FLAP - SHUFFLE - BALL CHANGE 2× ALT, STEP - SCUFF - HOP 2× ALT)**
   Counts: &1&2&3, &4&5&6, 1-2-3, 4-5-6
(B) Flap R - Shuffle - Ball Change L, Reverse All, Step R - Scuff L - Hop R - Step L, Hold 2 counts
   **(FLAP - SHUFFLE - BALL CHANGE, REVERSE ALL, STEP - SCUFF - HOP - STEP, HOLD 2 CTS)**
   Counts: &1&2&3, &4&5&6, 1-2-3-4, Hold: 5-6

17. **Double Shuffle Combination**
    Double Shuffle 3× R, Ball R, Heel (drops) 4× L-R-L-R
    **(DOUBLE SHUFFLE 3×, HEEL 4× ALT)**
    Counts: 1&a2, 3&a4, 5&a6, &7&a8

18. (A) Flap - Heel 8× R-L-R-L-R-L-R-L (travel forward), Back Flap - Heel 8× R-L-R-L-R-L-R-L (travel back)
    **(FORWARD: FLAP - HEEL 8× ALT, BACK: BACK FLAP - HEEL 8× ALT)**
    Counts: &a1&a2&a3&a4&a5&a6&a7&a8
    &a1&a2&a3&a4&a5&a6&a7&a8
    (B) Flap - Heel 4× R-L-R-L (travel forward), Back Flap - Heel 4× R-L-R-L (travel back)
    **(FORWARD: FLAP - HEEL 4× ALT, BACK: BACK FLAP - HEEL 4× ALT)**
    Counts: &a1&a2&a3&a4, &a5&a6&a7&a8
    (C) Flap - Heel 2× R-L (travel forward), Back Flap - Heel 2× R-L, (travel back), Flap - Heel 4× R-L-R-L (travel forward)
    **(FORWARD: FLAP - HEEL 2× ALT, BACK: BACK FLAP - HEEL 2× ALT, FORWARD: FLAP - HEEL 4× ALT)**
    Counts: &a1, &a2, &a3, &a4, &a5, &a6, &a7, &a8

19. Heel (bounce) L - Shuffle R - Heel (bounce) L, Toe Back R - Heel (bounce) L, Ball - Heel R - Heel Dig L, Reverse All & Repeat R, Ball Change - Kick - Step L, Clap
    **(HEEL - SHUFFLE - HEEL, TOE BACK - HEEL, BALL - HEEL - HEEL DIG, REVERSE ALL & REPEAT R, BALL CHANGE - KICK - STEP, CLAP)**
    Counts: 1&a2, &3&a4, 5&a6, &7&a8
    1&a2, &3&a4, &5-6-7-8

## 8. Extra Combinations

20. **Scissors (Fast)**
    Jump R (to R) - Cross (front) L - Jump R (to R) -
    Heel Dig L (to L) 4× R-L-R-L
    **(JUMP - CROSS - JUMP - HEEL DIG 4× ALT)**
    Counts: &1&2, &3&4, &5&6, &7&8

21. Flap Cramp Roll R 3×, Stamp R, Hold, Reverse All
    **(FLAP CRAMP ROLL 3×, STAMP, HOLD, REVERSE ALL)**
    Counts: &1&a2, &3&a4, &5&a6-7, Hold: 8
    &1&a2, &3&a4, &5&a6-7, Hold: 8

22. **Rolling Shuffle Combination**
    **(A)** Step R, Shuffle (front) - Jump 7× L-R-L-R-L-R-L
    **(STEP, SHUFFLE FRONT - JUMP 7× ALT)**
    Counts: 1, &a2, &a3, &a4, &a5, &a6, &a7, &a8
    **(B)** Shuffle (side) - Jump 8× R-L-R-L-R-L-R-L
    **(ROLLING SHUFFLE SIDE 8× ALT)**
    Counts: &a1, &a2, &a3, &a4, &a5, &a6, &a7, &a8
    **(C)** Shuffle (front) - Jump 2× R-L, Shuffle (side) - Jump 2× R-L,
    Shuffle (back) - Jump 2× R-L, Shuffle (front) - Jump R,
    Shuffle (back) - Jump L
    **(ROLLING SHUFFLE FRONT 2× ALT,**
    **ROLLING SHUFFLE SIDE 2× ALT,**
    **ROLLING SHUFFLE BACK 2× ALT,**
    **ROLLING SHUFFLE FRONT,**
    **ROLLING SHUFFLE BACK)**
    Counts: &a1, &a2, &a3, &a4, &a5, &a6, &a7, &a8
    **(D)** Shuffle (back) - Jump 2× R-L, Shuffle (side) - Jump 2× R-L,
    Shuffle (front) - Jump 2× R-L, Shuffle (back) - Jump R,
    Shuffle (front) - Jump L
    **(ROLLING SHUFFLE BACK 2× ALT,**
    **ROLLING SHUFFLE SIDE 2× ALT,**
    **ROLLING SHUFFLE FRONT 2× ALT,**
    **ROLLING SHUFFLE BACK,**
    **ROLLING SHUFFLE FRONT)**
    Counts: &a1, &a2, &a3, &a4, &a5, &a6, &a7, &a8

23. **(A)** Ball - Heel 3× R-L-R, Toe R (lift to R) - Heel R (bounce to R),
    Ball (tap) 2× L, Heel (bounce) 2× L, Toe L (lift to L),
    Heel L (bounce to L) 2×

(BALL - HEEL 3× ALT, TOE - HEEL, BALL 2×, HEEL 2×,
  TOE 2×, HEEL 2×)
  Counts: 1&, 2&, 3&, 4&, 5&, 6&, 7&, 8&

  **(B)** Cramp Roll R, Ball 4× R-L-R-L, Heel (drop) 4× R-L-R-L,
  Toe (lift - out) 4× R-L-R-L, Heel (drop - out) 4× R-L-R-L,
  Cramp Roll R (feet apart), Stamp R (feet together), Clap
  **(CRAMP ROLL, BALL 4×, HEEL 4×, TOE 4×, HEEL 4×,
  CRAMP ROLL, STAMP, CLAP)**
  Counts: 1&2&, 3e&a, 4e&a, 5e&a, 6e&a, 7e&a, 8-&

24. Reverse of #23
    **(A)** Heel Dig - Toe (drop) 3× R-L-R, Heel (bounce to R),
    Toe (lift to R), Heel (dig) 2× L, Toe (drop) 2× L,
    Heel L (bounce to L) 2×, Toe L (lift to L) 2×
    **(HEEL DIG - TOE 3× ALT, HEEL - TOE, HEEL DIG 2×,
    TOE 2×, HEEL 2×, TOE 2×)**
    Counts: 1&2&3&, 4&, 5&, 6&, 7&, 8&

    **(B)** Reverse Cramp Roll R, Weighted Heel Dig 4× R-L-R-L,
    Toe (drop) 4× R-L-R-L, Heel (bounce - out) 4× R-L-R-L,
    Toe (lift - out) 4× R-L-R-L, Reverse Cramp Roll R, Stamp R,
    Clap
    **(REVERSE CRAMP ROLL, WEIGHTED HEEL
    DIG 4× ALT, TOE 4× ALT, HEEL 4×, TOE 4×,
    REVERSE CRAMP ROLL, STAMP, CLAP)**
    Counts: 1&2&, 3e&a, 4e&a, 5e&a, 6e&a, 7e&a, 8-&

25. **(A)** 4 Count Riff R, Heel - Heel (bounces) R, Reverse All
    **(4 COUNT RIFF, HEEL - HEEL, REVERSE ALL)**
    Counts: 1&2&, 3-4, 5&6&, 7-8

    **(B)** Double Paradiddle R, Paradiddle 2× L-R
    (pause last count of the Paradiddle)
    **(DOUBLE PARADIDDLE, PARADIDDLE 2× ALT)**
    Counts: 1&2&3&, 4&5&6&7-8

26. **Triplet Combination**
    **(A)** Ball - Heel (drop) R - Heel (bounce) L 8×, Heel Dig -
    Toe (drop) R - Heel (bounce) L 8×
    **(BALL - HEEL - HEEL 8×, HEEL DIG - TOE DROP -
    HEEL 8×)**
    Counts: 1&a, 2&a, 3&a, 4&a, 5&a, 6&a, 7&a, 8&a
           1&a, 2&a, 3&a, 4&a, 5&a, 6&a, 7&a, 8&a

## 8. Extra Combinations

- **(B)** Ball - Heel (drop) R - Heel (bounce) L 4×, Heel Dig - Toe (drop) R - Heel (bounce) L 4×
  **(BALL - HEEL - HEEL 4×, HEEL DIG - TOE DROP - HEEL 4×)**
  Counts: 1&a, 2&a, 3&a, 4&a, 5&a, 6&a, 7&a, 8&a
- **(C)** Break: Ball - Heel (drop) R - Heel (bounce) L 2×, Heel Dig - Toe (drop) R - Heel (bounce) 2×, Ball - Heel (drop) R - Heel (bounce) L, Heel Dig - Toe (drop) R - Heel (bounce) 2×, Ball R - Heel (bounce) - Heel (drop) L-R
  **(BALL - HEEL - HEEL 2×, HEEL DIG - TOE DROP - HEEL 2×, BALL - HEEL - HEEL, HEEL DIG - TOE DROP - HEEL 2×, BALL - HEEL - HEEL)**
  Counts: 1&a, 2&a, 3&a, 4&a, 5&a, 6&a, 7&a, 8&a

27. **(A)** Step R - Heel Dig - Toe (drop) L 2×, Stamp R, Reverse All
    **(STEP - HEEL DIG - TOE 2×, STAMP, REVERSE ALL)**
    Counts: 1&2, &3&4, 5&6, &7&8
- **(B)** (Twisting to L) Step R - Heel L (lift to L) - Toe L (lift to L) 4×, Step - Step R-L
  **(TWISTING L: STEP - HEEL - TOE 4×, STEP - STEP)**
  Counts: 1&2, &3&, 4&5, &6&, 7-8
- **(C)** Repeat **(A)**
  **(STEP - HEEL DIG - TOE 2×, STAMP, REVERSE ALL)**
  Counts: 1&2, &3&4, 5&6, &7&8
- **(D)** (Twisting R) Ball - Heel (drop to R) - Toe (lift to R) - Heel (drop to R) R, Scuff - Step L, Crossing Shuffle R 2× (cross over L, uncross), Stamp - Stamp R-L
  **(TWIST R: BALL - HEEL - TOE - HEEL, SCUFF, CROSSING SHUFFLE 2×, STAMP - STAMP)**
  Counts: 1&2&, 3-4, &5&6, 7-8

QUOTABLE QUOTE

*"To watch us dance is to hear our hearts speak."*—Hopi Saying

# 9

# Beginning III / Intermediate / Advanced Levels

1. Shuffle R 31× (fast) - Step R, Reverse All
   **(SHUFFLE 31× - STEP, REVERSE ALL)**
   <u>Counts</u>: &1, &2, &3, &4, &5, &6, &7, &8
          &1, &2, &3, &4, &5, &6, &7, &8
          &1, &2, &3, &4, &5, &6, &7, &8
          &1, &2, &3, &4, &5, &6, &7-8

2. Shuffle R - Heel L 14× (fast) - Step R, Hold, Reverse All
   **(SHUFFLE - HEEL 14×, STEP - HOLD, REVERSE ALL)**
   <u>Counts</u>: &a1, &a2, &a3, &a4, &a5, &a6, &a7, &a8
          &a1, &a2, &a3, &a4, &a5, &a6, 7, Hold: 8

3. **Paradiddle (Or Paddle & Roll) Combination**
   **(A)** Paradiddle 3× R-L-R, Heel Dig L, Hold, Reverse All
       **(PARADIDDLE 3× ALT, HEEL DIG, HOLD, REVERSE ALL)**
       <u>Counts</u>: 1&2&, 3&4&, 5&6&, 7, Hold: 8
               1&2&, 3&4&, 5&6&, 7, Hold: 8
   **(B)** Paradiddle R, Heel Dig L, Hold, Reverse All, Hold
       **(PARADIDDLE - HEEL DIG, HOLD, REVERSE ALL, HOLD)**
       <u>Counts</u>: 1&2&, 3, Hold: 4, 5&6&-7, Hold: 8
   **(C)** <u>Break</u>: Paradiddle 2× R-L, Toe Back R - Heel (bounce) L - Step - Step R-L, Hold
       **(BREAK: PARADIDDLE 2× ALT, TOE BACK - HEEL - STEP - STEP, HOLD)**
       <u>Counts</u>: 1&2&, 3&4&, 5&6-7, Hold: 8)

### 9. Beginning III / Intermediate / Advanced Levels

4. **7-7 Combination**
   **(A)** Heel (bounce) L - Heel Dig R - Brush (back) R, Repeat 7×,
   Heel (bounce) L - Step (ball) R, Reverse All
   **(HEEL - HEEL DIG - BRUSH 7×, HEEL - STEP, REVERSE ALL)**
   Counts: &1&, a2&, a3&, a4&, a5&, a6&, a7&, a8
   &1&, a2&, a3&, a4&, a5&, a6&, a7&, a8
   **(B)** Heel (bounce) L - Heel Dig R - Brush (back) R, Repeat 3×,
   Heel (bounce) L - Step (ball) R, Reverse All
   **(HEEL - HEEL DIG - BRUSH 3×, HEEL - STEP, REVERSE ALL)**
   Counts: &1&, a2&, a3&, a4, &5&, a6&, a7&, a8
   **(C)** Heel (bounce) L - Heel Dig R - Brush (back) R,
   Heel (bounce) L - Step (ball) R, Reverse All,
   Heel (bounce) L - Heel Dig R - Brush (back) R, Repeat 3×,
   Heel (bounce) L - Step R
   **(HEEL - HEEL DIG, BRUSH - HEEL - STEP, REVERSE ALL, HEEL - HEEL DIG - BRUSH 3×, HEEL - STEP)**
   Counts: &1&, a2, &3&, a4, &5&, a6&, a7&, a8

5. **(A)** Shuffle - Ball - Heel 3× R-L-R, Tap L (to L) -
   Heel (bounce) R 2×, Reverse All
   **(SHUFFLE - BALL - HEEL 3× ALT, TAP - HEEL 2×, REVERSE ALL)**
   Counts: &1&2, &3&4, &5&6, &7&8
   &1&2, &3&4, &5&6, &7&8
   **(B)** Shuffle - Ball - Heel, Tap L (to L) - Heel (bounce) R 2×, Reverse,
   Shuffle - Ball - Heel 3× R-L-R, Tap L (to L) -
   Heel (bounce) R 2×
   **(SHUFFLE - BALL - HEEL, TAP - HEEL 2×, REVERSE, SHUFFLE - BALL - HEEL 3×, TAP - HEEL 2×)**
   Counts: &1&2, &3&4, &5&6, &7&8
   &1&2, &3&4, &5&6, &7&8

6. Brush (back) R - Heel (bounce) L - Shuffle - Toe - Heel R,
   Reverse & Repeat R, Shuffle Cramp Roll L, Reverse All
   **(BRUSH - HEEL - SHUFFLE - TOE - HEEL 3× ALT, SHUFFLE CRAMP ROLL, REVERSE ALL)**
   Counts: &a1&a2, &a3&a4, &a5&a6, &a7&a8
   &a1&a2, &a3&a4, &a5&a6, &a7&a8

## Tap Dance for All

7. **(A)** Hop L - Shuffle R - Hop L, Repeat, Hop L - Shuffle R 3×, Jump R, Reverse All
   **(HOP - SHUFFLE - HOP 2×, HOP - SHUFFLE 3×, JUMP, REVERSE ALL)**
   Counts: 1&a2, 3&a4, 5&a6&a7&a8
   1&a2, 3&a4, 5&a6&a7&a8

   **(B)** Hop L - Shuffle R - Hop L, Hop L - Shuffle - Jump R, Reverse All,
   Hop L - Shuffle R - Jump R, Reverse, Rolling Shuffle (Shuffle - Jump) 4× R-L-R-L
   **(HOP - SHUFFLE - HOP, HOP - SHUFFLE - JUMP, REVERSE ALL,**
   **HOP - SHUFFLE - JUMP, REVERSE, ROLLING SHUFFLE 4× ALT)**
   Counts: 1&a2, 3&a4, 5&a6, 7&a8
   1&a2, 3&a4, &a5&a6&a7&a8

8. Brush (back) R - Heel (bounce) - Shuffle - Step R, Reverse All & Repeat R, Heel (bounce) R, Ball - Heel L - Step R, Reverse All
   **(BRUSH - HEEL - SHUFFLE - STEP 3× ALT, HEEL - BALL - HEEL - STEP, REVERSE ALL)**
   Counts: &1&a2, &3&a4, &5&a6, &7&8
   &1&a2, &3&a4, &5&a6, &7&8

9. Heel (bounce) L - Flap R, Heel - Heel L-R, Heel Dig L, Reverse All & Repeat R, Heel (bounce) R - Ball - Heel L - Step R, Reverse All
   **(HEEL - FLAP - HEEL - HEEL - HEEL DIG 3× ALT, HEEL - BALL - HEEL - STEP, REVERSE ALL)**
   Counts: 1&2&3-4, 5&6&7-8
   1&2&3-4, 5-6-7-8

10. **(A)** Brush (back) R - Hop L, Flap 2× R-L, Step R - Heel Dig L, Reverse All
    **(BRUSH - HOP, FLAP 2×, STEP - HEEL DIG, REVERSE ALL)**
    Counts: &1, &2&3, &4, &5, &6&7, &8

    **(B)** Brush (back) R - Hop L, Flap 2× R-L, Ball - Heel R - Heel Dig L, Reverse All
    **(BRUSH - HOP, FLAP 2×, BALL - HEEL - HEEL DIG, REVERSE ALL)**
    Counts: &1&2, &3&a4, &5&6, &7&a8

## 9. Beginning III / Intermediate / Advanced Levels

11. Brush (front) R - Hop L, Brush (back) R - Hop L, Repeat 2×, Ball Change R 2×
    **(BRUSH - HOP 6×: FRONT - BACK - FRONT - BACK - BACK, BALL CHANGE 2×)**
    Counts: &1&2, &3&4, &5&6, &7&8

12. Flap 7× R-L-R-L-R-L-R, Heel (drop) R, Reverse All
    **(FLAP 7× ALT, HEEL, REVERSE ALL)**
    Counts: &1&2&3&4&5&6&7-8
    &1&2&3&4&5&6&7-8

13. **(A)** Brush (front) R - Hop L, Brush (back) R - Hop L, Shuffle R, Step - Step R-L, Heel (drop) L - Heel Dig R
    **(BRUSH - HOP 2×, SHUFFLE - STEP - STEP - HEEL - HEEL DIG)**
    Counts: &1&2, &a3&a4
    **(B)** Brush (back) R - Hop L, Flap 2× R-L, Ball - Heel R - Heel Dig L
    **(BRUSH - HOP, FLAP 2×, BALL - HEEL - HEEL DIG)**
    Counts: &5, &6&7, &a8

14. Flap - Heel R, Toe (back) L - Heel (bounce), Reverse, Flap - Heel 3× R-L-R, Toe (back) L - Heel (bounce) R
    **(FLAP - HEEL, TOE BACK - HEEL, REVERSE, FLAP - HEEL 3×, TOE BACK - HEEL)**
    Counts: &a1, &2, &a3, &4, &a5, &a6, &a7, &8

15. **(A)** Shuffle - Jump - Heel R, Toe Back L - Heel (bounce) R, Reverse All
    **(SHUFFLE - JUMP - HEEL, TOE BACK - HEEL, REVERSE ALL)**
    Counts: &1&2, 3-4, &5&6, 7-8
    **(B)** Shuffle - Toe-Heel 3× R-L-R, Toe Back L - Heel (bounce) R
    **(SHUFFLE - TOE - HEEL 3×, TOE BACK - HEEL)**
    Counts: &1&2, &3&4, &5&6, 7-8

16. 3 Count Riff - Back Flap - Heel 3× R-L-R, Flap - Heel 2× L-R, Reverse All
    **(3 COUNT RIFF - BACK FLAP - HEEL 3×, FLAP - HEEL 2×, REVERSE ALL)**
    Counts: &a1&a2, &a3&a4, &a5&a6, &a7, &a8

17. **<u>Gum Off the Shoe Combination</u>** (Drawback with an added Shuffle - Heel
    *Gum Off the Shoe was Mom's name for this combination - she*

*thought it felt like scraping gum off your shoe, and it gave her students a fun way to remember the combination.*

    **(A)** Brush (back) R - Heel (bounce) L - Shuffle R - Heel (bounce) L, Step (ball) R (rock L toe up as you step on R), Reverse All
    **(BRUSH - HEEL - SHUFFLE - HEEL - STEP, REVERSE ALL)**
    Counts: &a1&a2, &a3&a4

    **(B)** <u>Break</u>: Brush (back) R - Heel (bounce) L - Shuffle R - Heel (bounce) L - Step R (cross over L), Heel (drop) R - Toe Back L - Heel (bounce) R - Step L
    **(BREAK: BRUSH - HEEL - SHUFFLE - HEEL - CROSS, HEEL - TOE BACK - HEEL - STEP)**
    Counts: &a5&a6, &7&8

18. Shuffle (front) R - Hop L, Shuffle (side) R - Hop L, Repeat 2×, Ball Change R 2×
    **(SHUFFLE - HOP: FRONT & SIDE 3×, BALL CHANGE 2×)**
    Counts: &a1&a2, &a3&a4, &a5&a6, &7&8

19. **<u>Double Shuffle Combination</u>** (Accents are on 1-3-5)
    **(A)** Short Double Shuffle R 2×, Long Double Shuffle R (5 Shuffles), Repeat All
    **(SHORT DOUBLE SHUFFLE 2×, LONG DOUBLE SHUFFLE, REPEAT ALL)**
    Counts: <u>1</u>&a2, <u>3</u>&a4, <u>5</u>&a6&a7&a8
            <u>1</u>&a2, <u>3</u>&a4, <u>5</u>&a6&a7&a8

    **(B)** Long Double Shuffle 2×, Short Double Shuffle 2×, Long Double Shuffle
    **(LONG DOUBLE SHUFFLE 2×, SHORT DOUBLE SHUFFLE 2×, LONG DOUBLE SHUFFLE)**
    Counts: <u>1</u>&a2&a3&a4, <u>5</u>&a6&a7&a8
            <u>1</u>&a2, <u>3</u>&a4, <u>5</u>&a6&a7&a8

20. Brush (back) R - Heel (bounce) L, Shuffle R - Heel (bounce) L 2×, Ball R, Heel - Heel - Heel R-L-R, Reverse All
    **(BRUSH - HEEL, SHUFFLE - HEEL 2×, BALL - HEEL - HEEL - HEEL, REVERSE ALL)**
    Counts: &a, 1&a2&a, 3&a4, &a, 5&a6&a, 7&a8

21. **<u>Crossing Drawbacks Combination</u>**
    **(A)** Straight Drawback 2× R-L, Crossing Drawback 1× R, Straight Drawback 2× L-R, Crossing Drawback 1× L, Straight Drawback 2× R-L

### 9. Beginning III / Intermediate / Advanced Levels

(STRAIGHT DRAWBACK 2×, CROSSING DRAWBACK 1×, STRAIGHT DRAWBACK 2×, CROSSING DRAWBACK 1×, STRAIGHT DRAWBACK 2×)
Counts: &a1, &a2, &a3, &a4, &a5, &a6, &a7, &a8

(B) Break: Alternating Shuffle Cramproll (Shuffle - Ball R - Ball L - Heel L - Heel R) 4× R-L-R-L
(ALTERNATING SHUFFLE CRAMPROLL 4×)
Counts: &a1&a2, &a3&a4, &a5&a6, &a7&a8

22. (A) Shuffle R - Heel (bounce) L, Toe - Heel R - Step L, Drawback 2× R-L, Repeat All
(SHUFFLE - HEEL, TOE - HEEL - STEP, DRAWBACK 2×, REPEAT ALL)
Counts: &a1, &a2, &a3, &a4, &a5, &a6, &a7, &a8

(B) Shuffle R - Heel (bounce), Toe - Heel R - Step L, Repeat All, Drawback 4× R-L-R-L
(SHUFFLE - HEEL, TOE - HEEL - STEP, REPEAT ALL, DRAWBACK 4× ALT)
Counts: &a1, &a2, &a3, &a4, &a5, &a6, &a7, &a8

23. (Fast) Shuffle - Ball Change R, Ball R - Hop L, Repeat All 2×, Shuffle - Ball Change R 2×
(SHUFFLE - BALL CHANGE - BALL-HOP 3×, SHUFFLE - BALL CHANGE 2×)
Counts: e&a1&2, e&a3&4, e&a5&6, e&a7, e&a8

24. **12 Count Riff**
3 Count Riff 3×: Toe Back (inside edge) - Heel Scuff R - Heel Bounce L (front - cross over L - uncross), Heel Dig - Toe (drop) - Heel (bounce) R, Reverse All
(3 COUNT RIFF 3×: FRONT - CROSS - UNCROSS, HEEL DIG - TOE - HEEL, REVERSE ALL)
Counts: &a1&a2&a3&a4, &a5&a6&a7&a8

25. **24 Count Riff**
3 Count Riff 7×: Front - Cross - Uncross - Back - Front - Cross - Uncross, Heel Dig - Toe (drop) - Heel (bounce), Reverse All
(3 COUNT RIFF 7×: FRONT - CROSS - UNCROSS - BACK - FRONT - CROSS - UNCROSS, HEEL DIG - TOE - HEEL, REVERSE ALL)
Counts: &a1&a2&a3&a4&a5&a6&a7&a8
&a1&a2&a3&a4&a5&a6&a7&a8

26. **6 Count Riff Combination**
    *6 Count Riff = Toe Back (inside edge) - Scuff R - Heel (bounce) L - Heel Dig-Toe (drop) -Heel (bounce) R
    6 Count Riff, Back Flap - Heel 2× L-R, Reverse All & Repeat R Side, 6 Count Riff 2× L-R
    **(6 COUNT RIFF, BACK FLAP - HEEL 2× ALT, REVERSE ALL & REPEAT R SIDE, 6 COUNT RIFF 2× ALT)**
    Counts: &a1&a2, &a3&a4, &a5&a6, &a7&a8
    &a1&a2&a3&a4, &a5&a6, &a7&a8

27. **Slicing Combination**
    Brush (front) R - Hop L, Brush (cross over L) - Jump R, Reverse & Repeat R, Brush (front) - Jump L (kick R front), Brush (back) - Jump R (kick L back)
    **(BRUSH-HOP - BRUSH - JUMP 3× ALT, BRUSH - JUMP 2×)**
    Counts: &1&2, &3&4, &5&6, &7&8

28. Heel (bounce) L - Flap R, Heel - Heel L-R, Reverse All, Heel (bounce) L - Flap R, Reverse, Heel (bounce) L - Flap R, Heel - Heel L-R
    **(HEEL - FLAP, HEEL - HEEL, REVERSE ALL, HEEL - FLAP 2× ALT, HEEL - FLAP, HEEL - HEEL)**
    Counts: &a1, &2, &a3, &4, &a5, &a6, &a7, &8

29. Shuffle (side) - Step R, Heel (drops) 3× R-L-R, Reverse All, Shuffle - Step 3× R-L-R, Heel (drops) R-L-R
    **(SHUFFLE - STEP, HEEL 3× ALT, REVERSE ALL, SHUFFLE - STEP 3×, HEEL 3× ALT)**
    Counts: &a1, &a2, &a3, &a4, &a5, &a6, &a7, &a8

30. **Flap Cramp Roll Combination**
    *R Alternating Flap Cramp Roll = Flap R - Ball L - Heel L - Heel R, Reverse for L side
    **(A)** Flap Cramp Roll 3× R, Alternating Flap Cramp Roll R, Reverse All
    **(FLAP CRAMP ROLL 3×, ALTERNATING FLAP CRAMP ROLL, REVERSE ALL)**
    Counts: &1&a2, &3&a4, &5&a6, &7&a8
    &1&a2, &3&a4, &5&a6, &7&a8
    **(B)** Flap Cramp Roll R, Alternating Flap Cramp Roll R, Reverse All, Alternating Flap Cramp Roll 4×
    **(FLAP CRAMP ROLL, ALTERNATING FLAP CRAMP**

## 9. Beginning III / Intermediate / Advanced Levels

**ROLL, REVERSE ALL, ALTERNATING FLAP CRAMP ROLL 4×)**
Counts: &1&a2, &3&a4, &5&a6, &7&a8
&1&a2, &3&a4, &5&a6, &7&a8

31. Stomp - Brush (back) R - Heel (bounce) L, Ball - Heel (drop) R - Stomp - Brush (back) L, Stamp - Stamp L-R - Brush (back) L - Heel (bounce) L 2×
    **(STOMP - BRUSH - HEEL, BALL - HEEL - STOMP - BRUSH, STAMP - STAMP - BRUSH - HEEL 2×)**
    Counts: 1&2, &3&4, &5&6, &7&8

32. **Swing & Sway Plus Break** (Accents on **(A)** are counts 1-3-5-7 / **(B)** are 1-&-5-8)
    **(A)** Step R (to R) - Brush (back) - Step - Step L-R 4× Alt.
    **(STEP - BRUSH - STEP - STEP 4× ALT)**
    Counts: 1&2&, 3&4&, 5&6&, 7&8&
    **(B)** Break: Step (front) R - Toe Back L - Heel (bounce) R,
    Step (back) L, Toe Front R - Heel (bounce) L - Toe Back R -
    Heel (bounce) L, Step (back) R - Toe Front L -
    Heel (bounce) R - Toe Back L - Heel (bounce) R, Stamp - Stamp L-R
    **(BREAK: STEP - TOE BACK - HEEL, STEP -
    TOE FRONT - HEEL - TOE BACK - HEEL, STEP -
    TOE FRONT - HEEL - TOE BACK - HEEL,
    STAMP - STAMP)**
    Counts: 1, &2, &, 3&4&, 5, &6&7, &8

33. Brush (back) R - Heel (bounce) L - Toe Back R, Stamp - Stomp R-L, Reverse All, Brush (back) R - Heel (bounce) L, Shuffle R 2×, Ball R - Heel (drop) 3× R-L-R - Heel Dig L
    **(BRUSH - HEEL - TOE BACK, STAMP - STOMP, REVERSE ALL, BRUSH - HEEL, SHUFFLE 2×, BALL - HEEL 3× - HEEL DIG)**
    Counts: &1&a2, &3&a4, &5, &a6&, a7&a8

34. **Froggy** (Syncopated Rhythm / Accents are on counts 1-&-4-&7)
    Stomp R (turned in), Toe - Toe (lifts, Out-Out) L-R,
    Reverse All & Repeat Both Sides, Stomp R (turned in) -
    Toe (lift, Out) L - Stamp R
    **(STOMP - TOE - TOE 4×, STOMP - TOE - STAMP)**
    Counts: 1&2, &3&, 4&5, &6&, 7&8

101

35. **Riffle Combination**
    *Riffles = Toe (inside edge) - Scuff - Brush (back) R (Small Inward Ankle Circle)*
    (A) Riffle 3× R, Ball - Heel R, Reverse All
    **(RIFFLE 3×, BALL - HEEL, REVERSE ALL)**
    Counts: &a1, &a2, &a3, &4, &a5, &a6, &a7, &8
    (B) Riffle - Ball - Heel R, Reverse All, Riffle 3× R, Stamp - Stomp R-L
    **(RIFFLE - BALL - HEEL, REVERSE ALL, RIFFLE 3×, STAMP - STOMP)**
    Counts: &a1, &2, &a3, &4, &a5, &a6, &a7, &8

36. **Riffle Combination with Heel**
    (A) Riffle R - Heel L 3×, Ball - Heel - Heel L-R, Reverse All
    **(RIFFLE - HEEL 3×, BALL - HEEL - HEEL, REVERSE ALL)**
    Counts: 1&a2, 3&a4, 5&a6, 7&8
           1&a2, 3&a4, 5&a6, 7&8
           OR
           e&a1, e&a2, e&a3, &a4, e&a5, e&a6, e&a7, &a8
    (B) Riffle R - Heel L, Ball - Heel - Heel L-R, Reverse, Riffle R - Heel L 3×, Stamp - Stomp R-L
    **(RIFFLE - HEEL - BALL - HEEL - HEEL, REVERSE, RIFFLE - HEEL 3×, STAMP - STOMP)**
    Counts: 1&a2, 3&4, 5&a6, 7&8
           1&a2, 3&a4, 5&a6, 7-8
           OR
           e&a1, &a2, e&a3, &a4, e&a5, e&a6, e&a7, &8

37. **Shuffle Cramp Roll Combination**
    (A) Shuffle Cramp Roll R 3×, Alternating Shuffle Cramp Roll R, Reverse All
    **(SHUFFLE CRAMP ROLL 3×, ALTERNATING SHUFFLE CRAMP ROLL, REVERSE ALL)**
    Counts: &a1&a2, &a3&a4, &a5&a6, &a7&a8
           &a1&a2, &a3&a4, &a5&a6, &a7&a8
    (B) Shuffle Cramp Roll R, Alternating Shuffle Cramp Roll R, Reverse All, Alternating Shuffle Cramp Roll 4× R-L-R-L
    **(SHUFFLE CRAMP ROLL - ALTERNATING SHUFFLE CRAMP ROLL, REVERSE ALL, ALTERNATING SHUFFLE CRAMP ROLL 4×)**

## 9. Beginning III / Intermediate / Advanced Levels

<u>Counts</u>: &a1&a2, &a3&a4, &a5&a6, &a7&a8
&a1&a2, &a3&a4, &a5&a6, &a7&a8

38. Hop L - Heel Dig, Brush (back) - Jump R, Heel Dig L, Reverse All, Hop L, Heel Dig - Brush - Jump 3× R-L-R, Heel Dig L
**(HOP - DIG - BRUSH - JUMP - DIG, REVERSE ALL, HOP, DIG - BRUSH - JUMP 3× ALT, DIG)**
<u>Counts</u>: &1&a2, &3&a4, &5&a, 6&a, 7&a, 8

39. **Pick Ups & Pullbacks**
    (1) Shuffle R - Pick Up (Brush Back-Ball) L, Step - Step R-L, Repeat 3×
    **(SHUFFLE - PICK UP, STEP - STEP, REPEAT 3×)**
    <u>Counts</u>: e&a1, &2, e&a3, &4, e&a5, &6, e&a7, &8
    (2) Shuffle R - Swap Pullback (Brush Back L - Jump R) - Step - Step L-R 4× Alt
    **(SHUFFLE - SWAP PULLBACK - STEP - STEP 4× ALT)**
    <u>Counts</u>: e&a1, &2, e&a3, &4, e&a5, &6, e&a7, &8
    (3) Ball Change R - Separated Double Pullback R
    (Brush Back 2× R-L, Land - Land [balls] R-L), Repeat, Ball Change R, Separated Double Pullback R 3×
    **(BALL CHANGE - SEPARATED DOUBLE PULLBACK, REPEAT, BALL CHANGE, SEPARATED DOUBLE PULLBACK 3×)**
    <u>Counts</u>: &1, e&a2, &3, e&a4, &5, e&a6, e&a7, e&a8
    (4) Jump (two feet, front) - Double Pullback
    (Brush Back R & L Together, Land R & L Together), Repeat, Jump, Double Pullback 3×
    **(JUMP - DOUBLE PULLBACK 2×, JUMP, DOUBLE PULLBACK 3×)**
    <u>Counts</u>: 1&2, 3&4, 5&6&7&8

40. Flap - Pick Up R, Reverse, Flap 3× R-L-R, Pick Up R
**(FLAP - PICK UP, REVERSE, FLAP 3× ALT, PICK UP)**
<u>Counts</u>: &1&2, &3&4, &5, &6, &7, &8

41. Shuffle R - Swap Pullback L, Toe Back L - Hop R, Reverse All, Shuffle - Swap Pullback 3× R-L-R, Toe Back L - Hop R
**(SHUFFLE - SWAP PULLBACK, TOE BACK - HOP, REVERSE ALL, SHUFFLE - SWAP PULLBACK 3× ALT, TOE BACK - HOP)**
<u>Counts</u>: &1&a2, 3-4, &5&a6, 7-8
&1&a2, &3&a4, &5&a6, 7-8

42. Shuffle R - Swap Pullback L, Flap 2× L-R, Reverse All
    **(SHUFFLE - SWAP PULLBACK, FLAP 2×, REVERSE ALL)**
    Counts: &1&a2, &3&4, &5&a6, &7&8
43. Ball Change - Separated Double Pullback R, Repeat, Separated Double Pullback 4×
    **(BALL CHANGE - SEPARATED DOUBLE PULLBACK, REPEAT, SEPARATED DOUBLE PULLBACK 4×)**
    Counts: &1, e&a2, &3, e&a4, e&a5, e&a6, e&a7, e&a8
44. **Double Flap**
    (2 Flaps Run Together) R-L, Step - Step, Repeat 3×
    **(DOUBLE FLAP - STEP - STEP 4×)**
    Counts: e&a1, &2, e&a3, &4, e&a5, &6, e&a7, &8
45. Double Flap R-L, Step - Step R-L, Ball Change R, Separated Double Pullback R, Repeat All
    **(DOUBLE FLAP - STEP - STEP, BALL CHANGE - SEPARATED DOUBLE PULLBACK, REPEAT ALL)**
    Counts: e&a1, &2, &3, e&a4, e&a5, &6, &7, e&a8
46. **Wings**
    (1) **Double**
        Double Scape (both feet Out) - Double Brush (both feet In) - Double Land (both feet)
        **(DOUBLE SCRAPE - DOUBLE BRUSH - DOUBLE LAND)**
        Counts: &a1, &a2, &a3, &a4, &a5, &a6, &a7, &a8
    (2) **Single**
        Single Scrape R (Out) - Single Brush R (In) - Single Land R - Toe Back L
        **(SINGLE SCRAPE - SINGLE BRUSH - SINGLE LAND - TOE BACK)**
        Counts: e&a1, e&a2, e&a3, e&a4, e&a5, e&a6, e&a7, e&a8
    (3) **Crossing Double**
        Same as (1) but Land: 1st Wing R crossed over L, 2nd Wing feet parallel, 3rd Wing crossed L over R, and 4th Wing parallel
        **(DOUBLE SCRAPE - DOUBLE BRUSH - DOUBLE CROSS LAND, DOUBLE SCRAPE - DOUBLE BRUSH - DOUBLE PARALLEL LAND, REVERSE ALL)**
        Counts: &a1, &a2, &a3, &a4, &a5, &a6, &a7, &a8

## 9. Beginning III / Intermediate / Advanced Levels

(4) **Swap**
Scrape R (Out) - Single Brush R (In) - Single Land L - Toe Back R
**(SINGLE SCRAPE - SINGLE BRUSH - SINGLE LAND - TOE BACK)**
Counts: e&a1, e&a2, e&a3, e&a4, e&a5, e&a6, e&a7, e&a8

(5) **Pendulum**
Brush (front) R - Single Scrape L (Out) - Single Brush L (In) - Single Land L, Brush (back) R - Single Scrape L (Out) - Single Brush L (In) - Single Land L
**(BRUSH - SINGLE SCRAPE - SINGLE BRUSH - SINGLE LAND)**
Counts: 1&a2, 3&a4, 5&a6, 7&a8

47. **Wing Combinations**
(1) Crossing Double Wing 2 sets (Cross - Uncross - Cross - Uncross), Double Wing 4×
**(CROSSING DOUBLE WING 2×, DOUBLE WING 4×)**
Counts: &a1, &a2, &a3, &a4, &a5, &a6, &a7, &a8

(2) Single Wing 2× R, Swap Wing 2× R-L, Repeat All
**(SINGLE WING 2×, SWAP WING 2×, REPEAT ALL)**
Counts: e&a1, e&a2, &a3, &a4, e&a5, e&a6, &a7, &a8

(3) Swap Wing 3× R-L-R, Jump (two feet together), Double Wing 4×
**(SWAP WING 3×, JUMP, DOUBLE WING 4×)**
Counts: &a1, &a2, &a3-4, &a5, &a6, &a7, &a8

48. Jump R - Toe Back L - Hop R - Jump L - Toe Front R - Hop L - Toe Back R - Hop L, Jump R - Toe Front L - Hop R - Toe Back L - Hop R, Ball Change L
**(JUMP - TOE BACK - HOP - JUMP - TOE FRONT - HOP - TOE BACK - HOP, JUMP - TOE FRONT - HOP - TOE BACK - HOP, BALL CHANGE)**
Counts: 1&2&3&4&, 5&6&7, &8

49. **Bombershay Combination**
*Bombershay: Brush (back) L - Heel Dig L or Ball - Step R (to R)*
(A) Flap, Bombershay R 6×, Ball Change, Reverse All
**(FLAP, BOMBERSHAY 6×, BALL CHANGE, REVERSE ALL)**
Counts: &1, &a2, &a3, &a4, &a5, &a6, &a7, &8
&1, &a2, &a3, &a4, &a5, &a6, &a7, &8

(B) Flap, Bombershay 2× R, Ball Change L, Reverse All
   **(FLAP, BOMBERSHAY 2×, BALL CHANGE, REVERSE ALL)**
   Counts: &1, &a2, &a3, &4, &5, &a6, &a7, &8
(C) Flap R - Brush (back) - Ball Change L, Reverse All, Flap, Bombershay 2× R, Brush (back) - Ball Change L
   **(FLAP - BRUSH - BALL CHANGE, REVERSE ALL, FLAP, BOMBERSHAY 2×, BRUSH - BALL CHANGE)**
   Counts: &1&a2, &3&a4, &5, &a6, &a7, &a8

50. (A) Shuffle R - Hop L - Flap R, Flap 2× L-R, Reverse All
   **(SHUFFLE - HOP - FLAP, FLAP 2× ALT, REVERSE ALL)**
   Counts: &1&a2, &3&4, &5&a6, &7&8
   (B) Shuffle R - Step R - Ball Change L, Reverse & Repeat R Side, Flap 2× L-R
   **(SHUFFLE - STEP - BALL CHANGE, REVERSE & REPEAT R SIDE, FLAP 2×)**
   Counts: &1&a2, &3&a4, &5&a6, &7, &8

51. Brush (back) R - Heel (bounce) L, Brush (front) R - Heel (bounce) L, Back Flap - Heel R - Heel Dig L, Reverse All & Repeat R, Brush (back) L - Hop R, Rolling Shuffle 3× L-R-L
   **(BRUSH - HEEL 2×, BACK FLAP - HEEL - HEEL DIG, REVERSE ALL & REPEAT R, BRUSH - HOP, ROLLING SHUFFLE 3× ALT)**
   Counts: &1&2&3&4, &5&6&7&8
   &1&2&3&4, &5, &a6, &a7, &a8

52. Hop L - Shuffle R - Hop L - Step R, Flap - Heel 2× L-R, Shuffle L - Heel (bounce) R - Flap-Heel L, Reverse
   **(HOP - SHUFFLE - HOP - STEP, FLAP - HEEL 2× ALT, SHUFFLE - HEEL - FLAP - HEEL 2× ALT)**
   Counts: &1&a2, &a3&a4, &a5&a6, &a7&a8

53. Heel Dig - Brush (back) R - Heel (bounce) L, Flap R, Heel (drop) 3× L-R-L, Brush (back) R - Heel (bounce) L, Ball - Heel R - Heel Dig L, Back Flap L, Heel - Heel R-L
   **(HEEL DIG - BRUSH - HEEL, FLAP - HEEL - HEEL - HEEL, BRUSH - HEEL, BALL - HEEL - HEEL DIG, BACK FLAP - HEEL - HEEL)**
   Counts: 1&2, &3&a4, &5&a6, &7&8

54. Flap - Heel R, Back Flap - Heel L, Flap R - Scuff L - Heel R, Ball - Heel L, Repeat All

## 9. Beginning III / Intermediate / Advanced Levels

(FLAP - HEEL, BACK FLAP - HEEL, FLAP - SCUFF - HEEL - BALL - HEEL, REPEAT ALL)
Counts: &a1, &a2, &a3&, a4, &a5, &a6, &a7&, a8

55. **(A)** Flap - Heel R, Shuffle - Step L, Brush (back) R - Heel L, Repeat All
   (FLAP - HEEL, SHUFFLE - STEP - BRUSH - HEEL, REPEAT ALL)
   Counts: &1&, 2&3, &4, &5&, 6&7, &8
   **(B)** Flap R - Shuffle L, Ball L - Toe Back R - Heel (drop) L, Ball R - Brush (back) L - Heel (drop) R, Ball - Heel L, Shuffle R - Heel (bounce) L, Ball Change R
   (FLAP - SHUFFLE - BALL - TOE BACK - HEEL, BALL - BRUSH - HEEL, BALL - HEEL, SHUFFLE - HEEL, BALL CHANGE)
   Counts: &1&2, &3&, 4&5, &6, &a7, &8

56. **(A)** Heel (bounce) L - Flap R, Heel (drop) R - Shuffle L - Heel (bounce) R, Step L - Brush (back) R - Heel (drop) L - Toe front R, Repeat All
   (HEEL - FLAP, HEEL - SHUFFLE - HEEL, STEP - BRUSH - HEEL - TOE FRONT, REPEAT ALL)
   Counts: &a1, &2&a, 3&a4, &a5, &6&a, 7&a8
   **(B)** Step R - Scuff L, Alternating Cramproll L, Ball Change R, Repeat All
   (STEP - SCUFF, ALT CRAMPROLL - BALL CHANGE, REPEAT ALL)
   Counts: &1, 2&a3, &4, &5, 6&a7, &8

57. Hop L - Shuffle R, Hop L - Brush (front) R, Hop L - Step R - Ball Change L, Reverse All & Repeat R Side, Flap - Heel 4× L-R-L-R
   (HOP - SHUFFLE, HOP - BRUSH, HOP - STEP - BALL CHANGE, REVERSE ALL & REPEAT R SIDE, FLAP - HEEL 4× ALT)
   Counts: &1&a2, &3&4, &5&a6, &7&8
   &1&a2, &3&4, &a5, &a6, &a7, &a8

58. Brush (front) R - Hop L - Step R, Reverse, Ball Change R, Drawback 3× R-L R, Ball Change L
   (BRUSH - HOP - STEP 2× ALT, BALL CHANGE, DRAWBACK 3× ALT, BALL CHANGE)
   Counts: &1&, 2&3, &4, &a5, &a6, a&7, &8

## Tap Dance for All

59. **6 Count Riff Combinations**
    (1) 6 Count Riff 3× R-L-R, Back Flap - Heel 2× L-R, Reverse All
    **(6 COUNT RIFF 3× ALT, BACK FLAP - HEEL 2× ALT, REVERSE ALL)**
    Counts: &a1&a2, &a3&a4, &a5&a6, &a7, &a8
    &a1&a2, &a3&a4, &a5&a6, &a7, &a8
    (2) 6 Count Riff R, Ball - Heel L, Heel Dig - Brush (back) - Heel Dig R, Repeat All 2×, Flap - Heel R, Ball L - Heel (bounce) R, Flap - Heel L, Ball R - Heel (bounce) L
    **(6 COUNT RIFF, BALL - HEEL, HEEL DIG - BRUSH- HEEL DIG, REPEAT ALL 2×, FLAP - HEEL, BALL - HEEL 2× ALT)**
    Counts: &a1&a2, &a, 3&4, &a5&a6, &a, 7&8
    &a1&a2, &a, 3&4, &a5, &6, &a7, &8
60. Heel (bounce) L - Shuffle R - Heel (bounce) L - Ball R, Reverse All & Repeat R, Flap - Heel 2× L-R
    **(HEEL - SHUFFLE - HEEL - BALL 3× ALT, FLAP - HEEL 2×)**
    Counts: &1&a2, &3&a4, &5&a6, &a7, &a8
61. Hop L, Flap 3× R-L-R, Stomp L, Reverse All, Hop L, Flap 8× R-L-R-L-R-L-R-L
    **(HOP, FLAP 3× ALT, STOMP, REVERSE ALL, HOP, FLAP 8× ALT)**
    Counts: &a1&2&3-4, &a5&6&7-8
    &a1, &2, &3, &4, &5, &6, &7, &8
62. Shuffle R - Heel (bounce) L, Flap - Heel R, Shuffle Alternating Cramp Roll L, Repeat All
    **(SHUFFLE - HEEL, FLAP - HEEL, SHUFFLE ALTERNATING CRAMP ROLL, REPEAT ALL)**
    Counts: &a1, &a2, &a3&a4, &a5, &a6, &a7&a8
63. Drawback 3× R-L-R, Ball - Heel L - Heel Dig R, Repeat All
    **(DRAWBACK 3× ALT, BALL - HEEL - HEEL DIG)**
    Counts: &a1, &a2, &a3, &a4, &a5, &a6, &a7, &a8
64. Flap R - Shuffle - Ball Change, Reverse All, Step - Step R-L, Flap R - Shuffle - Ball Change, Reverse All, Step, Hold
    **(FLAP - SHUFFLE - BALL CHANGE, REVERSE ALL, STEP – STEP FLAP - SHUFFLE - BALL CHANGE, REVERSE ALL, STEP, HOLD)**
    Counts: &1&2&3, &4&5&6, 7-8
    &1&2&3, &4&5&6-7, Hold: 8

## 9. Beginning III / Intermediate / Advanced Levels

65. Flap R - Shuffle Swap Pullback L, Repeat All, Step - Step R-L, Repeat (end with only 1 Step R), Hold
    **(FLAP - SHUFFLE SWAP PULLBACK, REPEAT ALL, STEP - STEP, REPEAT ALL: FLAP - SHUFFLE SWAP PULLBACK, REPEAT ALL, STEP, HOLD)**
    Counts: &1, &2&a3, &4&5&a6, 7-8
    &1&2&a3, &4&5&a6-7, Hold: 8

66. **Rolling Shuffle Combination**
    (A) Rolling Shuffle 3× R-L-R, Shuffle L - Hop R, Reverse All
        **(ROLLING SHUFFLE 3×, SHUFFLE - HOP, REVERSE ALL)**
        Counts: &a1, &a2, &a3, &a4, &a5, &a6, &a7, &a8
    (B) Shuffle - Jump R, Shuffle L - Hop R, Reverse, Rolling Shuffle 4× R-L-R-L
        **(SHUFFLE - JUMP, SHUFFLE - HOP, REVERSE, ROLLING SHUFFLE 4× ALT)**
        Counts: &a1, &a2, &a3, &a4, &a5, &a6, &a7, &a8

67. Step L (to L) - Click R (to L Heel), Cramp Roll R, Reverse All, Step - Step L-R, Repeat All (end with only 1 Step), Hold
    **(STEP - CLICK - CRAMP ROLL, REVERSE ALL, STEP - STEP, REPEAT ALL: END WITH ONLY 1 STEP, HOLD)**
    Counts: 1-2, e&a3, 4-5, e&a6, 7-8
    1-2, e&a3, 4-5, e&a6-7, Hold: 8

68. **Stroll**
    *Mom created this combination, naming it the Stroll for how it should feel, easy like strolling down the street. Accents are on all numbers.*
    (A) Heel (bounce) L, Heel Dig - Toe (drop) R, Ball (cross back) - Heel (drop) L, Ball - Heel R, Heel Dig L, Reverse All
        **(HEEL, HEEL DIG - TOE, BALL - HEEL 2×, HEEL DIG, REVERSE ALL)**
        Counts: &<u>1</u>&, <u>2</u>&, <u>3</u>&, <u>4</u>, &<u>5</u>&, <u>6</u>&, <u>7</u>&, <u>8</u>
    (B) Break: Heel (bounce) L, Heel Dig - Toe (drop) - Heel (drop) R, Heel Dig L, Reverse All, Heel (bounce) L, Ball - Heel 3× R-L-R, Step L
        **(BREAK: HEEL, HEEL DIG - TOE-HEEL, HEEL DIG, REVERSE ALL, HEEL, BALL - HEEL 3× ALT, STEP)**
        Counts: &<u>1</u>&a<u>2</u>, &<u>3</u>&a<u>4</u>, &<u>5</u>&, <u>6</u>&, <u>7</u>&, <u>8</u>

69. **Train (Froggy Style)**
    Stamp R (over L), Toe - Toe (lifts) L-R, Reverse All, Stamp R - Toe (lift) L, Stamp R (over L), Toe - Toe (lifts) L-R, Reverse All, Step
    **(STAMP - TOE - TOE, REVERSE ALL, STAMP - TOE, STAMP - TOE - TOE, REVERSE ALL, STEP)**
    Counts: 1&2, &3&, 4&, 5&6, &7&, 8

70. **Paradiddle/Paddle & Roll Combination**
    **(A)** Paradiddle 4× R-L-R-L, Scuffle R - Heel (bounce) L, Shuffle R - Heel (bounce) L, Flap - Heel R, Paradiddle L, Hold, Repeat All 2× (no Hold on 3rd set)
    **(PARADIDDLE 4× ALT, SCUFFLE - HEEL, SHUFFLE - HEEL, FLAP - HEEL, PARADIDDLE, HOLD, REPEAT ALL 2×)**
    Counts: 1e&a, 2e&a, 3e&a, 4e&a, 5e&, a6e, &a7, e&a8, Hold: &
    1e&a, 2e&a, 3e&a, 4e&a, 5e&, a6e, &a7, e&a8, Hold: &
    1e&a, 2e&a, 3e&a, 4e&a, 5e&, a6e, &a7, e&a8
    **(B)** Break: Back Flap R, Step - Step L-R, Reverse All, Back Flap R, Heel - Heel (bounce) R-L, Shuffle R - Heel (bounce) L, Flap - Heel R, Stamp L
    **(BACK FLAP - STEP - STEP, REVERSE ALL, BACK FLAP - HEEL - HEEL, SHUFFLE - HEEL, FLAP - HEEL, STAMP)**
    Counts: &1&2, &3&4, &5&6, e&a, 7&a -8

71. **Weave Combination**
    **(A)** Shuffle - Ball - Heel, R (over L), Flap L - Back Flap R, Reverse All
    **(SHUFFLE - BALL - HEEL, FLAP - BACK FLAP, REVERSE ALL)**
    Counts: &1&2, &3&4, &5&6, &7&8
    **(B)** Break (Syncopated Rhythm): Shuffle - Step R (over L), Toe Back L - Heel (drop) R, Step L - Back Flap R, Toe Back L - Heel (drop) R, Step L - Brush (back) R - Heel (drop) L, Step - Step - Step R-L-R
    **(SHUFFLE - STEP - TOE BACK - HEEL, STEP - BACK FLAP, TOE BACK - HEEL, STEP - BRUSH - HEEL, STEP - STEP - STEP)**
    Counts: &1&, 2&, 3&4, &5, &6&, 7&8

## 9. Beginning III / Intermediate / Advanced Levels

72. **Shim Sham & Hard Break**
    **(A)** Shuffle - Step R, Reverse, Shuffle - Ball Change R, Shuffle - Step R, Reverse All & Repeat R
    **(SHUFFLE - STEP 2× ALT, SHUFFLE - BALL CHANGE, SHUFFLE - STEP, REPEAT ALL 2×)**
    Counts: &a1, &a2, &a3e, &a4, &a5, &a6, &a7e, &a8
    &a1, &a2, &a3e, &a4
    **(B)** Break: Flap L, Brush (front) - Ball Change R, Hop L - Step R (over L), Hop R, Step - Step - Step L-R-L, Hold
    **(FLAP - BRUSH - BALL CHANGE, HOP - CROSS, HOP - STEP - STEP - STEP, HOLD)**
    Counts: &1&a2, 3-4, &, 5-6-7, Hold: 8

73. **(A)** Hop L, Shuffle - Step R, Flap L, Shuffle - Step 2× R-L, Flap - Heel R, Heel Dig L, Reverse All, Hold
    **(HOP - SHUFFLE - STEP, FLAP, SHUFFLE - STEP 2× ALT, FLAP - HEEL, HEEL DIG, REVERSE ALL, HOLD)**
    Counts: 8&a1, &2, &3&4&5, &6&7,
    8&a1, &2, &3&4&5, &6&7, Hold: 8
    **(B)** Flap 2× R-L, Ball Change - Double Separated Pullback R, Repeat All, Ball Change - Double Separated Pullback R 2×, Double Separated Pullback R 4×
    **(FLAP 2× ALT, BALL CHANGE - DOUBLE SEPARATED PULLBACK, REPEAT ALL, BALL CHANGE - DOUBLE SEPARATED PULLBACK 2×, DOUBLE SEPARATED PULLBACK 4×)**
    Counts: &1, &2, &3, e&a4, &5, &6, &7, e&a8
    &1, e&a2, &3, e&a4, e&a5, e&a6, e&a7, e&a8

74. **(A)** Flap R - 3 Count Riff L, Back Flap Cramp Roll L, Reverse All
    **(FLAP - 3 COUNT RIFF, BACK FLAP CRAMP ROLL, REVERSE ALL)**
    Counts: &1, &a2, &3&a4, &5, &a6, &7&a8
    **(B)** Flap Cramp Roll - Back Flap Cramp Roll R, 3 Count Riff - Back Flap - Heel 2× R-L
    **(FLAP CRAMP ROLL - BACK FLAP CRAMP ROLL, 3 COUNT RIFF - BACK FLAP - HEEL 2× ALT)**
    Counts: &1&a2, &3&a4, &a5, &a6, &a7, &a8

75. Alternating Cramp Roll 4× R-L-R-L, Ball Change - Double Pullback R 2×

## Tap Dance for All

  (ALTERNATING CRAMP ROLL 4×, BALL CHANGE - DBL PULLBACK 2×)
  Counts: e&a1, e&a2, e&a3, e&a4, &5, e&a6, &7, e&a8

76. Double Shuffle - Ball - Heel 3× Alt. R-L-R, Back Flap 2× L-R
  (DOUBLE SHUFFLE - BALL - HEEL 3× ALT, BACK FLAP 2×)
  Counts: &a1&, a2, &a3&, a4, &a5&, a6, &7, &8

77. Hop L - Flap R, Step L - Scuffle R 2× Alt, Step L - Scuff R, Flap Bombershay R 2×, Brush (back) L - Heel (drop) R - Toe Back L
  (HOP - FLAP, STEP - SCUFFLE 2× ALT, STEP - SCUFF, FLAP BOMBERSHAY 2×, BRUSH - HEEL - TOE BACK)
  Counts: &a1, &2& a3&, a4, &5, &a6, &a7, &a8

78. **5 Count Shuffle**
  Shuffle R - Scuff R - Heel Dig R - Brush (back) R
  (SHUFFLE - SCUFF - HEEL DIG - BRUSH)
  Counts: &a1&2 OR 8&1&2 OR &1&a2 OR &1&2&
    (play around with this, there are more)

79. **Shuffle Double Pullbacks**
  Shuffle R, Pickup L, Land - Land R-L
  (SHUFFLE - PICKUP, LAND - LAND)
  Counts: &1, &a2, &3, &a4, &5, &a6, &7, &a8

80. **Alternating Shuffle Double Pullbacks**
  Shuffle R, Pickup L, Land - Land L-R, Reverse All & Repeat All
  (SHUFFLE - PICKUP, LAND - LAND, REVERSE ALL & REPEAT ALL)
  Counts: &1, &a2, &3, &a4, &5, &a6, &7, &a8

81. **Double Back Flaps**
  Both feet execute a Back Flap at the same time:
  Take off from both feet, Brush (back, in the air), Land (on both feet)
  (JUMP - BRUSH - LAND 8×)
  Counts: &1, &2, &3, &4, &5, &6, &7, &8

82. **Double Front Flaps**
  Both feet execute a regular front Flap at the same time:
  Take off from both feet, Brush (front, in the air), Land (on both feet)
  (JUMP - BRUSH - LAND 8×)
  Counts: &1, &2, &3, &4, &5, &6, &7, &8

QUOTABLE QUOTES

  *"The material for the dance is air, the movement is breath, and the source is love."—Unknown*

# 10

# Extra Combinations
## *(Beginning III / Intermediate / Advanced Levels)*

### *Beginning III Level*

1. **(A)** Brush (back) R - Hop L, Flap 2× R-L, Stamp R - Heel Dig L, Reverse All & Repeat R
   **(BRUSH - HOP, FLAP 2× ALT, STAMP - HEEL DIG 3× ALT)**
   Counts: &1&2&3&4, &5&6&7&8,
   &1&2&3&4
   **(B)** Brush (back) L, Heel (bounce) R, Stamp - Stomp L-R, Reverse All
   **(BRUSH - HEEL, STAMP - STOMP, REVERSE ALL)**
   Counts: &5&6, &7&8
2. **Rolling Shuffle Combination I**
   **(A)** Shuffle R - Hop L 7×, Shuffle - Jump R, Reverse All
   **(SHUFFLE - HOP 7×, SHUFLE - JUMP, REVERSE ALL)**
   Counts: &a1, &a2, &a3, &a4, &a5, &a6, &a7, &a8
   &a1, &a2, &a3, &a4, &a5, &a6, &a7, &a8
   **(B)** Shuffle R - Hop L, Shuffle - Jump R, Reverse All, Rolling Shuffle 4× R-L-R-L, Shuffle R - Hop L 7×, Shuffle - Jump R
   **(SHUFFLE - HOP, SHUFFLE - JUMP, REVERSE ALL, ROLLING SHUFFLE 4× ALT, SHUFFLE - HOP 7×, SHUFFLE - JUMP)**
   Counts: &a1, &a2, &a3, &a4, &a5, &a6, &a7, &a8
   &a1, &a2, &a3, &a4, &a5, &a6, &a7, &a8
3. **Rolling Shuffle Combination II**
   **(A)** Rolling Shuffle 3× R-L-R, Shuffle L - Hop R, Reverse All

(ROLLING SHUFFLE 3× ALT, SHUFFLE - HOP,
   REVERSE ALL)
   Counts: &a1, &a2, &a3, &a4, &a5, &a6, &a7, &a8
   (B) Shuffle - Jump R, Shuffle L - Hop R, Reverse All,
   Rolling Shuffle 4× R-L-R-L
   (SHUFFLE - JUMP, SHUFFLE - HOP, REVERSE ALL,
   ROLLING SHUFFLE 4× ALT)
   Counts: &a1, &a2, &a3, &a4, &a5, &a6, &a7, &a8
4. **Drawback Combination I (Slow)**
   *Be Sure to Note the Counts & Accents of Slow Drawbacks*
   Slow Drawback 3× R-L-R, Brush (back) L - Heel (drop), Ball -
   Heel L, Heel Dig R
   (SLOW DRAWBACK 3× ALT, BRUSH - HEEL, BALL - HEEL,
   HEEL DIG)
   Counts: &1-2, &3-4, &5-6, &7, &a8
5. **Drawback Combination II (Regular)**
   Drawback 3× R-L-R, Heel - Heel L-R, Heel Dig L, Reverse All
   (DRAWBACK 3× ALT, HEEL - HEEL, HEEL DIG,
   REVERSE ALL)
   Counts: &a1, &a2, &a3, &a4, &a5, &a6, &a7, &a8
6. Hop L, Shuffle - Step R, Reverse & Repeat R, Step - Step L-R,
   Reverse All
   (HOP - SHUFFLE - STEP 3× ALT, STEP - STEP,
   REVERSE ALL)
   Counts: 1&a2, 3&a4, 5&a6, 7-8
7. (A) Shuffle - Ball - Heel 3× R-L-R, Tap (side) L -
   Heel (bounce) R 2×, Reverse All
   (SHUFFLE - BALL - HEEL 3× ALT, TAP - HEEL 2×,
   REVERSE ALL)
   Counts: &1&2, &3&4, &5&6, &7&8
   (B) Shuffle - Ball - Heel R, Tap (side) L - Heel (bounce) R 2×,
   Reverse All
   (SHUFFLE - BALL - HEEL, TAP - HEEL 2× REVERSE ALL)
   Counts: &1&2, &3&4, &5&6, &7&8
   (C) Repeat (A): R side only
   (SHUFFLE - BALL - HEEL 3× ALT, TAP - HEEL 2×)
   Counts: &1&2, &3&4, &5&6, &7&8
8. (A) Heel Dig - Jump R - Heel Dig L, Heel (bounce) R - Step L,
   Repeat All

## 10. Extra Combinations

    (HEEL DIG - JUMP - HEEL DIG, HEEL - STEP,
    REPEAT ALL)
    Counts: 1&2, 3-4, 5&6, 7-8
    (B) Heel Dig - Jump R - Heel Dig L, Reverse, Heel Dig -
    Jump 2× R-L, Heel Dig R - Stamp - Stamp R-L
    (HEEL DIG - JUMP - HEEL DIG, REVERSE, HEEL DIG -
    JUMP 2× ALT, HEEL DIG - STAMP - STAMP)
    Counts: 1&2, 3&4, 5&6&, 7&8

9. Stamp R - Stomp L, Brush (back) L - Heel (bounce) R, Reverse All, Stamp - Stamp R-L, Double Chug 3×
    (STAMP - STOMP - BRUSH - HEEL, REVERSE ALL, STAMP - STAMP, DBL CHUG 3×)
    Counts: &1&2, &3&4, &5, &6&7&8

10. **Flap Cramp Roll Combination**
    Flap Cramp Roll R, Back Flap - Heel 2× R-L, Repeat All 2×, Ball Change R 2×, Heel (drop) L - Toe Back R - Step R
    (FLAP CRAMP ROLL, BACK FLAP - HEEL 2×, REPEAT ALL 2×, BALL CHANGE 2×, HEEL - TOE BACK - STEP)
    Counts: &1&a2, &a3&a4, &5&a6, &a7&a8
          &1&a2, &a3&a4, &5, &6, &7-8

11. Flap R (to R), Heel - Heel L-R, Brush (back) L - Heel (bounce) R - Toe Back L - Heel (bounce) R, Reverse All & Repeat R, Flap - Heel L - Dig (toe) R, Flap - Heel R - Dig (toe) L
    (FLAP - HEEL - HEEL, BRUSH - HEEL - TOE BACK - HEEL 3× ALT, FLAP - HEEL - DIG 2× ALT)
    Counts: &1, &2, &3&4, &5, &6, &7&8
          &1, &2, &3&4, &5&6, &7&8

12. Heel (bounce) L - Flap R - Heel - Heel L-R, Heel Dig L, Reverse & Repeat R, Ball - Heel L, Step (ball) R
    (HEEL - FLAP, HEEL - HEEL - HEEL DIG 3× ALT, BALL - HEEL, STEP)
    Counts: &a1, &a2, &a3, &a4, &a5, &a6, &7-8

13. Flap R, Heel - Heel L-R, Back Flap L, Heel - Heel L-R, Reverse All
    (FLAP - HEEL - HEEL, BACK FLAP - HEEL - HEEL, REVERSE ALL)
    Counts: &1&2, &3&4, &5&6, &7&8

14. Flap R, Heel - Heel L-R, Brush (back) L, Heel (bounce) R,
    Toe Back L, Heel (bounce) R, Flap L, Heel - Heel R-L -
    Heel Dig R, Flap R, Heel - Heel L-R, Heel Dig L
    **(FLAP - HEEL - HEEL, BRUSH - HEEL - TOE BACK - HEEL, FLAP - HEEL - HEEL - HEEL DIG 2× ALT)**
    Counts: &1&2, &3&4, &5&a6, &7&a8
15. Step (ball) R, Click (L to R), Heel (drop) R - Step L, Repeat All, Ball - Heel R, Reverse All (end: Step L, Hold, instead of Ball - Heel)
    **(STEP - CLICK - HEEL - STEP, REPEAT, BALL - HEEL, STEP - CLICK - HEEL - STEP, REPEAT, STEP)**
    Counts: 1-2&3, 4-5&6, 7-8
       1-2&3, 4-5&6, 7, Hold: 8
16. Step L, Cramp Roll R, Reverse All, Step - Step L-R, Repeat All (end: Step L, Hold, instead of Step - Step)
    **(STEP - CRAMP ROLL, REVERSE, STEP - STEP, STEP - CRAMP ROLL, REVERSE, STEP - HOLD)**
    Counts: 1-2&a3, 4-5&a6, 7-8
       1-2&a3, 4-5&a6, 7, Hold: 8
17. **Cincinnati**
    Brush (back) R - Hop L - Shuffle - Step R, Reverse, Flap 3× R-L-R, Step L - Stomp R
    **(BRUSH - HOP - SHUFFLE - STEP 2× ALT, FLAP 3×, STEP - STOMP)**
    Counts: &1&a2, &3&a4, &5, &6, &7, &8
18. Step - Step R-L, Scuffle R - Heel (bounce) L, Shuffle - Step R - Scuff L, Shuffle - Jump 2× L-R, Shuffle L - Heel (drop) R, Step L
    **(STEP - STEP, SCUFFLE - HEEL, SHUFFLE STEP - SCUFF, SHUFFLE - JUMP 2× ALT, SHUFFLE - HEEL, STEP)**
    Counts: 1&, 2&a, 3&a4, 5&a6&a, 7&a, 8
19. **Paradiddle or Paddle & Roll Combination I**
    **(A)** Reverse Paradiddle R, Toe (lift) L - Back Flap - Heel R, Paradiddle L - Heel (bounce) R, Brush (back) - Ball - Heel L
    **(REVERSE PARADIDDLE, TOE - BACK FLAP - HEEL, PARADIDDLE - HEEL, BRUSH - BALL - HEEL)**
    Counts: 1&2&, 3&4&, 5&6&, 7&8&
    **(B)** Heel (bounce) R - Back Flap - Heel L - Heel R, Back Flap - Heel L, Reverse Paradiddle R, Toe (lift) L - Back Flap - Heel R

## 10. Extra Combinations

(HEEL - BACK FLAP - HEEL - HEEL, BACK FLAP - HEEL, REVERSE PARADIDDLE, TOE - BACK FLAP - HEEL)
Counts: 1&2&3, &4&, 5&6&, 7&8&

20. **Paradiddle or Paddle and Roll Combination II**
Paradiddle R - Heel (bounce) L, Back Flap - Heel R - Heel L 6×, Back Flap - Heel R, Reverse All
(PARADIDDLE - HEEL, BACK FLAP - HEEL 6×, BACK FLAP - HEEL, REVERSE ALL)
Counts: 1e&a2, e&a3, e&a4, e&a5, e&a6, e&a7, e&a8, e&a
1e&a2, e&a3, e&a4, e&a5, e&a6, e&a7, e&a8, e&a

21. **(A)** Flap - Heel 2× R-L, Flap - Heel - Heel (drop / bounce) R, Stamp L
(FLAP - HEEL 2× ALT, FLAP - HEEL - HEEL, STAMP)
Counts: &1-2, &3-4, &5-6-7, 8

**(B)** Step R - Flap L (over R) - Step R, Shuffle L - Hop R, Shuffle - Step L, Shuffle - Jump R - Cross L (behind R), Step R (to R) - Drag (R & L together) - Stamp L
(STEP - FLAP - STEP, SHUFFLE - HOP, SHUFFLE - STEP, SHUFFLE - JUMP - CROSS, STEP - DRAG - STAMP)
Counts: 1&a2, &a3, &a4, e&a5, 6-7-8

22. **(A)** 4 Count Riff R, Heel - Heel - Heel (bounces) R, Reverse All
(4 COUNT RIFF, HEEL - HEEL - HEEL, REVERSE ALL)
Counts: 1&2&, 3&4, 5&6&, 7&8

**(B)** Slurp (Toe-Heel Dig-Toe Drop) - Heel R, Hold, Heel Dig L - Heel (bounce) R, Brush (back) L - Heel (bounce) R, Ball - Heel L, Heel Dig R - Brush (back) R - Heel Dig R - Toe (drop) R, Heel - Heel - Heel (bounces) R
(SLURP - HEEL, HOLD, HEEL DIG - HEEL - BRUSH - HEEL, BALL - HEEL, HEEL DIG - BRUSH - HEEL DIG - TOE, HEEL - HEEL - HEEL)
Counts: e&a1, Hold: &, 2&, 3&, 4&, 5&6&, 7&8

23. **(A)** 6 Count Riff 2× R-L (pause on last count)
(6 COUNT RIFF 2× ALT)
Counts: 1&2&3-4, 5&6&7-8

**(B)** Paradiddle or Paddle & Roll 3× R-L-R, Heel - Heel (bounces) R
(PARADIDDLE 3× ALT, HEEL - HEEL)
Counts: 1&2&, 3&4&, 5&6&, 7-8

24. **(A)** 4 Count Riff R, Heel - Heel (bounces) L-R, Paradiddle or Paddle & Roll 2× L-R, Heel - Heel (bounces) L-R

(4 COUNT RIFF, HEEL - HEEL, PARADIDDLE 2× ALT, HEEL - HEEL)
Counts: 1&2&, 3&, 4&5&, 6&7&, 8&

(B) 4 Count Riff 2× L-R, Heel (bounce) 6× L-R-L-R-L-R
(Pause before last Heel)
(4 COUNT RIFF 2×, HEELS 6× ALT)
Counts: 1&2&, 3&4&, 5&6&7-8

25. (A) Reverse Paradiddle or Paddle & Roll, 2 Count Riff - Scuffle L, Ball L, Heel - Heel (drops) L-R, Toe - Toe (lifts) L-R, Click (heels together)
(REVERSE PARADIDDLE, 2 COUNT RIFF - SCUFFLE, BALL, HEEL - HEEL, TOE - TOE, CLICK)
Counts: 1&2&, 3&4&, 5, &6, &7-8

(B) Ball - Heel L, Paradiddle or Paddle & Roll 3× R-L-R
(pause before the last count), Ball - Heel L,
Reverse Paradiddle or Paddle & Roll 3× R-L-R
(pause before the last count)
(BALL - HEEL, PARADIDDLE 3× ALT, BALL - HEEL REVERSE PARADIDDLE 3× ALT)
Counts: 1e, &a2e, &a3e, &a4-e, 5e, &a6e, &a7e, &a8-e

26. (A) Ball - Heel R, 2 Count Riff L, Paradiddle or Paddle & Roll L,
2 Count Riff R, Paradiddle or Paddle & Roll R, Ball - Heel L,
2 Count Riff R, Paradiddle or Paddle & Roll R,
2 Count Riff L, Paradiddle or Paddle & Roll L, Ball - Heel R
(BALL - HEEL, 2 COUNT RIFF, PARADIDDLE,
2 COUNT RIFF, PARADIDDLE, BALL - HEEL,
2 COUNT RIFF, PARADIDDLE, 2 COUNT RIFF,
PARADIDDLE, BALL - HEEL)
Counts: 1e, &a, 2e&a, 3e, &a4e, &a, 5e, &a6e, &a, 7e&a, 8&

27. (A) Shuffle R, 2 Count Riff R, Heel Dig - Brush (back) - Ball - Heel R, 2 Count Riff L, Heel Dig - Brush (back) - Ball - Heel L
(SHUFFLE, 2 COUNT RIFF, HEEL DIG - BRUSH - BALL - HEEL, 2 COUNT RIFF, HEEL DIG - BRUSH - BALL - HEEL)
Counts: 1&, 2&, 3&4&, 5&, 6&7&

(B) Shuffle R, 2 Count Riff R, Heel Dig - Brush (back) - Ball - Heel R, 2 Count Riff L, Heel Dig - Brush (back) - Ball - Heel L, Ball - Heel R

## 10. Extra Combinations

(SHUFFLE, 2 COUNT RIFF, HEEL DIG - BRUSH -
 BALL - HEEL, 2 COUNT RIFF, HEEL DIG - BRUSH -
 BALL - HEEL, BALL - HEEL)
Counts: 8&, 1&, 2&3&, 4&, 5&, 6&, 7-8

28. **(A)** Stomp R - Heel (bounce) L - Stamp R, Scuffle L -
 Heel (bounce) R, Train 2× L-R, Stomp L, Hold, Reverse All
 **(STOMP - HEEL - STAMP, SCUFFLE - HEEL,
 TRAIN 2× ALT, STOMP, HOLD, REVERSE ALL)**
 Counts: 1&2, &3&, 4&5&6&-7, Hold: 8
 1&2, &3&, 4&5&6&-7, Hold: 8

 **(B)** Stomp R - Heel (bounce) L - Stamp R, Scuffle L -
 Heel (bounce) R, Paradiddle or Paddle & Roll R 2× L-R,
 Stamp - Stamp L-R, Reverse All
 **(STOMP - HEEL - STAMP, SCUFFLE - HEEL,
 PARADIDDLE 2× ALT, STAMP - STAMP,
 REVERSE ALL)**
 Counts: 1&2, &3&, 4e&a, 5&6&, 7-8
 1&2, &3&, 4e&a, 5&6&, 7-8

29. Ball R - Heel - Heel L-R, Reverse All, Step R, Paradiddle or
 Paddle & Roll 2× L-R, Ball - Heel L, Step - Step R-L
 **(BALL - HEEL - HEEL, REVERSE ALL, STEP,
 PARADIDDLE 2× ALT, BALL - HEEL, STEP - STEP)**
 Counts: 1&2, &3&, 4, 5e&a, 6e&a, 7&, a8

30. **(A)** Brush - Brush (front - back) R, Heel (bounce) L - Toe Back R,
 Stamp R, Back Flap L, Stomp - Brush (back) R, Step - Step -
 Step R-L-R, Reverse All
 **(BRUSH - BRUSH, HEEL - TOE BACK, STAMP,
 BACK FLAP, STOMP - BRUSH, STEP - STEP - STEP,
 REVERSE ALL)**
 Counts: 1-2-3-4-5, &6, &7, &8&
 1-2-3-4-5, &6, &7, &8&

 **(B)** Brush - Brush (front - back) R, Heel (bounce) L - Toe Back R,
 Stamp R, Ball - Heel (drop) L - Heel (drop) R, Step L, Ball -
 Heel (drop) R - Heel (drop) L
 **(BRUSH - BRUSH, HEEL - TOE BACK, STAMP, BALL -
 HEEL - HEEL, STEP, BALL - HEEL - HEEL)**
 Counts: 1-2-3-4-5, &6&, 7, &8&

31. **(A)** Crossing Brush R - Heel (bounce) L 4× (brush: front - cross -
 uncross - back), Shuffle - Ball - Heel 2× R-L

(CROSSING BRUSH - HEEL 4×, SHUFFLE - BALL - HEEL 2×)
Counts: &1, &2, &3, &4, &5&6, &7&8

(B) Tap (side) - Drag (in) R, Step - Step R-L, Ball - Heel R, Shuffle - Ball Change L, Shuffle - Ball - Heel L, Stamp R
(TAP - DRAG, STEP - STEP - BALL - HEEL, SHUFFLE - BALL CHANGE, SHUFFLE - BALL - HEEL, STAMP)
Counts: 1-2, 3&a4, &5&6, &7&a8

32. **Paradiddle or Paddle & Roll: Playing with the 1st Count**
*Accent the 1st count of each Paradiddle or Paddle & Roll & reverse on L side*
(A) Paradiddle or Paddle & Roll 8× R-L-R-L-R-L-R-L
(PARADIDDLE 8× ALT)
Counts: 1e&a, 2e&a, 3e&a, 4e&a, 5e&a, 6e&a, 7e&a, 8e&a
(B) Brush (back) - Ball - Heel R, Heel Dig L 8× R-L-R-L-R-L-R-L
(BRUSH - BALL - HEEL - HEEL DIG 8× ALT)
Counts: 1e&a, 2e&a, 3e&a, 4e&a, 5e&a, 6e&a, 7e&a, 8e&a
(C) Ball - Heel R - Scuffle L 8× R-L-R-L-R-L-R-L
(BALL - HEEL - SCUFFLE 8× ALT)
Counts: 1e&a, 2e&a, 3e&a, 4e&a, 5e&a, 6e&a, 7e&a, 8e&a
(D) Heel (drop) L - Scuffle R - Ball R 7× L-R-L-R-L-R,
Break: Heel (drop) R - Brush (back) - Ball Change
(HEEL - SCUFFLE-BALL 7× ALT,
BREAK: HEEL - BRUSH - BALL CHANGE)
Counts: 1e&a, 2e&a, 3e&a, 4e&a, 5e&a, 6e&a, 7e&a, 8e&a

## *Intermediate / Advanced Levels*

1. (A) Flap - Heel R - Shuffle - Step L - Brush (back) R - Heel (drop) L, Repeat All
(FLAP - HEEL - SHUFFLE - STEP - BRUSH - HEEL, REPEAT ALL)
Counts: &1&2&3&4, &5&6&7&8
(B) Flap R, Shuffle (over R) - Step L, Toe Back R - Heel (drop) L - Step R, Brush (back) L - Heel (drop) R, Ball - Heel L, Shuffle R - Heel (bounce) L, Ball Change R
(FLAP - SHUFFLE - STEP - TOE BACK - HEEL, STEP,

## 10. Extra Combinations

BRUSH - HEEL, BALL - HEEL, SHUFFLE - HEEL, BALL CHANGE)
Counts: &1, &2&, 3&4, &5, &6, &a7, &8

2. **(A)** Step R, Shuffle Ball - Change - Step L, Scuff R - Heel (bounce) L - Step (ball) R, Hold
   **(STEP, SHUFFLE - BALL CHANGE - STEP, SCUFF - HEEL - STEP, HOLD)**
   Counts: 1&2&3-4, 5-6-7, Hold: 8

   **(B)** Heel (drop) R, Shuffle L - Heel R, Step - Step L-R, Stomp - Brush (back) L, Heel (bounce) R, Hold
   **(HEEL - SHUFFLE - HEEL, STEP - STEP, STOMP - BRUSH - HEEL, HOLD)**
   Counts: 1&2&3-4, 5-6-7, Hold: 8

   **(C)** <u>Syncopated Rolling Shuffle</u>: Step L, Shuffle - Jump 2× R-L, Shuffle R - Heel L 2×, Hold
   **(SYNCOPATED ROLLING SHUFFLE: STEP, SHUFFLE - JUMP 2× ALT, SHUFFLE - HEEL 2×, HOLD)**
   Counts: 1, &2&3&4, &5&6&7, Hold: 8

   **(D)** <u>Syncopated Rolling Shuffle</u>: Step R, Shuffle - Jump 2× L-R, Scuff L - Heel R - Step L, Hold
   **(SYNCOPATED ROLLING SHUFFLE: STEP, SHUFFLE - JUMP 2× ALT, SCUFF - HEEL - STEP, HOLD)**
   Counts: 1, &2&3&4, 5-6-7, Hold: 8

3. Stomp R - Heel (bounce) L, Flap - Heel R, Reverse All & Repeat R, Scuff L - Heel R - Stamp L
   **(STOMP - HEEL - FLAP - HEEL 3× ALT, SCUFF - HEEL - STAMP)**
   Counts: 1-2&a3, 4-5&a6, 1-2&a3, 4-5-6

4. **(A)** Heel (bounce) L - Heel Dig R, Brush (back) R - Heel (bounce) L - Shuffle R, Heel (bounce) L - Heel Dig R, Brush (back) R - Heel (bounce) L - Step R, Reverse All
   **(HEEL - HEEL DIG, BRUSH - HEEL - SHUFFLE, HEEL - HEEL DIG, BRUSH - HEEL - STEP, REVERSE ALL)**
   Counts: &1&a2&a3&a4, &5&a6&a7&a8

   **(B)** Heel (bounce) L - Heel Dig R - Brush (back) R - Heel (bounce) L - Step R, Reverse All, Heel (bounce) L - Heel Dig R - Brush (back) R 3×, Heel (bounce) L - Step R
   **(HEEL - HEEL DIG - BRUSH - HEEL - STEP,**

### Tap Dance for All

**REVERSE ALL, HEEL - HEEL DIG - BRUSH 3×, HEEL - STEP)**
Counts: &1&a2, &3&a4, &5&a6&a7&a8

5. **Weave** (cross over like a figure "8")
   (A) Shuffle - Ball - Heel R (cross over L), Back Flap 2× L-R, Reverse All
   **(SHUFFLE - BALL - HEEL, BACK FLAP 2×, REVERSE ALL)**
   Counts: &1&2, &3&4, &5&6, &7&8
   (B) Shuffle - Ball - Heel R 3× R-L-R, Back Flap 2× L-R
   **(SHUFFLE - BALL - HEEL 3× ALT, BACK FLAP 2× ALT)**
   Counts: &1&2, &3&4, &5&6, &7&8

6. **Flap Double Heel Combination**
   (A) Flap R, Heel - Heel L-R, Back Flap L, Heel - Heel L-R, Reverse All
   **(FLAP - HEEL - HEEL, BACK FLAP - HEEL - HEEL, REVERSE ALL)**
   Counts: &1&2, &3&4, &5&6, &7&8
   (B) Flap R, Heel - Heel L-R, Back Flap L, Heel - Heel R-L, Flap R, Heel - Heel L-R, Back Flap L, Heel - Heel L-R
   **(FLAP - HEEL - HEEL, BACK FLAP - HEEL - HEEL, FLAP - HEEL - HEEL, BACK FLAP - HEEL - HEEL)**
   Counts: &1&2, &3&4, &5&6, &7&8

7. (A) Heel (bounce) L, Heel Dig - Brush (back) R, Heel (bounce) L - Shuffle R, Heel (bounce) L, Heel Dig - Brush (back) R, Heel (bounce) L - Step (ball) R, Reverse All
   **(HEEL - HEEL DIG, BRUSH - HEEL - SHUFFLE, HEEL - HEEL DIG, BRUSH - HEEL - STEP, REVERSE ALL)**
   Counts: &1&a2&a3&a4, &5&a6&a7&a8
   (B) Repeat R Side,
   Break: Heel (bounce) R, Heel Dig-Brush L, Heel (bounce) R - Step (ball) L, Reverse
   **(HEEL - HEEL DIG, BRUSH - HEEL - SHUFFLE, HEEL - HEEL DIG, BRUSH - HEEL - STEP**
   **BREAK: HEEL - HEEL DIG - BRUSH - HEEL - STEP, REVERSE)**
   Counts: &1&a2&a3&a4, &5&a6, &7&a8

8. **Gum Off the Shoe (Drawback with Shuffle Combination)**
   Brush (back) R, Heel (bounce) L, Shuffle R, Heel (bounce) L,

## 10. Extra Combinations

Step (ball) R, Reverse All & Repeat R, Heel (drop) R, Toe Back L, Heel (drop) R, Step (ball) L
**(BRUSH - HEEL - SHUFFLE - HEEL - STEP, REVERSE & REPEAT R, HEEL - TOE BACK - HEEL - STEP)**
Counts: &a1&a2, &a3&a4, &a5&a6, &7, &8

9. Flap - Heel R, Back Flap - Heel L, Flap R - Scuff L - Heel (drop) R, Ball - Heel L, Repeat All
**(FLAP - HEEL, BACK FLAP - HEEL, FLAP - SCUFF - HEEL, BALL - HEEL, REPEAT ALL)**
Counts: &a1&a2&a3&a4, &a5&a6&a7&a8

10. Shuffle - Ball Change R, Step - Step R-L (or for speed replace Step - Step with Toe Dig R - Hop L), Repeat All, Shuffle - Ball Change 3× R, Step - Step R-L (or Toe Dig - Hop)
**(SHUFFLE - BALL CHANGE, STEP - STEP, REPEAT, SHUFFLE – BALL CHANGE 3×, STEP - STEP OR TOE DIG - HOP)**
Counts: e&a1&2, e&a3&4, e&a5, e&a6, e&a7, &8

11. Scuff R - Hop L, Step - Hop R, Shuffle - Step L, Step R, Flap - Ball Change L
**(SCUFF - HOP, STEP - HOP, SHUFFLE - STEP, STEP, FLAP - BALL CHANGE)**
Counts: 1-2-3-4, &a5-6, &7&8

12. Scuff R - Hop L, Back Flap - Hop R, Shuffle - Step L - Back Flap R, Flap - Ball Change L
**(SCUFF - HOP, BACK FLAP - HOP, SHUFFLE - STEP - BACK FLAP, FLAP - BALL CHANGE)**
Counts: 1-2, &3-4, &a5&6, &7&8

13. Back Flap 2× R-L, Shuffle - Stamp R - Stomp L, Reverse All
**(BACK FLAP 2×, SHUFFLE - STAMP - STOMP, REVERSE ALL)**
Counts: &1, &2, &3, &4, &5, &6, &7, &8

14. Back Flap 2× R-L, Shuffle - Stomp - Stamp R, Reverse All
**(BACK FLAP 2×, SHUFFLE - STOMP - STAMP, REVERSE ALL)**
Counts: &1, &2, &3&4, &5, &6, &7&8

15. **6 Count Riff Combination**
6 Count Riff R, Back Flap - Heel 2× L-R, Reverse All
**(6 COUNT RIFF, BACK FLAP - HEEL 2× ALT, REVERSE ALL)**
Counts: &a1&a2, &a3, &a4, &a5&a6, &a7, &a8

16. **3 Count Riff Combination**
    3 Count Riff - Back Flap - Heel R, Reverse & Repeat R, Flap - Heel 2× R-L
    **(3 COUNT RIFF - BACK FLAP - HEEL 3× ALT, FLAP - HEEL 2× ALT)**
    Counts: &a1, &a2, &a3, &a4, &a5, &a6, &a7, &a8
17. **7 Count Riff Combination**
    Brush (back) R - Heel (bounce) L, Shuffle R - Heel L, 7 Count Riff R, Reverse All
    **(BRUSH - HEEL - SHUFFLE - HEEL, 7 COUNT RIFF, REVERSE ALL)**
    Counts: &1, &a2, &a3e&a4, &5, &a6, &a7e&a8
18. Shuffle R - Hop L - Step R, Flap 2× L-R, Reverse All
    **(SHUFFLE - HOP - STEP, FLAP 2× ALT, REVERSE ALL)**
    Counts: &1&2, &3&4, &5&6, &7&8
19. Flap 2× R-L, Shuffle R - Hop L - Step R, Reverse All, Flap 3× R-L-R, Heel (drop) R - Heel Dig L, Reverse
    **(FLAP 2× ALT, SHUFFLE - HOP - STEP, REVERSE ALL, FLAP 3× ALT, HEEL - HEEL DIG, REVERSE)**
    Counts: &1, &2, &3&4, &5, &6, &7&8
    &1, &2, &3, &4, &5, &6, &7, &8
20. **Rolling Shuffle Combination**
    **(A)** Hop L - Shuffle R 6×, Hop - Double Chug R-L, Repeat All
    **(HOP - SHUFFLE 6×, HOP - DOUBLE CHUG, REPEAT ALL)**
    Counts: 1&a, 2&a, 3&a, 4&a, 5&a, 6&a, 7&8
    1&a, 2&a, 3&a, 4&a, 5&a, 6&a, 7&8
    **(B)** Hop L - Shuffle R 3×, Jump R, Reverse All, Hop L - Shuffle-Jump R, Reverse, Hop L, Rolling Shuffle 3× R-L-R
    **(HOP - SHUFFLE 3× ALT, JUMP, REVERSE ALL, HOP - SHUFFLE - JUMP, REVERSE, HOP, ROLLING SHUFFLE 3× ALT)**
    Counts: 1&a, 2&a, 3&a-4, 5&a, 6&a, 7&a-8
    1&a2, 3&a4, 5&a, 6&a, 7&a8
21. Heel Dig - Brush R - Heel (bounce) L 2× - Ball - Heel R, Toe Back L - Heel (bounce) R - Step L, Hold
    **(HEEL DIG - BRUSH - HEEL 2×, BALL - HEEL, TOE BACK - HEEL - STEP, HOLD)**
    Counts: 1&2, &3&, 4&, 5-6-7, Hold: 8

## 10. Extra Combinations

22. **Sentimental Journey**
    **(A)** Ball Change 2× R, Step R - Brush (forward) L - Hop R, Step L - Ball Change R, Back Flap 2× R-L, Shuffle R, Repeat All 2×
    **(BALL CHANGE 2×, STEP - BRUSH - HOP - STEP - BALL CHANGE, BACK FLAP 2× ALT, SHUFFLE, REPEAT ALL 2×)**
    <u>Counts</u>: &8, &1, &2&, 3&4, &5, &6, &7
    &8, &1, &2&, 3&4, &5, &6, &7
    &8, &1, &2&, 3&4, &5, &6, &7

    **(B)** <u>Break</u>: Shuffle - Step R, Shuffle, Ball Change - Ball 2× L, Hold, Ball Change 2× L, Hold
    **(SHUFFLE - STEP, SHUFFLE, BALL CHANGE 2×, HOLD, BALL CHANGE 2×, HOLD)**
    <u>Counts</u>: &a1, &2, &3, &4, Hold: 5, &6, &7, Hold: 8

23. **Back Essence Combination**
    Back Essence (Brush R, Cross Back R, Ball Change L, Reverse) 2× R-L, Back Flap 2× R-L, Shuffle R - Heel (bounce) L - Step R (over L), 3 Count Riff L
    **(BACK ESSENCE 2× ALT, BACK FLAP 2× ALT, SHUFFLE - HEEL - STEP, 3 COUNT RIFF)**
    <u>Counts</u>: &1, &2, &3, &4, &5, &a, 6&, a, 7, &a8

24. 5 Count Riff (two feet) R, Heel (bounce) R - Toe Back L - Heel (bounce) R - Step (ball) L, Heel (bounce) L - Heel Dig R 3×, Toe (drop) - Heel (bounce) R
    **(5 COUNT RIFF, HEEL - TOE BACK - HEEL - STEP, HEEL - HEEL DIG 3×, TOE - HEEL)**
    <u>Counts</u>: &a1&2, &3&4, &5, &6, &7, &8

25. Stomp R, Heel (bounce) L - Shuffle R 2×, Heel (bounce) L - Ball R, Heel R - Heel Dig - Brush (back) L - Heel (bounce) R - Toe Back L - Heel (bounce) R - Flap, Heel L - Stamp R
    **(STOMP, HEEL - SHUFFLE 2×, HEEL - BALL, HEEL - HEEL DIG, BRUSH - HEEL - TOE BACK - HEEL - FLAP, HEEL - STAMP)**
    <u>Counts</u>: 1&a2&a3, &4, &5&a6&a7, &8

26. **(A)** Cramp Roll R, Ball - Heel R, Reverse All, Reverse Cramp Roll R, Double Pullback R, Heel - Heel (drops) R, Heel - Heel (drops) L
    **(CRAMP ROLL, BALL - HEEL, REVERSE ALL,**

**REVERSE CRAMP ROLL, DOUBLE PULLBACK, HEEL - HEEL 2×)**
Counts: 1&a2, 3-4, 5&a6, 7-8
1&a2, 3&a4, 5-6, 7-8

(B) Out: Toe R (lift to R) - Toe L (lift to L), Heel R (bounce to R) - Heel L (bounce to L), Toe R (lift to R) - Toe L (lift to L), Cramp Roll R
In: Toe R (lift to L) - Toe L (lift to R), Heel R (bounce to L) - Heel L (bounce to R), Toe R (lift to L) - Toe L (lift to R), Cramp Roll R
**(OUT: TOE - TOE, HEEL - HEEL, TOE - TOE, CRAMP ROLL**
**In: TOE - TOE, HEEL - HEEL, TOE - TOE, CRAMP ROLL)**
Counts: 1&, 2&, 3&, 4e&a, 5&, 6&, 7&, 8e&a

(C) Double Paradiddle 2× R-L, Stomp - Stamp R, Reverse All
**(DOUBLE PARADIDDLE 2× ALT, STOMP - STAMP, REVERSE ALL)**
Counts: 1&2&3&, 4&5&6&, 7-8
1&2&3&, 4&5&6&, 7-8

27. (A) Heel (bounce) R - Toe (lift) L, Heel - Heel (bounces) R-L, Heel Dig R, Back Flap - Heel R, Toe - Toe (lifts) L-R, Heel (bounce) L - Heel Dig R, Back Flap 2× R-L, Flap R - Step L
**(HEEL - TOE, HEEL - HEEL, HEEL DIG, BACK FLAP, TOE - TOE - HEEL DIG, BACK FLAP 2× ALT, FLAP - STEP)**
Counts: &1&a2&a3&a4&, a5&6, &7-8

(B) Ball - Heel R, Flap L, Step R - Stomp L, Brush (back) L - Heel (bounce) R - Flap R, Shuffle - Ball - Heel R, Flap - Heel L, Tap R (to R) - Step R
**(BALL - HEEL, FLAP, STEP - STOMP, BRUSH - HEEL - FLAP, SHUFFLE - BALL - HEEL, FLAP - HEEL, TAP - STEP)**
Counts: &1, &2, &3, &a4&, a5&a, 6&a, 7-8

28. (A) Hold, Stamp - Stamp (out-out) R-L, Back Flap R (behind L), Step L (over R), Brush (front) R, Back Flap R, Heel - Heel R-L
**(HOLD, STAMP - STAMP, BACK FLAP, STEP, BRUSH, BACK FLAP, HEEL - HEEL)**
Counts: Hold: 1, 2-3, &4-5, 6, &7, &8

## 10. Extra Combinations

(B) Hold, 5 Count Riff (2 foot) R, Scuff L, Hold, Hop R,
Shuffle Alternating Double Pullback 3× L-R-L
**(HOLD, 5 COUNT RIFF, SCUFF, HOLD, HOP SHUFFLE ALT DOUBLE PULLBACK 3×)**
Counts: Hold: 1, e&a2&, 3, Hold: 4, 5, e&a6, e&a7, e&a8

29. (A) Stamp R, Ball L, Heel - Heel L-R, Stomp - Brush (back) - Step L, Ball - Heel R, Reverse All
**(STAMP, BALL - HEEL - HEEL, STOMP - BRUSH - STEP, BALL - HEEL, REVERSE ALL)**
Counts: 1, &a2, &3&, 4&, 5, &a6, &7&, 8&

(B) Repeat R Side, Stomp - Brush (back) - Step 3× L-R-L, Stamp R
**(STAMP, BALL - HEEL - HEEL, STOMP - BRUSH - STEP, BALL - HEEL, STOMP - BRUSH - STEP 3× ALT, STAMP)**
Counts: 1, &a2, &3&, 4&, 5&a, 6&a, 7&a-8

30. (A) Heel - Heel (weighted) R-L, Ball - Ball R-L, Paradiddle or Paddle & Roll R, Scuffle L - Heel (bounce) R, Heel - Heel (weighted) L-R, Ball - Ball L-R, Scuffle L - Heel (bounce) R, Shuffle L
**(HEEL - HEEL, BALL - BALL, PARADIDDLE, SCUFFLE - HEEL, HEEL - HEEL, BALL - BALL, SCUFFLE - HEEL, SHUFFLE)**
Counts: 1&, 2&, 3&a4, &a5, &a6&, a7&, a8

(B) Single Pickup R, Flap L, 3 Count Riff - Ball Change R, 5 Count Riff R, Heel - Heel (weighted) L-R, Click (front taps together), Toe - Toe (drops) L-R
**(SINGLE PICKUP, FLAP, 3 COUNT RIFF - BALL CHANGE, 5 COUNT RIFF, HEEL - HEEL, FLAP, HEEL - HEEL, CLICK - TOE - TOE)**
Counts: &1, &2, &a3&4, &5&a6, &7, &a8

31. (A) Stomp (front) - Drag (back) R, Step - Step R-L, Toe (outside edge of tap) R - Heel - Heel R-L, Scuffle R - Heel (bounce) L, Toe (inside edge of tap) R - Heel - Heel R-L, Scuffle R - Heel (bounce) L
**(STOMP - DRAG, STEP - STEP, TOE - HEEL - HEEL, SCUFFLE - HEEL, TOE - HEEL - HEEL, SCUFFLE - HEEL)**
Counts: 1-2, 3-4, 5&a, 6&a, 7&a, 8&a

(B) Stomp (front) - Drag (back) R, Step - Step R-L, Ball -

Heel (drop) R - Heel (bounce) L 3× (cross over L - R side - cross over L), Ball R - Heel - Heel L-R
**(STOMP - DRAG, STEP - STEP, BALL - HEEL - HEEL 3×: CROSS - OPEN - CROSS, BALL - HEEL - HEEL)**
Counts: 1-2, 3-4, 5&a, 6&a, 7&a, 8&a

(C) Reverse A & B (end Stamp L - no last Ball - Heel - Heel)
**(STOMP - DRAG, STEP - STEP, TOE - HEEL - HEEL, SCUFFLE - HEEL, TOE - HEEL - HEEL, SCUFFLE - HEEL ‖**
**STOMP - DRAG, STEP - STEP, BALL - HEEL - HEEL 3×: CROSS - OPEN - CROSS, STAMP)**
Counts: 1-2, 3-4, 5&a, 6&a, 7&a, 8&a
1-2, 3-4, 5&a, 6&a, 7&a-8

32. (A) Scuff R - Heel (bounce) - Toe (lift) L, Brush (back) R - Heel (bounce) L - Toe Back R, Toe (lift) L, Stamp - Stamp R-L, Hold, Back Flap 2× R-L
**(SCUFF - HEEL - TOE, BRUSH - HEEL - TOE BACK - TOE, STAMP - STAMP, HOLD, BACK FLAP 2× ALT)**
Counts: 1&2, &3&4, &5, Hold: 6, &7&8

(B) Scuff R - Hop L, Ball R - Heel - Heel (drops) R-L, Brush (back) R - Heel (bounce) L, Flap - Heel R - Flap L, Brush R 2× (front - back)
**(SCUFF - HOP, BALL - HEEL - HEEL, BRUSH - HEEL, FLAP - HEEL - FLAP, BRUSH 2×)**
Counts: 1-2, &a3, &4, &a5&6, 7-8

(C) Toe Stand R - Back Flap L, Flap R - Heel - Heel (drops) L-R, Ball L - Heel - Heel (drops) R-L, Ball R - Heel - Heel (drops) L-R, Step L
**(TOE STAND - BACK FLAP, FLAP - HEEL - HEEL, BALL - HEEL - HEEL 2×, STEP)**
Counts: 1&2, &3&4, &5&, 6&7-8

(D) Repeat (B) - End: Jump (two feet apart), Slide (two feet together)
**(SCUFF - HOP, BALL - HEEL - HEEL, BRUSH - HEEL, FLAP - HEEL - FLAP, JUMP - SLIDE)**
Counts: 1-2, &a3, &4, &a5&6, 7-8

33. Hop L, Shuffle - Ball - Heel R, Heel Dig - Toe (drop) L, Heel Dig - Brush (back) R, Ball - Heel R - Heel - Toe (lift) L, Heel Dig - Toe (drop) R

## 10. Extra Combinations

(HOP, SHUFFLE - BALL - HEEL, HEEL DIG - TOE,
HEEL DIG - BRUSH, BALL - HEEL - HEEL - TOE,
HEEL DIG - TOE)
Counts: 1, &2&3, &4, &5, &6&7, &8

34. **(A)** Double Shuffle R, Flap 2× R-L, Heel (bounce) 4× R-L-R-L - Stomp R, Back Flap 2× R-L
   **(DOUBLE SHUFFLE, FLAP 2× ALT, HEEL 4× - STOMP, BACK FLAP 2× ALT)**
   Counts: 1&a2, &3&4, &5&a6, &7&8
   **(B)** Click (heels), Heel - Heel R-L - Toe - Toe (lifts) R-L, Stamp - Stamp R-L, Stomp R, Back Flap 2× R-L, Stamp R
   **(CLICK, HEEL - HEEL - TOE - TOE, STAMP - STAMP, STOMP, BACK FLAP 2× ALT, STAMP)**
   Counts: 1, 2&a3, &4, 5, &6&7, 8

35. **Syncopated Combination**
   **(A)** Flap R - Step L 2×, Step - Step R-L, Flap R, Heel - Heel (drops) R-L - Toe - Toe (lifts) R-L 2×, Heel Dig R
   **(FLAP - STEP 2×, STEP - STEP, FLAP - HEEL - HEEL - TOE - TOE - HEEL - HEEL - TOE - TOE, HEEL DIG)**
   Counts: &1&, 2&3, &4, &5&a6&a7&a8
   **(B)** Back Flap 2× R-L, Flap R, Flap L - Step R 3×, Shuffle L
   **(BACK FLAP 2× ALT, FLAP, FLAP - STEP 3×, SHUFFLE)**
   Counts: &1&2, &3, &4&5&6&7&, 8&
   **(C)** Single Chug R, Step L (feet together), Heels - Heels (twist) R-L, Double Pullback R 4×
   **(SINGLE CHUG, STEP, HEELS - HEELS, DOUBLE PULLBACK 4×)**
   Counts: 1, 2, 3-4, 5&a6, 7&a8, 1&a2, 3&a4
   **(D)** Break: Heel (drop) R - Heel Dig L - Back Flap L - Stomp R, Drag (back) R - Single Chug L
   **(BREAK: HEEL - HEEL DIG - BACK FLAP - STOMP, DRAG - SINGLE CHUG)**
   Counts: &5&a6, 7-8

36. **(A)** Hop L, Flap 3× R-L-R, Stomp L, Reverse All
   **(HOP, FLAP 3× ALT, STOMP, REVERSE ALL)**
   Counts: &a1&2&3-4, &a5&6&7-8
   **(B)** Hop L, Flap 2× R-L, Shuffle Swap Grab Off R, Flap R, Shuffle Swap Grab Off L, Stomp L

### Tap Dance for All

### (HOP, FLAP 2× ALT, SHUFFLE SWAP GRAB OFF, FLAP, SHUFFLE SWAP GRAB OFF, STOMP)
<u>Counts</u>: &a1&2, &3&a4, &5, &6&a7, 8

QUOTABLE QUOTE

*"We should consider every day lost on which we have not danced at least once."—Friedrich Wilhelm Nietzsche*

… 11 …

# Intermediate / Advanced, Advanced Levels

1. Ball Change - Double Pullback R, Step R - Toe Back L - Heel (drop) R - Step L, Ball Change R, Double Pullback 3× R, Reverse All
   **(BALL CHANGE - DOUBLE PULLBACK, STEP - TOE BACK - HEEL - STEP, BALL CHANGE, DOUBLE PULLBACK 3×, REVERSE ALL)**
   Counts: &1e&a2, &3&4, &5, e&a6, e&a7, e&a8
         &1e&a2, &3&4, &5, e&a6, e&a7, e&a8
2. Step - Step R-L - 3 Count Riff R, Repeat, Step - Step R-L, Heel - Heel L-R, Toe Back L - Heel (bounce) R, Step - Step L-R
   **(STEP - STEP - 3 COUNT RIFF, REPEAT, STEP - STEP, HEEL - HEEL, TOE BACK - HEEL, STEP - STEP)**
   Counts: &1&a2, &3&a4, &5&6&7&8
3. Hop L, Scuffle - Jump 2× R-L, Scuffle R - Heel (drop) L, Scuffle R - Hop L, Scuffle - Jump R, Scuffle - Step (ball) L, Heel (drop) 4× R-L-R-L
   **(HOP, SCUFFLE - JUMP 2×, SCUFFLE - HEEL, SCUFFLE - HOP, SCUFFLE - JUMP, SCUFFLE - STEP, HEEL DROP 4× ALT)**
   Counts: &1&a2&a3&a4&a, 5&a6&a7&a8
4. **Quadruple Combination**
   Shuffle - Shuffle - Ball - Heel R, Reverse & Repeat R, Flap - Heel 2× L-R
   **(SHUFFLE - SHUFFLE - BALL - HEEL, REVERSE & REPEAT R, FLAP - HEEL 2× ALT)**
   Counts: &a1&a2, &a3&a4, &a5&a6, &a7&a8

5. **Pullback Combination**
   Ball Change - Double Pullback 3× R, Swap Pickup (Shuffle R - Pickup L - Land R) 2× R-L,
   **(BALL CHANGE - DOUBLE PULLBACK 3×, SWAP PICKUP 2× ALT)**
   Counts: &1e&a2, &3e&a4, &5&6, &7&8

6. **Maxie Ford Combination**
   **(A)** Hop L - Shuffle R - Hop L, Maxie Ford with a Heel Drop 3×, Reverse All
   **(HOP - SHUFFLE - HOP, SHUFFLE - JUMP - HEEL - TOE BACK 3×, REVERSE ALL)**
   Counts 1&a2, &3&a4, 5&a6, &7&a8
   1&a2, &3&a4, 5&a6, &7&a8
   **(B)** Shuffle - Jump R, Ball - Heel L - Heel Dig R, Repeat All, Maxie Ford with a Heel Drop 2× R-L, Shuffle - Jump R, Ball - Heel L - Heel Dig R, Repeat All, Maxie Ford with a Heel Drop R, Stamp - Stamp L-R
   **(SHUFFLE - JUMP, BALL - HEEL - HEEL DIG, REPEAT ALL, MAXIE FORD WITH A HEEL DROP 2× ALT, SHUFFLE - JUMP, BALL - HEEL - HEEL DIG, REPEAT ALL, MAXIE FORD WITH A HEEL DROP, STAMP - STAMP)**
   Counts: &1e&a2, &3e&a4, &5&a6, &7&a8
   &1e&a2, &3e&a4, &5&a6, 7-8

7. **Double Flap & Pullback Combination**
   Double Flap R, Step - Step R-L, Ball Change - Double Pullback R, Outside Paddle Turn (no turn: Back Brush - Ball Change R - Back Brush R, Ball Change 2× R)
   **(DOUBLE FLAP, STEP - STEP, BALL CHANGE - DOUBLE PULLBACK, OUTSIDE PADDLE TURN: NO TURN)**
   Counts: e&a1, &2, &3e&a4, &5&6&7&8

8. **Scuffle Cramp Roll Combination**
   Scuffle Alternating Cramp Roll 3× R-L-R,
   Heel (drops) 6× L-R-L-R-L-R
   **(SCUFFLE ALTERNATING CRAMP ROLL 3×, HEELS 6× ALT)**
   Counts: &a1&a2, &a3&a4, &a5&a6, &a7&a8

## 11. Intermediate / Advanced, Advanced Levels

9. **<u>Riffle - Heel Cramp Roll Combination</u>**
   Riffle R - Heel L, Alternating Cramp Roll R, Reverse All & Repeat R, Same Side Cramproll 2× L
   **(RIFFLE - HEEL, ALTERNATING CRAMP ROLL, REVERSE ALL & REPEAT R, SAME SIDE CRAMP ROLL 2×)**
   <u>Counts</u>: e&a1, e&a2, e&a3, e&a5, e&a6, e&a7, e&a8

10. Heel (bounce) L - Flap R, Heel - Heel R-L, Shuffle R - Jump R - Toe Back L - Step L - Ball Change R, Repeat All
    **(HEEL - FLAP, HEEL - HEEL, SHUFFLE - JUMP - TOE BACK - STEP - BALL CHANGE, REPEAT ALL)**
    <u>Counts</u>: &a1&a2&a3&a4, &a5&a6&a7&a8

11. Flap R, Heel - Heel L-R, Brush (back) L - Heel (bounce) R - Toe Back L - Heel (bounce) R, Flap L, Heel - Heel R-L, Shuffle Alternating Cramp Roll R
    **(FLAP - HEEL - HEEL, BRUSH - HEEL - TOE BACK - HEEL, FLAP - HEEL - HEEL, SHUFFLE ALTERNATING CRAMP ROLL)**
    <u>Counts</u>: &1&2&3&4, &5&6, &a7&a8

12. Flap R, Shuffle 2× L, Ball Change L, Back Flap L - Shuffle - Ball Change R - Heel (bounce) L - Step R
    **(FLAP, SHUFFLE 2×, BALL CHANGE, BACK FLAP - SHUFFLE – BALL CHANGE - HEEL - STEP)**
    <u>Counts</u>: &1&2&3&4, &5&6&7&8

13. Heel (bounce) L - Riffle R - Heel (bounce) L, Back Flap R, Shuffle 2× L - Heel (bounce) R - Step L, Riffle R - Heel (bounce) L - Back Flap R, Riffle L - Heel (bounce) R - Back Flap L
    **(HEEL - RIFFLE - HEEL, BACK FLAP, SHUFFLE 2× - HEEL - STEP, RIFF, RIFFLE - HEEL - BACK FLAP 2× ALT)**
    <u>Counts</u>: &e&a<u>1</u>, &2, &a3&a4, e&a<u>5</u>&6, e&a<u>7</u>&8

14. Back Flap 2× R-L, Shuffle R - Heel (bounce) L - Step - Heel (drop) R - Scuff L, Brush (back) L - Heel (bounce) R - Toe Back - Jump L - Heel Dig R, Reverse
    **(BACK FLAP 2× ALT, SHUFFLE - HEEL - STEP - HEEL - SCUFF, BRUSH - HEEL - TOE BACK - JUMP - HEEL DIG 2×)**
    <u>Counts</u>: &1&a2&a3&4, &5&a6, &7&a8

15. **(A)** Step R - Scuff L - Heel (drop) R, Back Flap 2× L-R, Shuffle L - Heel (bounce) R, Step L (over R), Hold

  (STEP - SCUFF - HEEL, BACK FLAP 2× ALT, SHUFFLE - HEEL - CROSS, HOLD)
  Counts: 1-2-3, &4&5&6&7, Hold: 8
 (B) Ball Change 2× R (L over R), Heel (drop) L - Step R (over L) - Heel (drop) R - Toe Back L - Slide R (to L) - Step L
  (BALL CHANGE 2×, HEEL - CROSS - HEEL - TOE BACK - SLIDE - STEP)
  Counts: &1&2, 3-4-5-6-7-8

16. Heel (drop) L - Heel Dig (weighted) R, Step - Step L-R, Reverse All, Heel (drop) L, Ball - Heel 3× (Jazz Square or Grapevine) R-L-R, Dig (toe) L
  (HEEL - HEEL DIG, STEP - STEP, REVERSE ALL, HEEL, BALL - HEEL 3× ALT, DIG)
  Counts: &1&2, &3&4, &5&6&7&8

17. Shuffle R - Hop L 2×, Shuffle - Jump R, Shuffle L - Hop R, Reverse All & Repeat R, Rolling Shuffle (Shuffle - Jump) 4× L-R-L-R
  (SHUFFLE - HOP 2×, SHUFFLE - JUMP, SHUFFLE - HOP, REVERSE ALL & REPEAT R, ROLLING SHUFFLE 4× ALT)
  Counts: &a1&a2, &a3, &a4, &a5&a6, &a7, &a8
      &a1&a2, &a3, &a4, &a5&a6&a7&a8

18. (A) Flap - Heel R - Toe Back L - Heel (bounce) R - Step (back) - Brush (back) R - Heel (bounce) L, Heel Dig - Toe (drop) R - Step L 2×, Heel (bounce) L, Heel Dig R
  (FLAP - HEEL - TOE BACK - HEEL - STEP - BRUSH - HEEL, HEEL DIG - TOE - STEP 2×, HEEL - HEEL - DIG)
  Counts: &1&2&3&4, &5&6&7&8
 (B) Repeat 1st 4 counts, Ball Change - Step R, Ball - Heel L, Step R, Hold
  (FLAP - HEEL - TOE BACK - HEEL - STEP - BRUSH - HEEL, BALL CHANGE - STEP - BALL - HEEL - STEP, HOLD)
  Counts: &1&2&3&4, &5&6&7, Hold: 8

19. (A) Brush (forward) R - Hop L, Step - Step R-L, Brush (forward) R - Hop L, Step 3× R-L-R, Shuffle - Ball - Heel 3× L-R-L, Ball - Heel (drop) R, Reverse All
  (BRUSH - HOP - STEP - STEP, BRUSH - HOP, STEP 3× ALT, SHUFFLE - BALL - HEEL 3× ALT, BALL - HEEL, REVERSE ALL)

## 11. Intermediate / Advanced, Advanced Levels

    Counts: &a1&2&3&4, e&a5, e&a6, e&a7, &8
    &a1&2&3&4, e&a5, e&a6, e&a7, &8

  (B) Repeat 1st 4 counts, Alternating Cramp Roll 4× L-R-L-R, Reverse All
    **(BRUSH - HOP - STEP - STEP, BRUSH - HOP, STEP 3× ALT, ALTERNATING CRAMP ROLL 4×, REVERSE ALL)**
    Counts: &a1&2&3&4, e&a5, e&a6, e&a7, e&a8
    &a1&2&3&4, e&a5, e&a6, e&a7, e&a8

20. Brush (back) R - Heel (bounce) L, Shuffle R - Heel (bounce) L, Ball - Heel R, Heel Dig L, Stamp - Stomp L-R, Brush (back) R - Heel (bounce) L - Stamp - Stomp R-L, Reverse Brush (back) R - Heel (bounce) L - Stamp - Stamp R-L, Chug - Chug R-L
    **(BRUSH - HEEL, SHUFFLE - HEEL, BALL - HEEL, HEEL DIG - STAMP - STOMP, BRUSH - HEEL - STAMP - STOMP, REVERSE, BRUSH - HEEL - STAMP - STAMP, CHUG - CHUG)**
    Counts: &a1&a, 2&a3&, a4&a, 5&a6, &a7&, a8

21. **Pullback Combination**
  (A) Flap - Single Pullback 2× R-L, Flap 3× R-L-R, Single Pullback R
    **(FLAP - SINGLE PULLBACK 2× ALT, FLAP 3×, SINGLE PULLBACK)**
    Counts: &1&2, &3&4, &5&6&7, &8
  (B) Flap - Single Pullback 2× L-R, Flap 2× L-R, Ball Change - Double Pullback L
    **(FLAP - SINGLE PULLBACK 2× ALT, FLAP 2× ALT, BALL CHANGE – DOUBLE PULLBACK)**
    Counts: &1&2, &3&4, &5&6, &7e&a8

22. Heel - Heel (weighted) R-L, Click (toes together) - Toe - Toe (drops) R-L 2×, Ball Change R, Step R - Click L (to R) - Heel (drop) R, Reverse, Ball Change R - Click R (to L) - Ball Change R
    **(HEEL - HEEL, CLICK - TOE - TOE 2×, BALL CHANGE, STEP - CLICK - HEEL 2× ALT, BALL CHANGE - CLICK - BALL CHANGE)**
    Counts: &1&a2&a3, &4, &5&a6&, a7&a8

23. Stomp R - Heel (bounce) L - Flap - Heel R, Reverse All & Repeat R, Scuff L - Heel (bounce) R - Stamp L

(STOMP - HEEL - FLAP - HEEL 3× ALT, SCUFF - HEEL - STAMP)
Counts: 1-2&a3, 4-5&a6, 1-2&a3, 4-5-6

24. Stomp R - Heel (bounce) L, Shuffle R - Heel (bounce) L 2×, Ball - Heel R, Heel Dig L - Brush (back) L - Heel (bounce) R - Toe Back L - Heel (bounce) R, Flap - Pause - Heel L - Stamp R
(STOMP - HEEL, SHUFFLE - HEEL 2×, BALL - HEEL, HEEL DIG - BRUSH - HEEL - TOE BACK - HEEL, FLAP - PAUSE - HEEL - STAMP)
Counts: 1&, 2&a3&a, 4&5&a6&a7, &8

25. 5 Count Riff (two feet) R, Heel (bounce) R - Toe Back L - Heel (bounce) R - Step L, Heel (bounce) L - Heel Dig R 3× (out - cross front - out), Toe (drop) R - Heel (drop) R
(5 COUNT RIFF, HEEL - TOE BACK - HEEL - STEP, HEEL - HEEL DIG 3×: OUT - CROSS - OUT, TOE - HEEL)
Counts: &a1&2, &3&4, &5&6&7, &8

26. Flap R, Heel - Heel L-R, Heel Dig L, Brush (back) L - Heel (bounce) R - Toe Back L - Heel (bounce) R, Flap L, Heel - Heel R-L, Heel Dig R, Back Flap R, Heel - Heel L-R, Heel Dig L
(FLAP - HEEL - HEEL - HEEL DIG, BRUSH - HEEL - TOE BACK - HEEL, FLAP - HEEL - HEEL - HEEL DIG, BACK FLAP - HEEL - HEEL - HEEL DIG)
Counts: &1&a2, &3&4, &5&a6, &7&a8

27. Ball Change - Flap R, Maxie Ford (Shuffle - Jump L - Toe Back R), Ball Change - Flap - Heel R, Back Flap - Heel L, Step - Step R-L
(BALL CHANGE - FLAP, MAXIE FORD, BALL CHANGE - FLAP - HEEL, BACK FLAP - HEEL, STEP - STEP)
Counts: &1&2&3&4, &5&a6&a7, &8

28. Ball Change - Flap R, Maxie Ford (Shuffle - Jump L - Toe Back R), Ball Change - Double Pullback R, Heel - Heel (weighted) R-L, Reverse Double Pullback R
(BALL CHANGE - FLAP, MAXIE FORD, BALL CHANGE - DOUBLE PULLBACK, HEEL - HEEL, REVERSE DOUBLE PULLBACK)
Counts: &1&2&3&4, &5e&a6, &7e&a8

29. Ball Change - Double Pullback R, Double Wing, Step R - Scuff L, Reverse All

## 11. Intermediate / Advanced, Advanced Levels

(BALL CHANGE - DOUBLE PULLBACK, DOUBLE WING,
STEP - SCUFF, REVERSE ALL)
Counts: &1e&a2, &a3, &4, &5e&a6, &a7, &8

30. **Mock Wing Time Step Combination**
    (A) Mock Wing Time Step 2× R-L
    (MOCK WING TIME STEP 2×)
    Counts: &1&a2, &3&a4, &5&a6, &7&a8
    (B) Double Flap R, Step - Step R-L, Double Pullback R, Step - Step R-L, Mock Wing Time Step R
    (DOUBLE FLAP, STEP - STEP, DOUBLE PULLBACK, STEP - STEP, MOCK WING TIME STEP)
    Counts: e&a1, &2, e&a3, &4, &5&a6, &7&a8

31. Flap Bombershay R, Brush (back) L - Heel (drop) R - Shuffle L - Heel (drop) R - Step L, 3 Count Riff R, Back Flap - Heel R, Back Flap L, Heel - Heel - Heel L-R-L, Heel Dig R
    (FLAP BOMBEERSHAY, BRUSH - HEEL - SHUFFLE - HEEL - STEP, 3 COUNT RIFF, BACK FLAP - HEEL, BACK FLAP, HEEL - HEEL - HEEL, HEEL DIG)
    Counts: &1&a2, &a3&a4, &a5, &a6, &a, 7&a, 8

32. Brush (back) R - Heel (bounce) L, Stamp - Stomp R-L, Reverse All
    Brush (back) R - Heel (bounce) L - Shuffle R - Heel (bounce) L, 6 Count Riff R
    (BRUSH - HEEL, STAMP - STOMP, REVERSE ALL
    BRUSH - HEEL - SHUFFLE - HEEL, 6 COUNT RIFF)
    Counts: &1&2, &3&4, &5&a6, &a7&a8

33. Stomp - Brush (back) R - Heel (bounce) L, Flap R, Heel - Heel R-L, Brush (back) R - Heel (bounce) L, Flap R, Heel - Heel L-R, Heel Dig, L
    (STOMP - BRUSH - HEEL, FLAP - HEEL - HEEL, BRUSH - HEEL, FLAP - HEEL - HEEL, HEEL DIG)
    Counts: 1&2, &3&4, &5&6&7-8

34. (A) Heel (bounce) L - Shuffle R - Heel (bounce) L - Step (ball) R, Heel (bounces) 4× L-R-L-R, Reverse All
    (HEEL - SHUFFLE - HEEL - STEP, HEELS 4× ALT, REVERSE ALL)
    Counts: &1&a2, &3&4, &5&a6, &7&8
    (B) Heel (bounce) L - Shuffle R - Heel (bounce) L - Toe Dig R, Heel (bounce) L - Shuffle R - Heel (bounce) L - Step (ball) R,

Heel (drop) R - Shuffle L 2×, Heel (bounce) R - Ball L, Heel - Heel R-L, Heel Dig R
**(HEEL - SHUFFLE - HEEL - TOE DIG, HEEL - SHUFFLE - HEEL - BALL, HEEL - SHUFFLE 2×, HEEL - BALL - HEEL - HEEL - HEEL DIG)**
Counts: &1&a2, &3&a4, &5&a6&a7&a8

35. Heel (bounce) L - Heel Dig - Toe (drop) R - Heel (bounce) L, Heel Dig - Brush (back) R - Heel (bounce) L - Step (ball) R, Heel (drop) R - Heel Dig - Toe (drop) L - Heel (bounce) R, Heel Dig L - Heel (bounce) R 2×
    **(HEEL - HEEL DIG - TOE - HEEL, HEEL DIG - BRUSH - HEEL - BALL, HEEL - HEEL DIG - TOE-HEEL, HEEL DIG - HEEL 2×)**
    Counts: 1&2&3&4, &5&6&7&8

36. **(A)** Ball Change - Double Flap R 2×, Ball Change R, Double Pullback R 3×
    **(BALL CHANGE - DOUBLE FLAP 2×, BALL CHANGE, DOUBLE PULLBACK 3×)**
    Counts: &1e&a2, &3e&a4, &5, e&a6, e&a7, e&a8
    **(B)** Ball Change - Double Flap R 2×, Back Flap R - Ball Change L, Heel (drop) R - Ball-Heel L - Step R
    **(BALL CHANGE - DOUBLE FLAP 2×, BACK FLAP - BALL CHANGE, HEEL - BALL - HEEL - STEP)**
    Counts: &1e&a2, &3e&a4, &5&6, &7&8

37. **(A)** Hop L - Shuffle R - Hop L - Step (ball) R, Flap - Heel 2× L-R, Reverse All
    **(HOP - SHUFFLE - HOP - STEP, FLAP - HEEL 2×, REVERSE ALL)**
    Counts: &1&a2, &a3, &a4, &5&a6, &a7, &a8
    **(B)** Hop L - Shuffle R - Hop L - Step (ball) R, Reverse All & Repeat R Side, Flap Cramp Roll L
    **(HOP - SHUFFLE - HOP - STEP, REVERSE ALL & REPEAT R SIDE, FLAP CRAMP ROLL)**
    Counts: &1&a2, &3&a4, &5&6, &7&a8

38. **(A)** Flap R, Heel - Heel R-L, Heel Dig R, Brush (back) R - Heel (bounce) L - Toe Back - Jump - Heel (drop) R - Heel Dig L

## 11. Intermediate / Advanced, Advanced Levels

    (FLAP - HEEL - HEEL - HEEL DIG, BRUSH - HEEL - TOE BACK - JUMP - HEEL - HEEL DIG)
    Counts: &1&a2&a3&a4

  (B) Brush (back) L - Heel (bounce) R, Stamp - Stomp L-R, Reverse & Repeat L
    (BRUSH - HEEL, STAMP - STOMP 3× ALT)
    Counts: &a5&, a6&a, 7&a8

39. (A) Brush (back) R - Heel (bounce) L, Shuffle - Ball - Heel R, Back Flap - Heel 2× L-R, Reverse All
    (BRUSH - HEEL, SHUFFLE - BALL - HEEL, BACK FLAP - HEEL 2×, REVERSE ALL)
    Counts: &a1&a2&a3&a4, &a5&a6&a7&a8

  (B) Brush (back) R - Heel (bounce) L, Shuffle - Ball - Heel R, Reverse All & Repeat R Side, Flap L, Step - Step (ball) R-L, Heel (drop) R - Heel Dig L
    (BRUSH - HEEL, SHUFFLE - BALL - HEEL, REVERSE ALL & REPEAT R SIDE, FLAP - STEP - STEP - HEEL - HEEL DIG)
    Counts: &a1&a2, &a3&a4, &a5&a6, &a7&a8

40. Shuffle R - Hop L 5×, Double Shuffle R - Hop L - Shuffle R - Hop L - Jump R
    (SHUFFLE - HOP 5×, DOUBLE SHUFFLE - HOP - SHUFFLE - HOP - JUMP)
    Counts: &a1&a2&a3&a4&a5, &a6&a7&a8

41. Flap 2× L-R, Toe Dig L - Heel (drop) R - Heel Dig L - Ball Change L, Heel (drop) R - Step (ball) L, Heel - Heel R-L - Heel Dig R, Reverse
    (FLAP 2×, TOE DIG - HEEL - HEEL DIG - BALL CHANGE, HEEL - STEP - HEEL - HEEL - HEEL DIG, REVERSE)
    Counts: &1&2&3&a4, &5&a6, &7&a8

42. (A) Back Flap R, Double Shuffle L - Heel (drop) R - Toe Back L - Heel (bounce) R - Jump L - Heel Dig R
    (BACK FLAP, DOUBLE SHUFFLE - HEEL - TOE BACK - HEEL - JUMP - HEEL DIG)
    Counts: &1, &a2&, a3&a4

  (B) Brush (back) R - Heel (drop) L - Toe Back R, Stamp - Stomp R-L, Reverse All

(BRUSH - HEEL - TOE BACK, STAMP - STOMP,
REVERSE ALL)
Counts: &5&a6, &7&a8

43. **(A)** Heel (bounce) L - Heel Dig R - Brush (back) R -
Heel (bounce) L - Toe Back R - Heel (bounce) L, Toe -
Heel R, Step (ball) L
**(HEEL - HEEL DIG - BRUSH - HEEL - TOE BACK - HEEL,
BALL - HEEL, STEP)**
Counts: &1&2&3&a4

   **(B)** Heel (drop) L - Toe Back R - Heel (bounce) L - Step (ball),
Reverse All
**(HEEL - TOE BACK - HEEL - STEP, REVERSE ALL)**
Counts: &5&6, &7&8

44. **Pickup Combination**
   **(A)** Scuff R - Heel (bounce) L, Brush R - Heel (bounce) L 3×
(Brushes: cross over L, uncross, back),
Syncopated Rhythm: Toe Back R - Pickup L, Brush (front) R -
Pickup L, Brush R (cross over L) - Pickup L
**(SCUFF - HEEL, BRUSH - HEEL 3×,
<u>SYNCOPATED</u>: TOE BACK - PICKUP, BRUSH -
PICKUP 2×)**
Counts: 1&, 2&3&4&, Sync: <u>5</u>&6, &7&, 8&1

   **(B)** Brush R (uncross) - Pickup, Brush (back) R - Heel (bounce) L -
Toe Back R - Heel (bounce), Toe Stand R - Toe Stand L,
Heel - Heel (weighted) R-L, Toe - Toe (drops) R-L
**(BRUSH - PICKUP, BRUSH - HEEL - TOE BACK - HEEL,
TOE STAND 2× ALT, HEEL - HEEL, TOE - TOE)**
Counts: &2&, 3&4&, 5&, &6, 7-8

45. **Ball - Heel Combination**
Ball - Heel 2× R-L, Ball - Heel - Toe (lift) - Heel R, Ball -
Heel 2× L-R, Ball - Heel - Toe (lift) - Heel L, Ball - Heel 2× R-L,
Ball - Heel - Toe (lift) - Heel R, Reverse All
**(BALL - HEEL 2× ALT, BALL - HEEL - TOE - HEEL, BALL -
HEEL 2× ALT, BALL - HEEL - TOE - HEEL, BALL -
HEEL 2× ALT, BALL - HEEL - TOE - HEEL, REVERSE ALL)**
Counts: 1&2&, 3e&a, 4&5&, 6e&a, 7e&a, 8e&a
1&2&, 3e&a, 4&5&, 6e&a, 7e&a, 8e&a

46. **(A)** Double Paradiddle or Paddle & Roll R, Stomp L -
Brush (back) L - Heel (bounce) R - Toe Back L,

## 11. Intermediate / Advanced, Advanced Levels

Heel (bounce) R - Flap 3× L-R-L, Heel (drop) - Toe R (lift to L) - Stamp L
**(DOUBLE PARADIDDLE, STOMP - BRUSH - HEEL - TOE BACK, HEEL - FLAP 3×, HEEL - TOE - STAMP)**
<u>Counts</u>: 1&a2&a, 3&a4, &a5&6&7, &a8

**(B)** Flap 3× R-L-R, Heel (drop) - Toe L (lift to R), Stamp R, Back Flap 2× L-R, Shuffle R - Hop L, Scuff - Heel Dig - Toe (drop) L - Stamp R, Reverse All
**(FLAP 3×, HEEL - TOE, STAMP, BACK FLAP 2× ALT, SHUFFLE - HOP, SCUFF - HEEL DIG - TOE - STAMP, REVERSE ALL)**
<u>Counts</u>: &1&2&3, &a4, &5&a, 6&a, 7&a8
&1&2&3, &a4, &5&a, 6&a, 7&a8

47. **(A)** Ball R - Heel - Heel (drops) R-L, Scuffle R - Heel (bounce) L, Heel Dig - Toe (drop) R - Heel (bounce) L, Scuffle R - Heel (bounce) L, Reverse Scuffle R - Heel (bounce) L, Scuffle R - Heel (bounce) L, Ball R - Heel - Heel (drops) L-R, Scuffle L - Heel (bounce) R, Reverse All
**(BALL - HEEL - HEEL, SCUFFLE - HEEL, HEEL DIG - TOE - HEEL, SCUFFLE - HEEL, REVERSE SCUFFLE - HEEL, SCUFFLE - HEEL, BALL - HEEL - HEEL, SCUFFLE - HEEL, REVERSE ALL)**
<u>Counts</u>: 1&a2&a, 3&a4&a, 5&a6&a, 7&a8&a
1&a2&a, 3&a4&a, 5&a6&a, 7&a8&a

**(B)** Reverse Scuffle R - Heel (bounce) L, Scuffle R - Heel (bounce) L, Heel Dig - Toe (drop) R - Heel (bounce) L, Scuffle R - Heel (bounce) L, Reverse Scuffle R - Heel (bounce) L, Scuffle R - Heel (bounce) L, Heel Dig - Toe (drop) R - Heel (bounce) L, Scuffle R - Heel (bounce) L
**(REVERSE SCUFFLE - HEEL, SCUFFLE - HEEL, HEEL DIG - TOE - HEEL, SCUFFLE - HEEL, REVERSE SCUFFLE - HEEL, SCUFFLE - HEEL, HEEL DIG - TOE - HEEL, SCUFFLE - HEEL)**
<u>Counts</u>: 1&a2&a, 3&a4&a, 5&a6&a, 7&a8&a

**(C)** Reverse Scuffle R - Heel (bounce) L - Toe (lift) L - Back Flap R 3× R-L -R, Stamp - Stamp L-R
**(REVERSE SCUFFLE - HEEL - TOE - BACK FLAP 3× ALT, STAMP - STAMP)**
<u>Counts</u>: 1&a2&a, 3&a4&a, 5&a6&a, 7-8

# Tap Dance for All

48. **(A)** Shuffle Paradiddle or Paddle & Roll R, Heel Dig - Brush (back) L - Heel (bounce) R, Shuffle - Ball - Heel L, Paradiddle or Paddle & Roll R, 5 Count Riff L
    **(SHUFFLE PARADIDDLE, HEEL DIG - BRUSH - HEEL, SHUFFLE - BALL - HEEL, PARADIDDLE, 5 COUNT RIFF)**
    Counts: 1&a2&a, 3&a, 4&a5, &a6&, a7&a8
    **(B)** Shuffle - Stomp R, Drag R + Single Chug (front) L, Flap Alternating Cramp Roll R, Stomp L, Brush (back) - Step L - Stomp R, Back Flap R, Shuffle - Step L - Stamp R
    **(SHUFFLE - STOMP, DRAG + SINGLE CHUG, FLAP ALT CRAMP ROLL, STOMP, BRUSH - STEP - STOMP, BACK FLAP, SHUFFLE - STEP - STOMP)**
    Counts: &a1-2, &3e&a4, &a5, &6, &7&8

49. Reverse Cramp Roll R, Scuffle R - Toe (lift) L - Toe Back R, Heel (bounce) L - Shuffle - Flap R, Back Flap L, Scuffle - Cramp Roll R, Scuffle R - Toe (lift) L - Toe Back R - Heel (bounce) L, Shuffle - Ball - Heel R - Scuffle L
    **(REVERSE CRAMP ROLL, SCUFFLE - TOE - TOE BACK, HEEL - SHUFFLE - FLAP, BACK FLAP, SCUFFLE - CRAMP ROLL, SCUFFLE - TOE - TOE BACK - HEEL, SHUFFLE - BALL - HEEL - SCUFFLE)**
    Counts: 1e&a, 2e&a, 3e&a4, e&, a5e&a6, e&a7e, &a8e&a

50. Shuffle - Ball - Heel R, Paradiddle or Paddle & Roll L, Heel Dig - Toe (drop) R - Ball - Heel L, Heel Dig - Back Flap - Heel (drop) R, Stomp L - Heel (bounce) R - Stomp L
    **(SHUFFLE - BALL - HEEL, PARADIDDLE, HEEL DIG - TOE - BALL - HEEL, HEEL DIG - BACK FLAP - HEEL, STOMP - HEEL - STOMP)**
    Counts: 1&a2, &a3&, a4&a, 5&6&, 7&8

51. Brush (back) R - Hop L - Heel (drop) L - Toe Back R - Heel (bounce) L, 6 Count Riff R, Ball Change L, Crossing Double Pullback L (end R over L), Uncrossing Double Pullback R (end parallel), Ball Change L
    **(BRUSH - HOP - HEEL - TOE BACK - HEEL, 6 COUNT RIFF, BALL CHANGE, CROSSING DOUBLE PULLBACK, UNCROSSING DOUBLE PULLBACK, BALL CHANGE)**
    Counts: &1&a2, &a3&a4, &5, e&a6, e&a7, &8

## 11. Intermediate / Advanced, Advanced Levels

52. **(A)** <u>Twist L</u>: Shuffle R - Toe (lift) L, Shuffle - Heel (bounce) L, Repeat All, Maxie Ford With a Pickup R, Heel (drop) R, Ball Change L
    **(TWIST L: SHUFFLE - TOE, SHUFFLE - HEEL, REPEAT ALL, MAXIE FORD WITH A PICKUP, HEEL, BALL CHANGE)**
    <u>Counts</u>: &a1&a2&a3&a4, &5&a6, 7, &8
    **(B)** Flap L, Rolling Shuffle 3× R-L-R, Flap L, Bombershay 2× R (travel L), Brush (back) - Ball Change R
    **(FLAP, ROLLING SHUFFLE 3× ALT, FLAP, BOMBERSHAY 2×, BRUSH - BALL CHANGE)**
    <u>Counts</u>: &1, &a2&a3&a4, &5, &a6&a7, &a8
53. Brush (back) - Step R - Step L, Drag R (over L) - Heel (bounce) L - Drag R (uncross), Toe (lift) L - Brush (back) R - Heel (bounce) L - Toe Back R - Toe (lift) L, 5 Count Riff R, Stomp L
    **(BRUSH - STEP - STEP, DRAG - HEEL, DRAG, TOE - BRUSH - HEEL - TOE BACK - TOE, 5 COUNT RIFF, STOMP)**
    <u>Counts</u>: &a1, 2-3-4, &5&a6, &a7&a, 8
54. Back Flap L - Stomp R, Drag (back) R, Heel (bounce) L - Toe Back R – Swap Grab Off L - Heel (drop) R, Flap L, Bombershay R (to L) 2×, Back Flap R - Stamp L
    **(BACK FLAP - STOMP, DRAG, HEEL - TOE BACK - SWAP GRAB OFF - HEEL, FLAP, BOMBERSHAY 2×, BACK FLAP - STAMP)**
    <u>Counts</u>: &a1, 2, &3&a4, &5, &a6&a7, &a8
55. Hold, Chug - Chug R-L, Toe (lift) L - Ball - Heel R - Stomp L, Brush (back) - Ball Change L, Toe Back L - Heel (bounce) R 2×, Stomp L
    **(HOLD, CHUG - CHUG, TOE - BALL - HEEL - STOMP, BRUSH - BALL CHANGE, TOE BACK - HEEL 2×, STOMP)**
    <u>Counts</u>: Hold: 1, &2, &3&4, &5&, &6&7&, 8
56. Jump (both hands / feet), Hold, Riffle R - Heel (bounce) L, Heel Dig - Toe (drop) - Heel (bounce) R, Hold, Stamp - Stamp L-R, Double Pullback L, Heel (drop) L - Toe Dig (inside edge) R
    **(JUMP, HOLD, RIFFLE - HEEL, HEEL DIG - TOE - HEEL,**

**Tap Dance for All**

**HOLD, STAMP - STAMP, DOUBLE PULLBACK, HEEL - TOE DIG)**
<u>Counts</u>: 1, Hold: 2, e&a3, &a4, Hold: 5, &6, e&a7, &8

QUOTABLE QUOTE

*"He who cannot dance puts the blame on the floor."*—*Hindu Proverb*

# 12

# Time Steps / Time Step Breaks

*(Beginning III / Intermediate / Advanced Levels)*

1. **Buck Time Step**
   **Single**: Shuffle R - Hop L, Step R - Flap L - Step R, Reverse All, Repeat R side, Add Break (See Time Step Breaks)
   **(SHUFFLE - HOP, STEP - FLAP - STEP, REVERSE ALL, REPEAT R SIDE, ADD BREAK)**
   Counts: 8&1, 2&3&, 4&5, 6&7&, 8&1, 2&3&
   **Double**: Shuffle R - Hop L - Toe Back R, Step R - Flap L - Step R, Reverse All, Repeat R Side, Add Break (See Time Step Breaks)
   **(SHUFFLE - HOP - TOE BACK, STEP - FLAP - STEP, REVERSE ALL, REPEAT R SIDE, ADD BREAK)**
   Counts: 8&1&2&3&, 4&5&6&7&, 8&1&2&3&
   **Double II**: Shuffle R - Hop L - Flap R, Flap L - Step R, Reverse All, Repeat R Side, Add Break (See Time Step Breaks)
   **(SHUFFLE - HOP - FLAP, FLAP - STEP, REVERSE ALL, REPEAT R SIDE, ADD BREAK)**
   Counts: 8&1&2&3&, 4&5&6&7&, 8&1&2&3&
   **Triple**: Shuffle R - Hop L, Shuffle - Step R, Flap L - Step R, Reverse All, Repeat R Side, Add Break (See Time Step Breaks)
   **(SHUFFLE - HOP, SHUFFLE - STEP, FLAP - STEP, REVERSE ALL, REPEAT R SIDE, ADD BREAK)**
   Counts: 8&1&a2&3&, 4&5&a6&7&, 8&1&a2&3&
   **Triple II**: Shuffle R - Hop L - Toe Back R - Heel (drop) L - Step R, Flap L - Step R, Reverse All, Repeat R Side, Add Break (See Time Step Breaks)

### Tap Dance for All

**(SHUFFLE - HOP - TOE BACK - HEEL - STEP, FLAP - STEP, REVERSE ALL, REPEAT R SIDE, ADD BREAK)**
Counts: &a1&a2, &3-4, &a5&a6, &7-8, &a1&a2, &3-4

2. **Stomp Time Step**
   **Single**: Stomp R - Hop L, Step R - Flap L - Step R, Reverse All, Repeat R Side, Add Break (See Time Step Breaks)
   **(STOMP - HOP, STEP - FLAP - STEP, REVERSE ALL, REPEAT R SIDE, ADD BREAK)**
   Counts 1-2, 3&4&, 5-6, 7&8&, 1-2, 3&4&
   
   **Double**: Stomp R - Hop L - Toe Back R, Step R - Flap L - Step R, Reverse All, Repeat R Side, Add Break (See Time Step Breaks)
   **(STOMP - HOP - TOE BACK, STEP - FLAP - STEP, REVERSE ALL, REPEAT R SIDE, ADD BREAK)**
   Counts: 1-2&, 3&4&, 5-6&, 7&8&, 1-2&, 3&4&
   
   **Double II**: Stomp R - Hop L, Flap 2× R-L - Step R, Reverse All, Repeat R Side, Add Break (See Time Step Breaks)
   **(STOMP - HOP, FLAP 2× ALT, STEP, REVERSE ALL, REPEAT R SIDE, ADD BREAK)**
   Counts: 1-2, &3&4&, 5-6, &7&8&, 1-2, &3&4&
   
   **Triple**: Stomp R - Hop L, Shuffle - Step R, Flap L - Step R, Reverse All, Repeat R Side, Add Break (See Time Step Breaks)
   **(STOMP - HOP, SHUFFLE - STEP, FLAP - STEP, REVERSE ALL, REPEAT R SIDE, ADD BREAK)**
   Counts: 1-2, &a3, &4&, 5-6, &a7, &8&, 1-2, &a3, &4&

3. **Fundamental Time Step**
   **Single**: Hop L, Shuffle - Step R, Flap L - Step R - Stomp L, Reverse All, Repeat R Side, Add Break (See Time Step Breaks)
   **(HOP - SHUFFLE - STEP, FLAP - STEP - STOMP, REVERSE ALL)**
   Counts: 1&a2, &3&4, 5&a6, &7&8
   
   **Double**: Brush (back) R, Hop L, Shuffle - Step R, Flap L - Step R - Stomp L, Reverse All
   **(BRUSH - HOP - SHUFFLE - STEP, FLAP - STEP - STOMP, REVERSE ALL)**
   Counts: &1&a2, &3&4, &5&a6, &7&8
   
   **Double II**: Brush (back) R, Hop L, Shuffle - Step 2× R-L, Step R - Stomp L, Reverse All, Repeat R Side, Add Break (See Time Step Breaks)

## 12. Time Steps / Time Step Breaks

**(BRUSH - HOP, SHUFFLE - STEP 2× ALT, STEP - STOMP, REVERSE ALL, REPEAT R SIDE, ADD BREAK)**
Counts: &1, &a2&a3, &4, &5, &a6&a7, &8, &1, &a2&a3, &4
**Double III**: Brush (back) R, Hop L, Shuffle - Step 2× R-L, Toe Back R, Step R - Stomp L, Reverse All, Repeat R Side, Add Break (See Time Step Breaks)
**(BRUSH - HOP, SHUFFLE - STEP 2× ALT, TOE BACK, STEP - STOMP, REVERSE ALL, REPEAT R SIDE, ADD BREAK)**
Counts: &1, &a2&a3, &a4, &5, &a6&a7, &8, &1, &a2&a3, &4

4. **Traveling Time Steps**
*NOTE: All Traveling Time Steps (Regular & Off Beat) Can Be Turned*
(R side Time Steps turn L on the Hop, L side Time Steps turn R on the Hop)

**Single Traveling Time Step**
Shuffle - Step R, Shuffle L, Ball Change 2× L, Brush (back) L - Hop R - Step L, Shuffle - Step R, Reverse All, Repeat R Side, Add Break (See Time Step Breaks)
**(SHUFFLE - STEP, SHUFFLE, BALL CHANGE 2×, BRUSH – HOP STEP, SHUFFLE - STEP, REVERSE ALL, REPEAT R SIDE, ADD BREAK)**
Counts: 8&1&2&3&4, &5-6, &7&, 8&1&2&3&4, &5-6, &7&, 8&1&2&3&4, &5-6, &7&

**Double Traveling Time Step I**
Shuffle - Step R, Shuffle L, Ball Change 2× L, Brush (back) L - Hop R - Toe Back - Step L, Shuffle - Step R, Reverse All, Repeat R Side, Add Break (See Time Step Breaks)
**(SHUFFLE - STEP, SHUFFLE, BALL CHANGE 2×, BRUSH - HOP - TOE BACK - STEP, SHUFFLE - STEP, REVERSE ALL, REPEAT R SIDE, ADD BREAK)**
Counts: 8&1&2&3&4&5&6&7&, 8&1&2&3&4&5&6&7&, 8&1&2&3&4&5&6&7&

**Double Traveling Time Step II**
Shuffle - Step R, Shuffle L, Ball Change 2× L, Brush (back) L - Hop R - Flap L, Shuffle - Step R, Reverse All, Repeat R Side, Add Break (See Time Step Breaks)
**(SHUFFLE - STEP, SHUFFLE, BALL CHANGE 2×,**

### Tap Dance for All

**BRUSH - HOP - FLAP, SHUFFLE - STEP,
REVERSE ALL, REPEAT R SIDE, ADD BREAK)**
Counts: 8&1&2&3&4&5&6&7&, 8&1&2&3&4&5&6&7&,
8&1&2&3&4&5&6&7&

**Triple Traveling Time Step**
Shuffle - Step R, Shuffle L, Ball Change 2× L, Brush (back) L - Hop R, Shuffle - Step 2× L - R, Reverse All, Repeat R Side, Add Break (See Time Step Breaks)
**(SHUFFLE - STEP, SHUFFLE, BALL CHANGE 2×,
BRUSH - HOP - SHUFFLE - STEP 2× ALT,
REVERSE ALL, REPEAT R SIDE, ADD BREAK)**
Counts: 8&1&2&3&4&5, &a6, &7&, 8&1&2&3&4&5, &a6, &7&,
8&1&2&3&4&5, &a6, &7&

5. **Off Beat Traveling Time Step**
**Single**: Shuffle - Step R, Shuffle L, Ball Change 2× L,
Brush (back) L - Hop R - Step L, Shuffle - Step R, Hold,
Reverse All, Repeat R Side, Add Break (See Time Step Breaks)
**(SHUFFLE - STEP, SHUFFLE, BALL CHANGE 2×,
BRUSH - HOP - STEP, SHUFFLE - STEP,
REVERSE ALL, HOLD, REPEAT R SIDE, ADD BREAK)**
Counts: &a1&2&3&4&5-6, &a7, Hold: 8, &a1&2&3&4&5-6,
&a7, Hold: 8,
&a1&2&3&4&5-6, &a7, Hold: 8

**Double I**: Shuffle - Step R, Shuffle L, Ball Change 2× L,
Brush (back) L - Hop R - Toe Back - Step L, Shuffle - Step R, Hold, Reverse All, Repeat R Side, Add Break (See Time Step Breaks)
**(SHUFFLE - STEP, SHUFFLE, BALL CHANGE 2×,
BRUSH - HOP - TOE BACK - STEP, SHUFFLE - STEP, HOLD, REVERSE ALL, REPEAT R SIDE,
ADD BREAK)**
Counts: &a1&2&3&4&5&6, &a7, Hold: 8, &a1&2&3&4&5&6,
&a7, Hold: 8,
&a1&2&3&4&5&6, &a7, Hold: 8

**Double II**: Shuffle - Step R, Shuffle L, Ball Change 2× L,
Brush (back) L - Hop R - Flap L, Shuffle - Step R, Hold,
Reverse All, Repeat R Side, Add Break (See Time Step Breaks)
**(SHUFFLE - STEP, SHUFFLE, BALL CHANGE 2×,**

## 12. Time Steps / Time Step Breaks

**BRUSH - HOP - FLAP, SHUFFLE - STEP, HOLD, REVERSE ALL, REPEAT R SIDE, ADD BREAK)**
Counts: &a1&2&3&4&5&6, &a7, Hold: 8, &a1&2&3&4&5&6, &a7, Hold: 8,
&a1&2&3&4&5&6, &a7, Hold: 8

**Triple**: Shuffle - Step R, Shuffle L, Ball Change 2× L, Brush (back) L - Hop R, Shuffle - Step 2× L - R, Hold, Reverse All, Repeat R Side, Add Break (See Time Step Breaks)

**(SHUFFLE - STEP, SHUFFLE, BALL CHANGE 2×, BRUSH - HOP - SHUFFLE - STEP 2× ALT, HOLD, REVERSE ALL, REPEAT R SIDE, ADD BREAK)**
Counts: &a1&2&3&4&5, &a6, &7&, Hold: 8,
&a1&2&3&4&5, &a6, &7&, Hold: 8, &a1&2&3&4&5,
&a6, &7&, Hold: 8

6. **Double / Triple**: Brush R - Hop L, Shuffle - Step R, Shuffle L, Step - Step L-R, Tap L, Reverse All, Repeat R Side, Add Break (See Time Step Breaks)

**(BRUSH - HOP, SHUFFLE - STEP, SHUFFLE, STEP - STEP - TAP, REVERSE ALL, REPEAT R SIDE, ADD BREAK)**
Counts: &1&a2, &3, &a4, &5&a6, &7, &a8, &1&a2, &3, &a4

7. **Mock Wing Time Step**
Brush (back) R - Hop L, Shuffle - Step R, Flap L & Brush (out) R, Brush (in) R, Step R, Heel Dig L, Reverse All, Repeat R Side, Add Break (See Time Step Breaks)

**(BRUSH - HOP - SHUFFLE - STEP, FLAP & BRUSH: OUT, BRUSH: IN, STEP - HEEL DIG, REVERSE ALL, REPEAT R SIDE, ADD BREAK)**
Counts: &1&a2, &3&a4, &5&a6, &7&a8, &1&a2, &3&a4

8. **Waltz Clog Time Step**
**Single**: Jump R - Shuffle - Ball Change L, Reverse All, Repeat R & L Sides, Add Break (See Time Step Breaks)

**(JUMP - SHUFFLE - BALL CHANGE, REVERSE ALL, REPEAT R & L SIDES, ADD BREAK)**
Counts: 1&2&3, 4&5&6, 1&2&3, 4&5&6

**Double**: Flap R - Shuffle - Ball Change L, Reverse All, Repeat R & L Sides, Add Break (See Time Step Breaks)

## Tap Dance for All

**(FLAP - SHUFFLE - BALL CHANGE, REVERSE ALL, REPEAT R & L SIDES, ADD BREAK)**
Counts: &1&2&3, &4&5&6, 1&2&3, 4&5&6

9. **Advanced Waltz Clog Time Step**
   Flap R, Shuffle - Step L, Heel - Heel (drops) L-R, Reverse All, Repeat R & L Sides, Add Break
   **(FLAP - SHUFFLE - STEP, HEEL - HEEL, REVERSE ALL, REPEAT R & L SIDES, ADD BREAK)**
   Counts: &1&2&a3, &4&5&a6, &1&2&a3, &4&5&a6

10. **Cramp Roll Time Step**
    **Single**: Brush (back) R - Hop L - Step R, Flap L - Step (ball), Heel R - Heel Dig L, Reverse All, Repeat R Side, Add Break (See Time Step Breaks)
    **(BRUSH - HOP - STEP, FLAP - STEP, HEEL - HEEL DIG, REVERSE ALL, REPEAT R SIDE, ADD BREAK)**
    Counts: &1-2, &3&a4, &5-6, &7&a8, &1-2, &3&a4
    **Double**: Brush (back) R - Hop L, Flap 2× R-L, Step (ball) - Heel R - Heel Dig L, Reverse All, Repeat R Side, Add Break (See Time Step Breaks)
    **(BRUSH - HOP, FLAP 2× ALT, STEP - HEEL - HEEL DIG, REVERSE ALL, REPEAT R SIDE, ADD BREAK)**
    Counts: &1, &2&3, &a4, &5, &6&7, &a8, &1, &2&3, &a4
    **Triple**: Brush (back) R - Hop L, Shuffle - Step R, Flap L - Step (ball) - Heel R, Heel Dig L, Reverse All, Repeat R Side, Add Break (See Time Step Breaks)
    **(BRUSH - HOP - SHUFFLE - STEP, FLAP - STEP - HEEL - HEEL DIG, REVERSE ALL, REPEAT R SIDE, ADD BREAK)**
    Counts: &1&a2, &3&a4, &5&a6, &7&a8, &1&a2, &3&a4

11. **Double / Triple Cramp Roll Time Step**
    Brush (back) R - Hop L, Shuffle - Step 2× R-L, Step (ball) - Heel R, Heel Dig L, Reverse All, Repeat R Side, Add Break (See Time Step Breaks)
    **(BRUSH - HOP, SHUFFLE - STEP 2× ALT, STEP - HEEL - HEEL DIG, REVERSE ALL, REPEAT R SIDE, ADD BREAK)**
    Counts: &1&a2&a3&a4, &5&a6&a7&a8, &1&a2&a3&a4

12. **Advanced Cramp Roll Time Step**
    Brush (back) R, Hop 2× L, Shuffle - Step R, Stamp L - Heel Dig R,

## 12. Time Steps / Time Step Breaks

Brush (back) R - Hop L, Flap R, Flap Cramp Roll L, Reverse All, Repeat R Side, Add Break (See Time Step Breaks)
**(BRUSH, HOP 2×, SHUFFLE - STEP - STAMP - HEEL DIG, BRUSH - HOP - FLAP - FLAP CRAMP ROLL, REVERSE ALL, REPEAT R SIDE, ADD BREAK)**
Counts: &1-2, &3&a4, &5&6&7&a8, &1-2, &3&a4,
&5&6&7&a8,
&1-2, &3&a4, &5&6&7&a8

## 13. Double / Triple Time Step

Shuffle R - Hop L, Shuffle - Step R, Shuffle L, Step - Step L-R, Reverse All, Repeat R Side, Add Break (See Time Step Breaks)
**(SHUFFLE - HOP, SHUFFLE - STEP, SHUFFLE - STEP - STEP, REVERSE ALL, REPEAT R SIDE, ADD BREAK)**
Counts: &a1&a2, &3&4, &a5&a6, &7&8, &a1&a2, &3&4

## 14. Bombershay Time Step

Brush (back) R, Hop 2× L, Shuffle - Step R, Stamp L - Heel Dig R, Flap R, Bombershay 3×, Reverse All, Repeat R Side, Add Break (See Time Step Breaks)
**(BRUSH, HOP 2×, SHUFFLE - STEP - STAMP - HEEL DIG, FLAP, BOMBERSHAY 3×, REVERSE ALL, REPEAT R SIDE, ADD BREAK)**
Counts: &1-2, &3&a4, &5&a6&a7&a8, &1-2, &3&a4,
&5&a6&a7&a8,
&1-2, &3&a4, &5&a6&a7&a8

## 15. Double Wing Time Step

**Single**: Brush (back) R - Hop L, Step - Step (balls) R-L, Double Wing, Tap (forward) L, Reverse All, Repeat R Side, Add Break)
**(BRUSH - HOP, STEP - STEP, DOUBLE WING, TAP, REVERSE ALL, REPEAT R SIDE, ADD BREAK)**
Counts: &1&2, &a3-4, &5&6, &a7-8, &1&2, &a3-4
**Double**: Brush (back) R - Hop L - Flap R - Step (ball) L, Double Wing, Tap (forward) L, Reverse All, Repeat R Side, Add Break (See Time Step Breaks)
**(BRUSH - HOP - FLAP - STEP, DOUBLE WING, TAP, REVERSE ALL, REPEAT R SIDE, ADD BREAK)**
Counts: &1&a2, &a3-4, &5&a6, &a7-8, &1&a2, &a3-4

## 16. Double Heel Time Step

Stamp L - Back Flap R, Scuffle - Step L - Scuff R, Heel (drop) L,

Ball R - Heel - Heel R-L 2×, Heel Dig R - Toe - Toe (drops) R-L, Ball R - Heel - Heel R-L, Reverse All, Repeat R Side, Add Break (See Time Step Breaks)
**(STAMP - BRUSH - STEP, SCUFFLE - STEP - SCUFF, HEEL, BALL - HEEL - HEEL 2×, HEEL DIG - TOE - TOE, BALL - HEEL - HEEL, REVERSE ALL, REPEAT R SIDE, ADD BREAK)**
<u>Counts</u>: 1&2, &3&4, &, 5&a, 6&a, 7&a, 8&a

## *Time Step Breaks*

1. **Buck Time Step Break** (Do either 3 or 7 Buck Time Steps + Break)
   **Single**: Shuffle L - Hop R, Flap - Ball Change R
      **(SHUFFLE - HOP - FLAP - BALL CHANGE)**
      <u>Counts</u>: 4&5, &6&7
   **Single II**: (Do either 3 or 7 Time Steps + Break)
      Shuffle R - Hop L, Step R, Shuffle - Step 3× L-R-L, Step R
      **(SHUFFLE - HOP, STEP, SHUFFLE - STEP 3×, STEP)**
      <u>Counts</u>: 8&1-2, &3&4&5&6&7
   **Double**: (Do either 3 or 7 Time Steps + Break)
      Shuffle L - Hop R, Flap - Ball Change L
      **(SHUFFLE - HOP - FLAP - BALL CHANGE)**
      <u>Counts</u>: 4&5&6&7
   **Triple**: (Do either 3 or 7 Time Steps + Break)
      Shuffle L - Hop R, Flap - Ball Change L
      **(SHUFFLE - HOP - FLAP - BALL CHANGE)**
      <u>Counts</u>: 4&5&6&7
   **Triple II**: (Do 3 or 7 Time Steps + Break)
      Shuffle L - Hop R, Flap - Ball Change L
      **(SHUFFLE - HOP - FLAP - BALL CHANGE)**
      <u>Counts</u>: 4&5&6&7
2. **Stomp Time Step Break** (Do 3 or 7 Stomp Time Steps + Break)
   **Single**: Stomp - Hop - Flap - Ball Change L
      **(STOMP - HOP - FLAP - BALL CHANGE)**
      <u>Counts</u>: 5-6, &7&8
   **Double**: (Do 3 or 7 Stomp Time Steps + Break)
      Stomp - Hop - Flap - Ball Change L

## 12. Time Steps / Time Step Breaks

   **(STOMP - HOP - FLAP - BALL CHANGE)**
   Counts: 5-6, &7&8
   **Triple**: (Do 3 or 7 Stomp Time Steps + Break)
   Stomp - Hop - Flap - Ball Change L
   **(STOMP - HOP - FLAP - BALL CHANGE)**
   Counts: 5-6, &7&8
3. **Fundamental Time Step Break** (Do 3 or 7 Fundamental Time Steps + Break)
   **Single**: Hop R, Flap - Ball Change L, Stamp R
   **(HOP - FLAP - BALL CHANGE, STAMP)**
   Counts: 5&6&7-8
   **Double I**: Brush (back) L, Hop R, Flap - Ball Change L, Stamp R
   **(BRUSH - HOP, FLAP - BALL CHANGE, STAMP)**
   Counts: &5&6&7-8
   **Double II**: Brush (back) L, Hop R, Flap - Ball Change L, Stamp R
   **(BRUSH - HOP, FLAP - BALL CHANGE, STAMP)**
   Counts: &5&6&7-8
   **Double III**: Brush (back) L, Hop R, Flap - Ball Change L, Stamp R
   **(BRUSH - HOP, FLAP - BALL CHANGE, STAMP)**
   Counts: &5&6&7-8
4. **Traveling Time Step Break** (Do 3 or 7 Traveling Time Steps + Break)
   **Single**: Shuffle - Step L, Shuffle R, Ball Change 2× R, Hold (or Clap), Ball Change 2× R
   **(SHUFFLE - STEP, SHUFFLE, BALL CHANGE 2×, HOLD or CLAP, BALL CHANGE 2×)**
   Counts: 8&1, &2, &3&4, Hold or Clap: 5, &6&7
   **Double I**: Shuffle - Step L, Shuffle R, Ball Change 2× R, Hold (or Clap), Ball Change 2× R
   **(SHUFFLE - STEP, SHUFFLE, BALL CHANGE 2×, HOLD or CLAP, BALL CHANGE 2×)**
   Counts: 8&1, &2, &3&4, Hold or Clap: 5, &6&7
   **Double II**: Shuffle - Step L, Shuffle R, Ball Change 2× R, Hold (or Clap), Ball Change 2× R
   **(SHUFFLE - STEP, SHUFFLE, BALL CHANGE 2×, HOLD or CLAP, BALL CHANGE 2×)**
   Counts: 8&1, &2, &3&4, Hold or Clap: 5, &6&7
   **Triple**: Shuffle - Step L, Shuffle R, Ball Change 2× R, Hold (or Clap), Ball Change 2× R

### Tap Dance for All

(SHUFFLE - STEP, SHUFFLE, BALL CHANGE 2×,
HOLD or CLAP, BALL CHANGE 2×)
<u>Counts</u>: 8&1, &2, &3&4, Hold or Clap: 5, &6&7

5. **Off Beat Traveling Time Step Break** (Do 3 or 7 Off Beat Traveling Time Steps + Break)
   **Single**: Shuffle - Step L, Shuffle R, Ball Change 2× R, Hold (or Clap), Ball Change 2× R, Hold
   (SHUFFLE - STEP, SHUFFLE, BALL CHANGE 2×,
   HOLD or CLAP, BALL CHANGE 2×, HOLD)
   <u>Counts</u>: a&1, &2, &3&4, Hold or Clap: 5, &6&7, Hold: 8
   **Double I**: Shuffle - Step L, Shuffle R, Ball Change 2× R, Hold (or Clap), Ball Change 2× R, Hold
   (SHUFFLE - STEP, SHUFFLE, BALL CHANGE 2×,
   HOLD or CLAP, BALL CHANGE 2×, HOLD)
   <u>Counts</u>: a&1, &2, &3&4, Hold or Clap: 5, &6&7, Hold: 8
   **Double II**: Shuffle - Step L, Shuffle R, Ball Change 2× R, Hold (or Clap), Ball Change 2× R, Hold
   (SHUFFLE - STEP, SHUFFLE, BALL CHANGE 2×,
   HOLD or CLAP, BALL CHANGE 2×, HOLD)
   <u>Counts</u>: a&1, &2, &3&4, Hold or Clap: 5, &6&7, Hold: 8
   **Triple**: Shuffle - Step L, Shuffle R, Ball Change 2× R, Hold (or Clap), Ball Change 2× R, Hold
   (SHUFFLE - STEP, SHUFFLE, BALL CHANGE 2×,
   HOLD or CLAP, BALL CHANGE 2×, HOLD)
   <u>Counts</u>: a&1, &2, &3&4, Hold or Clap: 5, &6&7, Hold: 8

6. **Double / Triple**: Shuffle L, Step - Step L-R, Tap L, Repeat All
   (SHUFFLE, STEP - STEP, TAP)
   <u>Counts</u>: &5&a6, &7&a8

7. **Mock Wing Time Step Break** (Do 3 or 7 Mock Wing Time Steps + Break)
   Brush (back) L, Hop R, Shuffle - Step L, Flap 2× R-L, Step R
   (BRUSH - HOP, SHUFFLE - STEP, FLAP 2× ALT, STEP)
   <u>Counts</u>: &5&a6, &7&a8

8. **Cramp Roll Time Step Break** (Do 3 or 7 Cramproll Time Steps)
   **Single**: Back Flap L, Step (ball), Heel R - Heel Dig L, Back Flap L, Step R - Stomp L
   (BACK FLAP, STEP - HEEL - HEEL DIG, BACK FLAP, STEP - STOMP)
   <u>Counts</u>: &5&a6, &7, &8

154

## 12. Time Steps / Time Step Breaks

**Double**: Back Flap L, Step (ball), Heel R - Heel Dig L, Back Flap L, Step R - Stomp L
**(BACK FLAP, STEP - HEEL - HEEL DIG, BACK FLAP, STEP - STOMP)**
Counts: &5&a6, &7, &8

**Triple**: Back Flap L, Step (ball), Heel R - Heel Dig L, Back Flap L, Step R - Stomp L
**(BACK FLAP, STEP - HEEL - HEEL DIG, BACK FLAP, STEP - STOMP)**
Counts: &5&a6, &7, &8

**Double / Triple**: Brush (back) L - Hop R, Shuffle - Step L, Brush (back) R - Hop L, Step R - Stomp L
**(BRUSH - HOP, SHUFFLE - STEP, BRUSH - HOP, STEP - STOMP)**
Counts: &5&a6, &7, &8

9. **Advanced Cramp Roll Time Step**
Flap Alternating Cramp Roll 2× L-R, Brush (back) L - Hop R, Shuffle - Jump L, Shuffle Alternating Cramp Roll R
**(FLAP ALT CRAMP ROLL 2×, BRUSH - HOP, SHUFFLE - JUMP, SHUFFLE ALT CRAMP ROLL)**
Counts: &1&a2, &3&a4, &5, &a6, &a7&a8

10. **Double / Triple Time Step** (Do 3 or 7 Double / Triple Time Steps + Break)
Shuffle L - Hop R, Shuffle - Step 2× L-R, Stamp - Stamp L-R
**(SHUFFLE - HOP, SHUFFLE - STEP 2× ALT, STAMP - STAMP)**
Counts: &a5, &a6&a7, &8

11. **Bombershay Time Step Break** (Do 3 or 7 Bombershay Time Steps + Break)
Flap L, Brush (back) - Ball Change R, Reverse, Flap Bombershay L, Brush (back) R, Heel (drop) L, Toe Back R, Heel (bounce) L, Stamp R, Stomp L
**(FLAP - BRUSH - BALL CHANGE 2× ALT, FLAP BOMBERSHAY, BRUSH - HEEL - TOE BACK - HEEL, STAMP - STOMP)**
Counts: &1&a2, &3&a4, &5&a6, &a7&, a8

12. **Soft Shoe Break** - Waltz Clog Time Step (Do 4 Waltz Clog Time Steps + Break)
*Can also be used as a break added to end any number of combinations*

Flap R, Brush L (over R) - Step - Step L-R, Shuffle L - Hop R, Shuffle - Step L - Brush (forward) R, Hop L - Step - Step - Step R-L-R, Brush (back) L - Hop R

**(FLAP - BRUSH - STEP - STEP, SHUFFLE - HOP, SHUFFLE - STEP - BRUSH, HOP - STEP - STEP - STEP, BRUSH - HOP)**

<u>Counts</u>: &1&a2, &a3e&a4, &5-6-7, &8

13. **Double Heel Time Step Break**

    Toe (outside edge) R - Heel - Heel (drops) R-L, Scuffle R - Heel (bounce) L, Toe (inside edge) R - Heel - Heel (drops) R-L, Scuffle R - Heel (bounce) L, Ball R - Heel - Heel (drops) L-R, Scuffle L - Heel (bounce) R 2×, Scuffle - Step L

    **(TOE - HEEL - HEEL, SCUFFLE - HEEL 2×, BALL - HEEL - HEEL, SCUFFLE - HEEL 2×, SCUFFLE - STEP)**

    <u>Counts</u>: 1&a, 2&a, 3&a, 4&a, 5&a, 6&a7&a, 8&a

Quotable Quotes

*"The dance—it is the rhythm of all that dies in order to live again, it is the eternal rising of the sun."—Isadora Duncan*

# 13

# Professional Physically Integrated Dancers Spotlight

### OBJECTIVE

- Understand how language and representation impact disabled people.
- Learn how nondisabled people can advocate and use their privilege to positively affect change for disabled people.
- Understanding of the difficulties disabled people face daily.
- Realization that disabled people are not only *very* capable, but sometimes even more capable than nondisabled people.

This chapter is dedicated to all the integrated dancers, disabled dancers, and mobility-impaired people out there who are showing the world the ability within their disability. I am eternally grateful to each of the four exceptional women featured in this chapter, and I am so excited to share their interviews with you. They have honestly and openly recounted their journeys, struggles, victories, and accomplishments, in order that you, the readers of this book, may better understand their world and just how important inclusivity, representation, and accessibility is to them. The goal and hope of this chapter is that everyone reading it will in turn help other nondisabled people see that focusing on someone's ability and capability is much more empowering than focusing on one's dis-ability. Strength, courage, and determination reside inside all of us, and as I have said many times as a dance competition judge, "It's not about the fall, it's about the recovery after the fall."

# Tap Dance for All

## *Ginger Lane*

I am starting with Ginger because I have known and loved this amazing woman since around the time I was in middle school. Both Ginger and my mom taught dance in the suburbs of Chicago at that time. Both dynamic women were unstoppable in their dedication to their art. Ginger's daughter Beth and I enjoyed dancing and performing together in our teen years. Ironically, I recently stumbled across a picture of Beth and I performing my mom's choreography to *Couple of Swells*, from the movie musical *Easter Parade*. That picture brought back a flood of wonderful memories of all the fun times I had with both of those prolific powerhouses. I always knew Ginger to be incredibly full of life, energy, and someone who had great enthusiasm and passion for the world of dance, no matter the form.

It was 1984, and I had just moved out to Hollywood from New York City to open the Los Angeles company of *42nd Street* when my mom called to give me the terrible news about Ginger. I was shocked and deeply saddened by the story of her accident. I was also distressed by the fact that I was on the other side of the county, unable to get away to be of any help or support. There were no computers, cell phones or iPads back in 1984! Can you even imagine? However, I took comfort in knowing that she had an incredible family standing behind her, one that would be there to help support her mentally and physically plus assist her in navigating through this life-altering time she now found herself in. It was not until

Ginger Lane, Founder of Counter-Balance—The Power of Integrated Dance, Recipient of the 3Arts Community Award in Dance, Recipient of a 3Arts Fellowship, UIC Disability Arts & Culture (courtesy Ginger Lane).

## 13. Professional Physically Integrated Dancers Spotlight

our interview that I understood what Ginger had gone through all those years ago, and how she has not only risen above her circumstances but helped so many others along the way. Since COVID-19 and the delta variant descended upon us over the past couple of years, we all have had to learn how to pivot in life and business to survive. Ginger Lane learned that survival lesson long ago, not only surviving her adversity but thriving through it. The accident may have robbed her of the use of her legs, but her infinite reservoir of creativity and talent was always there, ready and waiting for her to shift her perspective about what incredible opportunities her life still had in store for her. I am thrilled beyond words that in authoring this book I have been given the opportunity and gift of reconnecting with this fiercely talented and beautifully wise woman.

Thank you, Ginger.

### The Interview

**VICTORIA:** *What was it like going from having a full, physically active life, to having that life abruptly come to a halt?*

**GINGER:** On a personal level, it was having to learn about this whole new body, because my disability affected my entire body, and I wasn't born with it. If you're born with a disability, it's a whole other perspective. There are challenges to both, whether it's an acquired disability or congenital, or shortly after birth. They are just different perspectives.

I mean, from my own perspective, as a dancer, choreographer, and a teacher, when I became disabled, I never expected that I would be able to go back to dance. I felt that that world had closed, and I got very heavily into disability activism, independent living, and disability rights. I could not envision continuing my artistic work. But by becoming involved in the disability community I learned that anything is possible. My accident was in '84, and I sort of had to go through a period of rehabilitation and integrating myself into my life.

*How was it different coping in the world, going from nondisabled to disabled in the mid–1980s?*

Society-wise, there was this whole prolonged period of not understanding why buildings had steps, why sidewalks were slanted, why doors were not wide enough, why bathroom stall doors were too narrow for a wheelchair to get through. So, it was the physical barriers as well.

## Tap Dance for All

But over time I learned to either ignore them, work around them, or not to be bothered by them. You know, there's so much going on in the world that you have to deal with, that I don't need to deal with that [also].

***When and how did dance come back into your life?***
It wasn't until about 1990 when I was busy demonstrating [for] the passage of the ADA, the Americans with Disabilities Act. Shortly thereafter, I learned about a dance class that could include dancers in chairs. So, I went to that. I made myself be open to new experiences. Don't say "No." And so I was quickly disabused of that concept, that I could no longer do that, and that's kind of a critical factor. If you're not open to experiencing something new you're not ever going to be good at it. Starting at that point a lot of my effort went into convincing an audience that I could change their mind, I could make them more accepting, and I could challenge the stereotypes that exist for people with disabilities. I think we've come a long way since then. We no longer have to convince an audience, but what we do have to work on is making sure that we're judged on our merits and our ability, not on the fact that we have a disability and are pitied and accepted, but [with an] "Oh, that poor thing, look how hard she's trying." So, there's been a lot of progress towards an acceptance, but there's also been a change I think in the attitude of those of us professionals who have disabilities, in kind of saying, "We don't really care if you accept us or like us. We are doing this because this is what we were born to do. This is how I express myself. This is what I want to share with you, and this is my experience of the world." So, there isn't that kind of attitude of having to convince other people [now]. I don't make art to convince other people. I make art for myself, for my colleagues, and for people who love dance and who love the art form. And there's another aspect of it, which is whether we are disabled or not, we create and we perform in order to share our experience with the world.

Physically integrated dance, integrated tap dance, is a visible experience of our disability. It's the visible expression of our disability. It doesn't change who you are. My intent early on was to convince the world, and my intention now is to make work that I think is important and vital. Judge me as you wish, [but] judge me on the merit of my work.

***What is it like being an integrated dancer?***
If you love to move and you love to dance, you will find a way to make it work. The idea that you have an impairment, or some type of a

## 13. Professional Physically Integrated Dancers Spotlight

disability, does not stop you from being who you are, or wanting to perform, and wanting to share your life experience with others, the world, and with an audience.

It often isn't so much about how high you can jump, how fast you can tap, or how athletic you are, especially once you get a few years behind you. It's more about how do you communicate? How do you express yourself? Where does stillness and silence come in? And how important is that? Because we know that dance is all about movement, movement, movement. But there is a beauty in stillness, and it allows for breathing. I see dance as very empowering and freeing, and that dance should be accessible to everyone. The root of all art is the ability to express oneself.

*In integrated tap, the only limitations are traveling and turning. Would you agree?*

Now, wait a minute! Let's think about it. I choreographed a piece, maybe ten years ago, that was sort of like a country piece. I did it to a Chet Atkins song, and it included three nondisabled dancers and one guy in a wheelchair. He had been a basketball player. He is a bilateral,

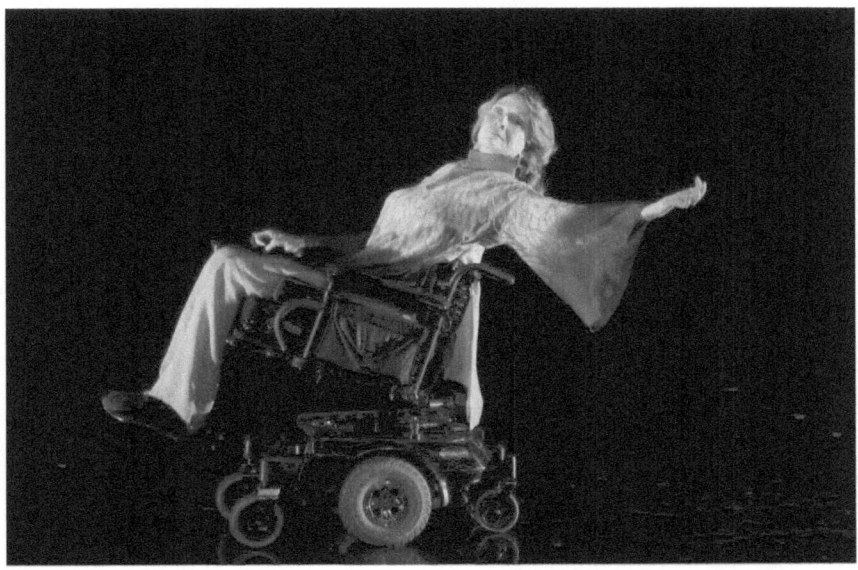

**Ginger Lane, from the piece titled *Paloma Triste*, choreographed by Ginger Lane (photograph by Lisa Green, courtesy Ginger Lane).**

above the knee amputee. But as a basketball player he was incredibly strong. Now, what did I have him do? He would do wheelies and bounce the front end of his chair on the floor. So, he was keeping rhythm that way, and he would start to turn and keep tapping. When I say "tapping" [I mean] he was actually tapping the front wheels on the floor, and that is a form of tapping. I didn't design it as a tap number, but it included that thumping, [so] it had rhythm. So, think about that!

***You are absolutely right. This unique perspective and way of seeing dance and tap is one of the main reasons behind me writing this book. Thank you for that clarity.***

***Tell me about your 30 years working at Access Living in Chicago***
When I started [there] I went back to school, and I focused on counseling people and helping them confront the physical barriers—access to jobs, no access to accessible apartments and housing, and accessible transportation. I don't know how many wheelchairs the airlines have broken. They've rolled over backwards on me several times. Things like that. So, I was dealing with a lot as far as the political and legal aspects of disability, as well as helping people get back into some form of life for themselves. In 1997 Access Living certainly knew that I had been a dancer, performer, and teacher.

When the Joffrey Ballet moved to Chicago, they wanted to do a benefit. We had an integrated dance number as part of that benefit. Gerry Arpino [choreographer and co-founder of the Joffrey] selected one of his premier dance masters to choreograph and collaborate along with us on a piece that we created together. That was a wonderful experience, and I went on quite a number of stops and talk shows with [Gerry]. I knew some of his dancers from my past life at Edna McKrae [known as the grand dame of the Chicago ballet community]. We had this wonderful repartee between the two of us, and he said, "Well, you know, Ginger, you are a member of the Joffrey [now]. You're a company member," which is very very cool. So, that was '96, '97, '98. After that I really became more aware of integrated dance and took a workshop with Access Dance.

Then in 2008, Access Living moved from the offices that we had been renting. We built our own office, our own building. Up on the fourth floor we created a big open space, well, relatively open, and we said, "Why don't we start an arts and culture project?" The "committee" that we had gotten together was saying, "Well, we can have poetry readings, and

## 13. Professional Physically Integrated Dancers Spotlight

theater, and comedy, and music." And I said, "And DANCE!" So, I began to produce annual dance events at Access Living. I had [already] choreographed some numbers for our company in Oak Park, Momenta Dance Company, [where] I became very good friends with Stephanie Clemens, the artistic director. I was in this piece that was choreographed for me and this other guy who was a bilateral amputee. And then I choreographed several [more] pieces for [Stephanie]. So, since 2003 I became very involved with [Momenta Dance Company], and still am. Every year we produce this annual dance concert that I call CounterBalance. The first year we called it Off Balance, but it's [been] CounterBalance [ever since]. I then branched out. I was in Israel where I met a dance company and worked on a community piece. I had them choreograph their part [in Israel] and send over the video. And then I choreographed the other part here. The next year I invited them to come and perform live. Then a company from Korea, a dance festival in Korea said, "We want to participate." So, they came! It became a sort of international event. So, my thinking shifted a bit, starting in around the early 2000s, from all this independent living and advocacy work, to getting back into the arts, which of course is my first love. And that's what I've been doing ever since. Now, just last year I retired from doing that. But we had that concert for ten or eleven years. However, I'm still involved in it.

**What do you think your legacy will be?**
Right now I am choreographing a piece that is going to be presented virtually, that really is a digital piece. [It is] the last major piece, besides the community pieces, that I choreographed. [It's] about generations, handing down a legacy, because part of my thinking and one of my intentions has been don't think about legacy when you are actively working. I was asked to give some artist talks, and as I looked back over my career, I realized I did create a legacy. One of my intentions and goals has been to teach and inspire the next generation of disabled artists to pursue their dreams and their goals. And so, I think about furthering the art of dance through the art of disability. And so, this important number about generations that I choreographed has me as the senior dancer who is beginning to slow down, thinking more about breath and stillness, because even I can no longer do what I did. I used to use a manual chair, [and] then I graduated to a power chair. The next dancer is a stand-up dancer, who is far more capable and a beautiful dancer [who is] about twenty-five or thirty-five years younger than I am. But she also is beginning to slow

down, has shoulder issues, you know, can't do what she did. Then a slightly younger dancer who uses a manual chair is the third generation. But that dancer has terrible shoulder problems [too right now]. And yesterday during rehearsal I said to her [jokingly], "Oh my God! What do you mean you can't reach your arm back? Do I really have to choreograph a cripple?" We both laughed about that. The fourth generation, the youngest dancer of this intergenerational piece is my granddaughter, who is at the height of her dance ability at 24 years old. So, she can do all the jumps, and has the marvelous extensions that my 55-year-old dancer can no longer do. You know, her knees are still good, and her hips are still good. It's passing down what you've learned, what your life experience has been, [and] that can [be] handed off to the next generation.

**What areas do you think dance studios and dance instructors need to look at and address to start moving the needle towards being more inclusive and welcoming to mobility challenged students?**

So, one of the things to think about to make it inclusive is to make the dance space physically accessible, like no steps getting in. If you have a step, you are eliminating people who use walkers, canes, or

**Susan Ojala Myers (left) and Ginger Lane perform *Imperfect*. Choreography by Ginger Lane (photograph by Lisa Green, courtesy Ginger Lane).**

## 13. Professional Physically Integrated Dancers Spotlight

wheelchairs. So, you don't want that. You definitely [do] want hard surface flooring because that's easier. Carpet is wonderful, but it is a drag on the feet and on the chairs. That's physical accessibility. Programmatic accessibility and programmatic inclusion are going to include, when possible, signage that is going to be easily readable, maybe larger print for those who don't have visual acuity, and maybe graphics instead of constant text. [Also], not eliminating somebody because they cannot do something, but challenging the teacher and the student to think outside of the box. So, that's physical access, programmatic access, and then [there's] attitudinal access. Disability culture includes all the different forms of art, music, dance, visual art, writing, and theater. Disability culture challenges you to think about what constitutes beauty, power, ability, and maybe acceptance, plus faith in yourself, your audience, and in your fellow students.

**What would you like the readers of this book to understand about those with disabilities?**

When you are writing this, if you can help the reader to understand that disability is a vantage point, a perspective, a way of experiencing the world. It may be about shattering stereotypes. It may be about sharing your disability experience, because let's face it, you're not going to be able to tap with your feet forever.

*That is one of the many reasons I am pivoting away from teaching so much nondisabled stand-up tap. After 50-plus years of beating my body up, I have undergone numerous surgeries. I have two cages in my lower back to stabilize my spine, and I have had two hip replacements, with the second as a revision to the first. I've also had the second toe of my left foot shortened, thanks to tap causing it to become what's known as a hammer toe. My right foot had to have a large pearl sized neuroma removed that was pinching a couple of the nerves in my right foot, again due to stand-up tapping. The human body is much like a car, the parts of both need constant maintenance, and sometimes replacing. As you said, even as a mature stand-up dancer there are moves that I just cannot execute well anymore. So, you are one hundred percent correct, I may not be in a wheelchair, but I do have some mild form of a disability going on between my bionic back and hip.*

So, we know that disability touches all of us at some point in our lives. Rather than fighting it we might as well make it work for us. The

## Tap Dance for All

three key words these days are diversity, inclusion, and equity, right? So, make things possible for ALL people. I think of dance as feeding your spirit. It's what keeps you alive. It's what we're meant to do. So, we just do it.

I want to underscore and expand upon an important moment in disability history that Ginger briefly touched on in our interview: the passing of the Americans with Disabilities Act, the ADA. Ginger, along with many other advocates, descended on Washington, D.C., in March of 1990 with the mission and goal of getting the ADA passed, which they accomplished in an astonishingly short amount of time. This iconic rally made history for the rights of disabled people from coast to coast in the United States. When the advocates, who had traveled far and wide to be there, were denied access to their legislators, they would not be deterred. They got out of their wheelchairs and literally crawled up the steps of the Capitol building. This is what Ginger participated in and was talking about earlier in our interview. Also not mentioned was that 104 of those advocates, including Ginger, were arrested that day. Ginger thought that was a wonderful thing. When the 104 arrestees were taken into the rotunda, they all began chanting. When the police told them that chanting was not allowed in the Capitol

Ginger Lane (left) and Anita Fillmore Kenney performing *Prayer*. Choreography by Ginger Lane (courtesy Ginger Lane).

rotunda, everyone of the 104 locked their chairs and refused to budge. Passive resistance was the name of their game, only this was no game. They were there to make sure the disabled community finally had a voice, and that that voice was heard across our nation. To remove the 104 protestors the police had to drag them out. Through the tunnels beneath the Capitol building, the 104 activists were towed to a large room where they were photographed and fingerprinted. Once that routine police booking procedure was finished, they were all put into a row and told not to move or talk. Well, as you can guess they did the exact opposite. They were eventually released and instructed to be present at the D.C. courthouse the next day for their arraignment. When they all showed up at the courthouse the following day, they discovered that the building was... again, not accessible. And so, one more time, all 104 of them demonstrated right there at the bottom of the courthouse steps! To quote John Lewis, "Get into good trouble, necessary trouble." Because Ginger Lane and the other 103 protestors did exactly that in 1990, those with disabilities now have more accessibility to basic functionality in their daily lives, things that nondisabled individuals who are able to climb stairs, fit through doorways and bathroom stalls, and so much more, never have to even think about.

### CHALLENGE

Assess your studio, or where you take or give classes. Make a list of the things Ginger has mentioned regarding accessibility. Are there places that could be made more accessible, welcoming, and inviting for those that use crutches or a wheelchair? Talk about what changes you would suggest implementing so that the space would no longer be difficult or impossible for disabled and mobility-impaired students to take class there. As Ginger said, "Dance should be accessible for everyone, so make things possible for ALL people," not just for some.

## *Mindy Kim*

Next up is a 42-year-old chair tap instructor from North Carolina. Mindy has been teaching for over 20 years and has a rare condition called myotonic dystrophy, which is a form of muscular dystrophy that affects many muscles and organs in the body. The dictionary defines myotonia, with myotonic being the adjective of myotonia, as the "inability to relax

# Tap Dance for All

voluntary muscle after vigorous effort." The progressive muscle deterioration and weakness seen in regular muscular dystrophy is also seen in myotonic dystrophy. During our interview Mindy goes into further detail about the disorder and how it has not stopped her from continuing to do what she was born to do: dance.

## The Interview

**VICTORIA:** *Where do you teach?*

**MINDY:** In North Carolina. I grew up in southern California, [and] I was in Keller, Texas [before moving to North Carolina]. I've kind of been a little bit of everywhere. If we have to move east for a job again, we're going to end up in the middle of the Atlantic Ocean.

Mindy Kim, Virtual Chair Dance Instructor for Dance for All Bodies, and Chair One Fitness Instructor (courtesy Mindy Kim).

*Tell me about how you got into dance and when you were diagnosed with myotonic dystrophy.*

I grew up dancing. I started at three years old. My mom put me in this little pre-dance class, and that is where I fell in love with tap. I was supposed to be a ballet dancer but fell in love with tap and I've been doing it ever since. I danced all throughout high school and college. I never danced professionally, that just wasn't the path for me. I just liked doing it. So, after university, and moving, and getting married, I started teaching little kids regular nondisabled tap. Fast forward about eight years, [to] around 2010. My son was two years old [at that time], and I hadn't lost any weight. I had lost strength with him for about the first three or four months. My muscles were not coming back, and I was very confused. I went to the doctor, X-ray—nothing. MRI—nothing. It turned out that I have myotonic dystrophy, which is a type of muscular dystrophy. There are a thousand things going wrong with my body, [but] the main one that is affecting me the most is that my muscles are

## 13. Professional Physically Integrated Dancers Spotlight

dissolving basically, [which is the best way] to think of it. So, I do not have strength. I can't even stand on my tip toes anymore.

I was sitting at home one night feeling sorry for myself, running a dance company at the time, and realizing this is a career-ending diagnosis. I noticed, as I was sitting there sulking, that my feet were moving. I thought, "Wait a minute!" I've always been tap dancing, [and] I don't want to stop tap dancing, plus I'm doing this perfectly well in a chair. So, that's where I got the idea for chair tap. I started teaching at the senior center and a couple of assisted living facilities. So, the students that took the class were able to move their feet.

*How did you get into hand tap?*

Ten years later, it's 2021 now, and I'm in North Carolina. I found DFAB [Dance for All Bodies] through a friend. She said, "Have you seen this?" [After] I took a class or two I filled out their teacher form and thought, what the heck, maybe they can use me. Getting this job [and] adjusting the class for people who are not mobile below the waist was a good thing. I [even] had one [student] that had no legs in one class, so it was all hands and all movement. It's been a learning experience for me [just] as much as it has been for the students who are learning to tap for the first time. [In regular stand-up tap] we like to put our hands down, or on our hips, or maybe clap, so we can focus on our feet. When I first looked into it, I went online looking for resources, but there were none. There was, however, one teacher who was disabled that had made herself tap gloves. She'd sit at the head of [her] class and show the students what to do with her hands and they would copy her, [but] with their feet. That was my first introduction as to how to do this. I'm still learning, and I'm constantly improving and doing more. For people who don't want to buy the taps to sew onto the gloves, I encourage them to use a wooden cutting board and spoons, or something else metal to give the same idea of the sound. They can drum it, they can shuffle it, or Heel-Toe it you know, things like that. So, they can use their hands, spoons, or feet of course.

*That is true outside-of-the-box thinking, Mindy.*

I've had to jump outside of the box like 18 times! I'm getting there.

*You obviously have an amazing support system in your husband. Did you ever feel that society treated you differently after your*

## Tap Dance for All

*diagnosis? Were there any obstacles that you had to find work arounds for along the way?*

After running my dance company for a few years, and about six months before moving to North Carolina, I stopped and handed [the company] over to my other teacher. I hadn't been teaching anyone except my advanced tappers because they understood [the] terminology in tap and I could tell them or demonstrate in my chair what [I wanted] them to do. I was also teaching at a senior center and an assisted living facility. It was simple: they were nondisabled below the waist, so they could move their feet how I needed them to. I brought the tap shoes every time, and cutting boards, lots of cutting boards. So, at that time I don't think that there was a huge adjustment, just doing less of the kids, and more of the older community.

***Can you tell me a bit more about your myotonic dystrophy? I am sure many who are reading this, like me, have never heard of this disorder.***

Myotonic dystrophy is pretty rare. It is a form of muscular dystrophy, which I'm sure you've heard of from the Jerry Lewis telethon [yearly fundraiser for MDA that ran from 1966 to 2010]. We're part of that. Basically, like when I clench my fist, and I'm engaging every little muscle in my hand and fingers, this is how fast I can open it. (Mindy was extremely slow to open her hand back up) That's myotonia, the inability to release your muscles. It's progressive, so it's continually getting worse. Like I said, the [muscles] are dissolving, for lack of a better term. There's [also] heart issues, [because] the heart is a big old muscle [too]. There are lung issues because there are all these muscles around the lungs that make them work. There are GI issues [as well]. For the people that get it younger, there are cognitive issues. It's a whole-body system problem. I was diagnosed at 32 [years old]. I have what's called adult onset. There's juvenile onset and congenital [onset], which means you're born showing symptoms. [With juvenile and congenital onset,] there are learning disabilities. I have never been in those categories, just physical body changes. [As] it was getting worse, and by the time we arrived in North Carolina, I realized I couldn't teach standing up any longer. I just don't have the ability to effectively show something, you know, for someone to copy me, because I can't do it physically. So, I got hired to teach chair tap at the YMCA. The class didn't take off as much as they wanted it to. So, even though they were still making money, the

### 13. Professional Physically Integrated Dancers Spotlight

class ended after a while. I also teach now [for] Chair One Fitness at the senior center. [Unfortunately] that's ended since COVID. My mobility has gotten worse since then, and I'm not even sure if I [could] physically get there and teach the class [now]. Getting out of my house is the hardest thing, so I don't know if that will continue. But then I got the job teaching at Dance for All Bodies, and it's been great. I teach right from this chair. It's all virtual.

**Have you found varying degrees of ability, both physically and mentally in your classes? I know you said you only teach adults these days, but would you like to teach children again?**

I would love to teach children. My class is open to children, but right now I currently have all adults. They're not necessarily older [though]. My mom is probably the oldest one there, and she's seventy-two. Most of them are younger but disabled. They heard about me through the disabled communities and disabled groups.

**Have you ever had a multi-platform class? One where some students are doing hand tap, and other students are doing chair tap?**

That's what I'm currently doing. They are all seated, and I have my cutting board on my lap to teach hand tap. A lot of times, though, I'm using my hands and feet at the same time while teaching.

**Once studios open again, would you ever integrate all three types of tap into one class: hand, chair, and stand-up?**

I will not say someone should not come to my class. If that class is the only time and day that you can come and it's a chair class, still come. You can do it standing up. Especially if you are a new learner or have any balance issues, it's good to

Mindy Kim, a true warrior for myotonic dystrophy (courtesy Mindy Kim).

start in the chair before you start standing up. Also, people with injuries or professional tap dancers that can't put weight on their feet due to getting hurt [can] take a chair tap class until [they] can get back up on [their] feet. At least your dancing can continue developing in your brain, and your body will catch up when it's ready.

**For college graduates who are majoring in dance, what advice or tips could you offer them as far as teaching someone with disabilities, or those who are mobility impaired?**

I would say plan your classes (a) as if the student has never had a class before, and (b) as if they have never even moved, really. You want to start with the bare minimum. I had a student come to me and say, "I don't really have use of my feet." I [replied], "Oh that's fine because we use our hands. But can you move your legs?" And she [responded], "No, it's like the whole thing." You have to [first] understand what you are dealing with. She couldn't even lift her knees up and down.

Never think that you can't teach somebody, because everybody is teachable. Everyone has something; even if you can only move your chin, and that's all you've got, you can still do it. You just have to figure out how to teach that. Don't ever forget that you're not just a dancer, you're [also] a musician, which is encouraging to my students when I tell them that. Tap is fun and rhythmic, and there's so much more to it than the physical body movement that you have to know. You still have to learn rhythm, and you've still got to learn the attitude, the personality of tap. I've never seen a sad tap dancer. I've never had a bad day tap dancing.

**What would you say has been your biggest victory since your diagnosis?**

My biggest win is that I haven't had to stop. I never had to stop tap dancing. I had to modify, but I didn't have to stop it. So, that's huge, because when I was running my own company and everything, I felt like I was fulfilling God's calling with my life. I am supposed to be a dance teacher. So, when that opportunity was threatened there was a huge, "What am I supposed to do with that now," you know? But I managed to be able to keep going. I just had to do it in a different way.

**That took a lot of strength, fortitude, and determination.**

Determination and stubbornness. I knew that there had to be a way. There just had to be a way.

## 13. Professional Physically Integrated Dancers Spotlight

***Stories like yours are sure to be very empowering and enlightening to others. Is there anything that you'd like to add before we close?***

When you asked me about integrating, I just think that I would encourage teachers not to have just a chair tap [class], and not to have just a hand tap [class], but to put it all together. Bring everybody together. You can come up with some really cool choreography, especially when you have a range of abilities there. If you have a student that you think you can't teach, challenge yourself. Maybe all they can do is snap their fingers, and that's fine. But get them in there and challenge yourself to make them feel included and get them to dance in some form. You can use spoons, cutting boards, and real instruments too, like castanets. I cannot wait for the day when I pick up a pamphlet from the dance company down the street and it includes chair tap. That's what I'm waiting for.

### CHALLENGE

Create an integrated tap piece utilizing all three types of tap: hand, chair, and stand-up. How creative can you be in incorporating all three of these modalities? Do not forget what Mindy suggested as far as thinking outside of the box by including other instruments. Mix it up and let your creativity soar.

## *Lindy Dannelley*

Lindy had an extensive career with Full Radius Dance as a physically-integrated dancer. Now retired, she has unreservedly shared her knowledge of the disabled community with me to educate the non-disabled dance world on how to do better and be better with respect to disabled people. Lindy graciously opened her world to me with true southern hospitality so that I may better understand what disabled people face daily. She shared real-life stories, frustrations, and recommendations, which should no longer be ignored. Change can only happen when we step outside of our comfy, cozy, safe little box and educate ourselves on issues that are going on all around us every day. Turning a blind eye can no longer be an option, especially for those of us with privilege.

Lindy was born and bred in Atlanta, Georgia. She is half Native American and half Irish, which according to Lindy is common in the

# Tap Dance for All

**Lindy Dannelley (also known as Oji), professional integrated dancer, writer, published author, and living her most audacious life (courtesy Lindy Dannelley).**

South. If you want to see everything possible to do with a wheelchair as an integrated dancer, look for Lindy's YouTube channel under the name Oji, which, according to Lindy, is the pronounceable version of her Native American name. Lindy is the least-butchered version of her Gaelic birth name, her name in the professional dance world, and what she was known by when she was performing with Full Radius Dance.

Performing has been in Lindy's life since the age of five. She was a "theater baby" from that incredibly early age all the way through adulthood. Lindy has studied directing at Georgia State University, been a stage manager, owned her own company, and done about every job there is to do in the theater. Around 2005, at the age of 40, Lindy noticed some changes in her body. Even though the degenerative progression began 16 years earlier, she was only accurately diagnosed around the

## 13. Professional Physically Integrated Dancers Spotlight

end of 2019, beginning of 2020. Lindy has sacroiliac joint dysfunction and mononeuritis multiplex. She shared with me that 90 percent of disabled people do not get a correct real diagnosis for ten or more years, and half of that is due to doctors not believing them. Lindy realized that she was going to have to take responsibility for her own mobility when she experienced the frustrating guessing game the doctors were playing with her.

Sacroiliac joints are located on either side of the base of the spine. These joints have strong ligaments to connect the pelvis to the spine. There are as many as a dozen different causes of sacroiliac joint dysfunction, so narrowing down the root cause can be difficult because the pain can mimic other conditions. Pain can manifest anywhere below the waist, from the buttocks all the way down to the feet, on only one side or both sides.

Mononeuritis multiplex is a type of peripheral neuropathy. Mononeuritis multiplex is not a disease of its own, but a group of symptoms. Depending on which type of nerves are damaged, difficulty in controlling movement, numbness, tingling, paralysis of part of the body, lack of sensation, and abnormal sensation are all typical symptoms of mononeuritis multiplex. The extent of disability can range from extraordinarily little to complete loss of feeling or movement.

Lindy began her journey as a disabled person using canes and crutches, but soon came to realize that because of her fierce independence and the inaccessibility of the world, that she was injuring herself more by using those canes and crutches to get where she wanted to go. She fought against using a wheelchair in the beginning because she bought into typical ableist thought patterns: you are *bound* to a wheelchair, you *give in* to a wheelchair. Lindy explained that these are terms that should never be used. She is not "bound" or "confined" to a wheelchair. Language and terminology are vitally important key pieces to be aware of when you are looking to become better at communicating with the disabled community.

Lindy has given us a wealth of information to digest, comprehend, and put into application, to help the nondisabled community become better advocates for disabled people. Lindy, thank you for your generosity, expertise, and breaking it all down with an unvarnished truth and a pinch of humor.

Tap Dance for All

## The Interview

**VICTORIA:** *Can you please help those of us that are nondisabled understand what you mean when you talk about the importance of the language we use when communicating, with not only disabled dancers, but disabled people in general?*

**LINDY:** First, the word is disabled. We are not handy capable, [and] anything that is not disabled, or any [word] that makes an able-bodied person feel warm and fuzzy inside, is probably the wrong word. When an able-bodied person and a person with a disability dance together, that is called physically integrated dance. We are not wheelchair dancers, because our chairs don't dance. Often, we are not even in our wheelchairs. All chair users are [just that], chair users, period. Anybody who says anything else [is using] ableist language. We have to have a whole hashtag on Instagram, #AmbulatoryWheelchairUsersExist, because we can be in our chairs going about our day, [but if] we move a toe someone is going to come and scream at us for being lazy, for trying to milk the system, or "How dare you not be walking." All paralyzed people use chairs. And that's it! I will tell you that I've had many able-bodied people get all bent out of shape when we call them able-bodied, because they'll say things like, "I have problems too. My knee hurts sometimes." I used to call them bipedal, but then I was reminded that my deaf friends are also bipedal. So, I came up with bio-typical. Trust me, able-bodied people love labels. Disabled is what you call anybody with a disability. [As I mentioned], physically integrated dance is the term when an able-bodied person and a disabled person dance together. When a disabled person dances [alone], that's just dance. I dance because I am a dancer, and I fall like I'm a dancer.

When we did so much traveling [with Full Radius] I started to understand the problems, with not only accessibility but [also] language. Words we do not want to hear [are]: "special" and "inspirational." We really, really don't want to exist to inspire you, period. The word is disabled, and it is perfect just the way it is.

Part of what I do now, working for social media, is teaching language. Douglas [Scott, the artistic and executive director of Full Radius] has helped me with that. We realized there was a problem with some of the terms that we used at the beginning of my tenure in that journey. It was like, what is the essence? If I'm taking what an able-bodied person is doing and I'm going to put it on my body, what do I have access to, and

## 13. Professional Physically Integrated Dancers Spotlight

what is the essence of that movement? Is it a sweep? Is it up and down? What's the most important part of that movement? And that's what I need to transpose onto my chair.

For my journey, it was trying to always remain professional while being completely frustrated and flabbergasted by the people who were temporarily hiring us. For one to be so blinded by their own ableist agendas, which I'm not saying are based in malice, as I may be the first disabled person they've ever met, but there are other people that are just not going to cut you any slack. After one performance I went out in the lobby, and some guy actually said to me, "Well, I'm just so glad that I'm not in a wheelchair. I'd have to kill myself every day. I wouldn't be able to do anything. I would just leap off a building. You're so brave." I was like, "Yeah okay, thanks for coming to the show. I hope you paid full price for your ticket." We don't want to be "brave." We don't want to live in a world where we have to be brave. I would love to not be brave. Brave is an [okay] word, but it depends on how it's being used. I guess the rule you should think about when you're using any noun or adjective is, "Would you use that exact same noun or adjective if you were talking about an able-bodied dancer only?" If you would have used that word anyway, then okay. Just that whole idea: are they brave because the moves were so difficult for any human body, or are they brave because they got out of bed today, and they danced and entertained you. It's that idea of why you are choosing that word. For me, instead of saying that move was so brave, [try instead using] that move was so disciplined. That would be better. Or, that move was so professional. Those are words I would use for anyone. I hone my craft just like any stand-up dancer does, maybe even more so. Representation means **"nothing about us without us."**

My first interview when I became a dancer was with a guy that used the term wheelchair bound, and I said, "No, it's wheelchair user." And then he did it again, "wheelchair bound." So, again I responded, "No, it's wheelchair user." My reply after the third time he said wheelchair bound was, "No, only on date night and only if you have duct tape." It was like, I'm sorry, I gave you three chances. Douglas [Scott] would say, "I'm sorry, they don't allow me to duct tape them to their chairs anymore. They're not having that." It's that idea that you are confined. A mobility device is the exact opposite.

I [also] hate the word "overcome." I don't overcome my physical body. We're not here to overcome our physical bodies. I don't believe in that use of the word, but I can overcome my fears. Most of the things

## Tap Dance for All

I have to overcome are because society is so ableist. And that is something that I really shouldn't have to overcome. I should not have to overcome the stares, and the "God bless you," and "Oh look, you took something off a shelf." And then there's the opposite, "I saw you move a toe, you're in the disabled parking spot, you're a faker." This would be the disability police. The term "overcoming" is another very dangerous, slippery trough that we don't need because what we're overcoming is not something inside of us, we're overcoming what's going on out there.

***I've read a piece that you wrote called Border Gimp. Can you explain what that is all about?***

When I first wrote Border Gimp, it was right before I joined Full Radius Dance. I don't think the internet was ready for Border Gimp when I first wrote it. It just came out as a stream of thought. I mean, I look back now because I was an English major in college and think, "Wow, that essay was really horribly constructed." It was [based on] what I was starting to notice in Full Radius Dance, how those dancers approached this [subject]. I always start by saying that I use the term "gimp," but a nondisabled person should **never** use this term. [Like] there are certain words that Native Americans use amongst themselves, and I might use with my family, but I would never use them out in public. Why? Because I look Caucasian [not Native American], and so that other people don't [then] look at me and say, "She's not Native American," and I respect that.

For the cradle gimp, their thing is that they've never had any other normal [than being disabled]. So, they just figure out ways to do things, how to get around. They don't have to unlearn anything because they came into the world that way.

Then there's the instant gimp; this person is thrust into that emotional journey extremely abruptly. They have that whole grief process to deal with, and on top of that they have society wanting that Lifetime [TV] moment of them getting out of the chair and being their old self again. They want you to be happy. They want you to get a computer job. They want you to fit into a niche, and you have had no time to prepare for that, and you are probably thinking the same things. So, it takes them even longer [to acclimate]. I was working with a brilliant dancer once, he was an instant gimp, and it was ten years [post-accident for him]. There was no medical hope that this guy was ever going to walk [again]. It was just not going to happen. But there would be moments he

### 13. Professional Physically Integrated Dancers Spotlight

would say, "Well, maybe." And that was his journey, but there was still that part of him that thought, "I'm not going to be better until I walk."

With the border gimp, like me, we are slowly losing things. There are things that I have marked in my life, just personally, that this is going to be the last time I am going to be able to do this. I started going gimp around 2005-ish. That's when I really started to notice that something was really going wrong with my body, that I wasn't just overdoing it. One of the things I love to do here in Atlanta is called Stone Mountain. Once a year I would go, get up to the top of the mountain, have my moment and do my thing, then go back down. But I realized there was a point when it was going to be the last time. So, I got a really strong friend to go with me and we took forever. As a border gimp you have those opportunities: this is going to be the last time I'm going to be able to do this, this way. Now, I could easily take the little trolley they have up at Stone Mountain, trolley it up there and sit in the little accessible thing, but it's not the same as being out there on the rock. I'll probably take my granddaughter up there eventually.

When you translate those three types of disabled into dance, for the cradle gimps, physically integrated dance is all they've known in dance, and they just figure it out. An instant gimp is really terrified of falling because they've not had a slow gradual progression into this. They've lost the autonomy of their body in such an immediate, instant way, unless they're young. We've had a couple [of dancers] that were really young when they had their accident, and [you know] 17-year-old boys will try anything. For the border gimp, well I know for me, when I felt that sensation of spinning—I was in! Douglas [Scott] first spotted me at one of those Full Radius Fridays, coming up to me saying that he wanted to do some partnering, real actual partnering to show them all how to do it correctly. So, we counter spun. The dancing I do now, and the things I choreograph on myself, are all about spinning. My first video was called Fly, and it is all about the spinning. I really wanted Fly to be about exploring all the ways my chair could move. In Fly I was just by myself, exploring every conceivable way I could move that chair. I could push myself by [manipulating] my wheel like this, or I could grab the wheel and just keep my hand in that one place, and how does that differ? And that's how I ended up coming up with a move where I do the spin and pop up on the foot plate. When we first did it, Douglas had two dancers take me by the arms and put me in the position. I realized as time went on that I could hold it [myself]. And then it was, "can I get myself into it?" Well, I do have access to a big toe on my right side, so that was all I needed. The key was that tiny thing, plus figuring out how to pull my body. I'm strapped in so that allows me to pull, and [with] that one toe as the pendulum, the pivot point, and then pulling on it, I had just enough torque. Then I learned how to hold it.

***Tell me about when you went from canes and crutches to your first wheelchair.***
When I finally got my first wheelchair it literally made me a better artist. I mean, that wheelchair changed everything in a completely 100 percent positive way. Most [disabled] people will tell you that like me, they fought it. There are no Lifetime TV movies where a person in a wheelchair gets out of it in the end. And [so] we're really just fighting that scenario. So, I fought it and fought it, and when I got in my chair I thought, "What the heck was I doing to myself?" When it comes to adapting the chair, it usually takes four wheelchairs before you figure out what you need in a chair. Your first one's always a buggy with a wheel broken that you got at a grocery store. That's always your first chair. Your second chair is just a slightly better buggy. The third one, okay, now you're starting to realize what you need and what you don't need. On my fourth one I was incredibly lucky to have it custom made by a guy who watched my video, saw exactly what I needed out of the chair, and also saw exactly what I didn't need out of the chair. He custom built my chair for ⅓ of the cost of what any insurance company is going to give you. I would say never get a chair from your insurance company because you're going to have to pay a lot of it out of pocket. You can take that same money and go to an independent sports chair builder and get exactly what you need, and never have even one bolt in it that would inevitably break or come out. I don't believe in bolts in wheelchairs. When it's all just a frame and no bolts, then the wheels can pop off. Usually, they're made from aero-grade aluminum, but who has $10,000 for a chair?

Our chairs took damage while performing. I ended up finding a guy who would come weld my chair at my house. He wasn't cheap, but he was quick, there when I needed him, and really good. He would always ask me how I broke the weld. I would say, "Well, I had three dancers on me, all on one side of my chair, as I was holding us all in a tilt. Yeah, I needed a chair that could hold up to 600 pounds, so it took the plate right out." He was like, "Yeah, that'd do it." I have almost no back to my

## 13. Professional Physically Integrated Dancers Spotlight

chair compared to most chairs. You have to have at least a little, just so you have something to push back on when you do a wheelie or have a full-grown human in your lap.

***Tell me about your time with Full Radius and how you became a member of that company.***

If there had not been a Full Radius Dance, I could not have become a professional dancer. There was no place for me to be a physically integrated dancer. So, I'm in my chair and I'm building back my life, rejoining society. I had been a fan of Full Radius because I had a friend who was in it. Full Radius Fridays are held by the company and are open to the public. So, I go to the Full Radius Friday, and I keep going. I realize I am learning skills that I'm able to apply, [like] how to get through a crowd, how to get off a curb, [and] how to maneuver my chair. Douglas offered me an apprenticeship in 2011. I was in! [At the end of] my apprenticeship he offered me a permanent space in the company.

I was with Full Radius for ten years. [Over that time] there were 20 to 25 people that came and went through my tenure, with one dancer who was there longer than myself. A lot of times [at Full Radius Fridays, the audience] would warm up with us for a while, spin us around, hopefully not injuring us, and they would then give donations. We could tell they just wanted to feel good. We call that "inspirational porn" by the way. That's what [the audience] wanted. That's what they were buying. They wanted that picture they could put on their Instagram and show what a "good" person they are. They danced with a disabled person who could dance circles around them.

As my tenure went on, we had tap dancers, a martial artist, and even an aerialist over that time. Whatever the dancers had, that's what Douglas used. So, the vastly different shows that we did [were] based on what everybody in the company could do.

***When you were touring around the globe with Full Radius, did you encounter any difficulties with the various venues you played in?***

If the world was accessible, we, [disabled people], would have the same playing field just like in any group. Ninety percent of the time we can't [even] get onto the stage. Half the time during my ten years with Full Radius Dance [the venue] booked a company that they knew used wheelchairs, and it never occurred to them until we arrived that there was no way [for us] to get onto the stage that they wanted us to perform on. Now, we made the choice that we would figure it out for ourselves.

## Tap Dance for All

Sometimes I would throw my chair off, shimmy my rear end up the stairs, grab my chair and pull it up with me. I'm a professional, and this was where we had to go and what had to be done.

Then there was the time we were on this one stage that they didn't allow us to see ahead of time. I'm in a line in this tight little hallway, and suddenly six people are grabbing my chair, picking me up four feet [high], and just kind of shoving me onstage. Of course, I've got to keep going, I've got to keep performing. You can imagine that that would be terrifying for certain disabled people: to not have autonomy over their chairs.

We've been brought into spaces with five minutes to set up and a carpet that is 3½" thick. When we went on tour in smaller countries, like Spain, they would send tour buses that were just death traps. And these people [that] were so eager to help us were going to get us injured. So, Douglas finally had to learn how to say, "Stop touching my dancers" in Spanish. Our able-bodied company people know how to help us. We're like, we're good. Please stop helping us. Common things I say on any given day are, "Please don't pray on me spontaneously," "Please don't touch me," and "I'm not a piece of furniture." And don't assume I'm not intelligent. I have to remind people constantly that there are real people in those chairs.

We're about to have the Atlanta Peachtree Road Race for the first time in person, and they are still calling it the wheelchair race. I'm like, do you call it the shoe race, because there are people in shoes, right? So again, wheelchair user [is the language that should be used].

When we fly, we have to give our wheelchairs to the airline to store, and if they break it they are not going to pay for it. Do you know that they break 26 wheelchairs every day in this country? And they pay for none of them. If we were to show up in Spain, New York, or any of the places we flew out to with no chair, what would we do? That right there just killed my livelihood. You can't just go to the store and buy another one. Airlines don't see that chair as our legs. They expect us to just get out and crawl. I have many horror stories [with airlines]. One time they tried to make me get out and crawl because they said they couldn't find my chair. I said, "I'm not getting off this plane without my chair. You'll have to take me out kicking and screaming, and my friend here is going to film it for YouTube. I'm not getting off this plane." It took them 15 minutes of trying several times to force me onto a gurney. I reminded them again that they'd have to take me kicking and screaming… and oh look, they found my chair.

## 13. Professional Physically Integrated Dancers Spotlight

*That's got to be so frustrating. This is something that nondisabled people don't have to think about or deal with and don't understand. All we have to gripe about is slow or lost luggage.*

It's because of the language. Unless we're in the chair they don't put it together, and when they do put us together with our chairs, they don't see us as human. It's the chair, the chair is the problem, the chair is an issue, the chair is something we're adapted for. There's the infamous "you people" that gets used a lot, "What do you people want?" One time I finally responded, "In. What we want is in. I see where you got confused there."

Even in the disability community, we're using our platforms on social media to show us just living our lives. I'm a big proponent of the best way to get back to any "normality" is to just go out and be normal. People will literally walk up to me and ask what's wrong with me? And I go, "Hi, I'm Lindy." Suddenly they see there's an actual person sitting in the wheelchair. One of the gimp rules is: If you don't know my name, you don't get to ask what my disability is. I do not owe you my disability story. I'm just here to pick up my Chinese food. I really don't care that you had to push your grandmother in her wheelchair for the day. Seriously, I don't.

There's a great series on YouTube called My Gimpy Life. It was done by the amazing Teal Sherer. She writes for wheelchair magazines, she's an actor, and has just done lots of stuff. She was also in Full Radius for a while. She is a lovely human being. In the show she's just a person, she's just living her life. In the very first shot she gets up, makes her bed, gets her coffee, gets dressed, gets in her car, takes her chair apart and puts it in the trunk. She then gets in the car, drives, takes the chair back out and puts it together. Just as she is about to transfer herself into the chair her phone rings. She lets go of the chair, and as she's on her phone she sees her wheelchair roll down the street. We have all done that! When it happened to me this guy jumped out of his car to help me but forgot to put his car in park. One of my wheels went like this, and the other wheel went like that. My chair was in pieces. The carriage came down, pinning me to the ground, and my tires went bouncing away like cartoon characters. The guy finally puts his car in park and goes after my wheels. As he's standing there with my wheels in his hands, I'm lying on the ground laughing. I was like, "This is a funny situation, sir, you're allowed to laugh. This is not, 'oh, don't laugh at the poor crippled girl,' this is comedy right here. Thanks for the wheels." Putting it out there

## Tap Dance for All

that we are just living our lives is needed. My granddaughter, who is three, loves all my devices and is so relaxed in this chair. She loves to sit in my chair and dance with me. Her friends are fascinated by whatever mobility device I am using that day. And she's like, "Yeah, my grandma's in a wheelchair, yours is not? That must be boring, let's go play." It's the idea of making it so normal.

***Tell me what it was like for you to take a dance class in a nondisabled studio.***

If I wanted to go to a ballet class and roll into the class with my chair, everybody in that class would freak the bejesus out. When I roll into a class and they've never seen me before, they'd want to push me far in a corner because they think that I'm going to take out everybody, but I'm actually nimbler than they are. I have to remind able-bodied people all the time that their feet are not my responsibility. If we're dancing together you've got to be responsible for your own darn feet. They also expect me to just use my hands. No, we figure out a way to use not just the hands, but also the wheels. I can make my chair do lots of things. I can bounce it off those wheels, or balance on my foot plate with no wheels on the ground at all. I have always explored what else I could do.

Once we did a [piece] called Rain Dance, where we're supposed to be two kids playing in the rain. As we were playing in the rain I thought, "What if it really started pouring down?" So, I popped myself onto one hand, pulled off my wheel, and now [that wheel] is an umbrella. Then the other dancer got underneath me, took the umbrella away from me, and continued playing in the rain with the "umbrella." That's what we want to do. We want to change how people see a performance like that. Success is when people suddenly forget they're looking at someone who is using crutches or chairs and see that we go beyond the mobility device.

There is a difference between physically-integrated dance as therapy, and physically-integrated dance as a profession. They really are two different things. Yes, all bodies should dance. Every disabled person should get out there and dance. Every human on this planet should dance for therapy. Not everybody is equipped mentally and emotionally to be a [professional] dancer though. The issue is that there are so few [professional] companies out there. If I try, I can maybe come up with 14 companies on this side of the planet. I know of one in Spain, and one in Italy. There's just so little opportunity.

Being a dancer is more than just having the right [facility] for dance. People often say that when I'm just doing my thing that I move like a dancer. That's how I learned to push a shopping cart while in my wheelchair. I have a large family, so I need a lot of food, and I don't have time for a tiny little basket. [Grocery shopping] is no different than dancing with another person in a chair. It took about a year of me shopping that way before people stopped taking the cart out of my hands. Obviously, I'm struggling and need help, but I don't want that, nor do I want to be prayed over spontaneously.

***Is the performance pay equal to that of a professional nondisabled dancer?***

Back when I was an actor and director, you would get paid stipends if you were lucky. As a disabled dancer most [venue owners] think, "Surely you'll [perform] for me for the pure enjoyment of inspiring this audience." Yeah, no! Douglas always made sure we were paid like any professional dancer. The few times we did a pro-bono performance he would ask us if we wanted to do it. If you like what I do, if you stop seeing my chair, that is what I'm wanting. It's my profession, it's what I do for a living, and it's not any different from what a regular dancer does. The standards are the same.

***Are there any debates within the disabled dance community about performing professionally?***

There are some things that come with disability. There is one argument even amongst the physically-integrated dance companies. There are some people who feel that you can only be this disabled [to be a professional performer]. That you must have access to at least this much of your body to even be considered a professional dancer. You must be an athlete. You must be able to do handstands. You must be [muscularly] ripped. And that's one train of thought. I do not personally subscribe to that. However, I do think there's a certain amount of that, but again I don't think it's about your disability. I think it's about you as a person: do you have the discipline to be in a profession where you must push your body to do certain things?

The deaf community has their own line of dancers, and the blind community has their own line of dancers [as well]. It's all about what you have access to and what you are going to do with it. Is it going to help me just love life, because that's a wonderful thing, or is the discipline and desire at that next level? If we don't have opportunities for the first one, we're never going to build up the opportunities for the second one.

## Tap Dance for All

When we would audition new able-bodied dancers for Full Radius, I could always recognize in the very first minutes whether the dancer would ever be able to get over their hesitancy or their ableism, or whether it was not going to be an issue. I could also see something in someone who maybe has never touched a disabled person before, but I can tell that they're going to be able to get over it. It was also like that with people in my life. Some people just got onboard with the program and off we went. Some people were like, it took me a little while to not be constantly afraid that you were going to fall and kill yourself. And then I saw you fall, and you didn't kill yourself. You got back up and got back in your chair, so I guess you're fine. And then there were those people who were never going to be able to get over it, and I bless them way the heck away from me. It was hurtful at first. Although, disability is a great way of weeding people out of your life that were never any good for you anyway. And it does that quickly. Even though it hurts, you come to find out that it saves a whole lot of time.

***Do you feel a responsibility to act as representation for young ones with disabilities?***

My ten years with Full Radius really opened up what representation is for me. I was already a professional performer and I already had the discipline, but what changed was that there were little kids [in the audience] now. The moment that it really hit home was when we had a little girl named Zoe come to the shows. She was about eight years old when I first met her, and she was in a chair. She would come to every show her mom could get her to. There was a meme out there where there was a little girl in a wheelchair looking in the mirror at an able-bodied ballet dancer doing the same arm [pose]. Her mom called me and said, "Zoe saw this. She was [so mad]! And she said, 'When I look in the mirror, I don't see that stand-up dancer, I see Lindy.'" And that's when I discovered that I did not realize that that was part of the gig. I am representing for all those kids that you can grow up to be a professional dancer if that dancer part of you is part of your spirit.

***Are there places that young disabled kids can go to get the training to become an integrated dancer?***

There are no places for young people to go. Even at Full Radius we were not covered by insurance to work with people under 18, which is terrible. How are we going to train and capitalize on the drive and ingenuity of childhood when we're not even allowed to spin them or put

## 13. Professional Physically Integrated Dancers Spotlight

Lindy Dannelley describes this picture as "inspirational porn," and not an appropriate role model for a child with a disability (courtesy Lindy Dannelley).

them in a wheelie until they are 18? When performing professionally, it was just standard for us to sign away all our insurance rights. One time when I was on stage, I told them how they had us getting on and off the stage with zero lighting, in a pitch-black condition, that somebody was going to fall off the stage. And I did exactly that in the middle of the performance. When it happened, I just popped back up and made it part of the show, but I injured myself seriously. We have to go into it thinking, if you make this space dangerous for me there's nothing I can do about it, because then I can't dance, perform, and ultimately make a living. So, it's a choice I have to carefully consider.

**Victoria**: *What advice would you give to teachers and studio owners about how to teach disabled students that are using chairs or crutches?*

**Lindy**: First, you're going to have to invite us, because we won't know we're welcome. And don't dumb it down for us. If you're doing ballet steps with your feet, let us decide if we want to stay or go, or how we want to transpose those steps, or if we can transpose them. We need the dance studios not to be terrified and make us sign our rights away so that a kid under the age of 18 can come and move. Twice I was brought into a high school where they were doing their senior play and they had somebody who was in a chair. I was like, "All right, is your mom going to be okay? Are you afraid of falling? Because I just need to know what your boundaries are before we get started. Okay, not afraid of falling? Not afraid. You guys that are going to dance with him are going to get your toes run over. Is that a problem?" After that it was like they totally forgot this kid was in a chair. He was just part of the musical. And that is what we've got to do. We've got to open the spaces, open people's minds.

Lindy Dannelley (left) and Zoe (Laryssa) Crossman show the proper representation for disabled youth (courtesy Lindy Dannelley).

Just let them move. Let them figure out ways to move and watch how they can move. Because Douglas pushed us over those ten years I was with Full Radius Dance, I've found so many ways to move my chair. Well, how many ways can you move a chair? I can move it with only two fingers. I can move it by pulling my chair up. I can move it by flipping myself up backwards. If you really want to see, go to the Full Radius site, and watch a piece called Do You Know What You're Doing Now. If you want to see almost every single way a disabled body can move, check out me, Lisa, and Eric in that number, because we did it all.

I think that all kids in chairs should get into physically-integrated dance, or at least wheelchair-using dance, because it will teach them things about how their chair moves. I don't even know how [disabled] non-dancers get around in their chairs in the world. Dance will teach you how to push up a hill, how to adjust your weight, how to get into spaces, and give you the confidence that when the elevator's out to just grab the escalator and go up it.

If you are going to teach a person with a disability on a professional level, they have got to trust that disabled person to know the limits of their body. We've learned to phrase it like this when we get new dancers and we're trying to get them to do more complicated moves, especially the first time they try the move: "What do you need to feel safe to do this?" And the same is true for the able-bodied dancer. In the last piece I did for Full Radius, I worked with a new dancer and she did this move where I'm laying on the ground in my chair on my back and she does a cartwheel landing on my knees, and then I pop us up. She was terrified! Of course she was. I asked her, "What do you need?" First, we did it with spotters, but then she realized that gravity was on her side, and that I was strong enough. It was then that she realized we were going to be fine. The trust [factor] in physically-integrated dance is huge. That's the difference between being in charge and responsible for your own body, but also trusting your partner. The repetition you get in rehearsals are key in any live art form, but I think having a slightly longer rehearsal period is even more important in physically integrated dance because we have to trust so much more muscle memory. We must know where and how much you can hold, because even though I'm in a wheelchair and you're in a wheelchair, the physical capacity that we each have available in our bodies could be vastly different. Where is the weight? We might even look the same size, but all the other dancer's weight might be in his legs, whereas all my weight is in my butt, which gives me a good center of gravity and a center in my chair, allowing me to just pull my axle right up under my butt.

**Were there ever times when putting a piece together that you felt like, "I don't know if I can pull that move off?"**

When I first started, I couldn't do a wheelie, and now I do wheelies without even realizing I'm in a freaking wheelie. It's our way of leaning because when you're [sitting up] like this all day your posture is great, but sometimes you just want to take a moment and take the pressure off your back. When I'm popping a wheelie, I'm moving my center of gravity off my spinal cord for a few minutes. At first, I couldn't do a wheelie and was afraid of some of the moves. You can see my progression [in my videos]. First, I had to find a partner that I trusted. Shawnee is tiny, but freakishly strong for such a tiny man. I mean really, freakishly strong! Douglas wanted to do this thing in one piece called Gut Instinct where the [able-bodied dancers] lean down and pick us up. So, we are wrapped around them like sideways koalas, and they're walking with us because it's a comedy piece. The fact that Shawnee could do it, first of all, was crazy, but I realized that I felt like I was fine, and mostly it was just getting to trust my own body. Dancers get injured all the time, but it was like once I had that trust, if I fall, I fall. The hardest thing for disabled dancers is a fall backwards because that is when we have the least control. We've all taken a tumble backwards though.

**When I think about dance studios and their layouts, I recall having seen some entrances that would make it exceedingly difficult for someone in a wheelchair to be able to enter because there were one, two, or three steps.**

Even though I have the capacity to get over those two or three steps, some businesses use the excuse that "no disabled people come here" for not making the building accessible. Do you remember back in history when there was a time where they had a sign that said only a certain ethnic group could be in certain places? I guess there must not be anybody of this particular ethnic group in the entire world. You know, disabled people have money, and it spends just as well as other people's money. This is why I came up

Lindy Dannelley exudes power, grace, focus, and complete control while in rehearsal (courtesy Lindy Dannelley).

## 13. Professional Physically Integrated Dancers Spotlight

with the gimp rules, and #6 is: "If I cannot get into your building, it's not accessible."

If you want me to come out with you, like go to a bar or something, what you don't realize is that I have to call every place I go ahead of time and ask, "Are you accessible?" First, they're going to panic and say yes before they even know if they are because they're terrified I'm with the ADA and I'm going to give them a ticket. I then follow up with, "Okay, let's talk about this accessibility you speak of. How wide is your door?" Well, it is four feet wide, but it has a pole right in the middle of it. That might be a problem. "When you say accessible, do you mean that I can go up and down that chute you have for the garbage in the back of the restaurant?" Eighty percent of the time that is what they mean. I have been through the back of more restaurants than you could ever imagine.

Large events are terrible for not knowing their accessibility. If you ask any event organizer what the accessibility of the event is, they won't know. They don't know because it has never even occurred to them to know. They just assume that all buildings are ADA accessible. I had a job for a while at some of the big conventions we have here in Atlanta. It's like okay, so you say your event is accessible. Let's give it a go. If I can't get in, what's rule #6 again? If I can't get in, it's not accessible. And I'm sorry, but those little electric lifts with the key? Well, nobody knows where that key is, so that doesn't count. I tell able-bodied people to just imagine if every time you needed to use the stairs, every time, you had to wait between 20 and 45 minutes, and then flip a coin that half the time the lift was broken or didn't work anyway. **Every time you needed to use the stairs!** This is why we don't like lifts. It's called a ramp, it's a board and everyone can walk on it and use it. It's a technological amazement!

### How can the nondisabled community better help the disabled community?

This is what the barriers are, the barriers of society. Able-bodied people, just like with the Black Lives Matter movement that had the support of the white community and others, need to use their privilege to protect us. We're begging able-bodied people to please use your privilege. If you go and patronize that bar that doesn't have accessibility, they're never going to change. But if you get forty people to say, "You know what? We're leaving with all of our money because our friend can't

## Tap Dance for All

come in," [just watch how they change their tune]. And yes, I have those kinds of friends.

If I come to a two-hundred-year-old building that has an obstruction blocking my entry, I have the choice of having my friends pick me up over the obstacle, and that's my choice. A lot of disabled people don't have that option. The thing that's got to change is the way the able-bodied community sees it. Accessibility can be fixed, but because it's not, opportunities don't exist right now. Why is Ali Stocker the only disabled actor on Broadway? I know lots of disabled actors. I have asked countless friends who are casting directors for major movies why they wouldn't hire a disabled person for a disabled part. Their response is always about how the sets are built, making it difficult for the disabled to maneuver. They could fix that because accessibility really doesn't cost anything. It just costs your time and you caring about it. Nondisabled casting for disabled parts has got to stop. If it doesn't stop it will never get better.

When it comes to how to treat a disabled dancer, it's disrespectful and self serving to treat them like they don't have to get the movements right. And anything that is done solely to make the able-bodied person feel good about themself by creating puppy dog and butterfly moments is also disrespectful and self serving. Disabled dancers don't do that to able-bodied dancers. Every time you should stop and think, would I have done that with an able-bodied dancer? And if you wouldn't have, then there's your problem.

The main thing is the language, the representation, and being willing to use your platform to open the proverbial door for us. Use that able-bodied privilege as teachers. Able-bodied people right now have the privilege, and we need you to use it. Climbing up the Capitol steps back in 1990 is what it took to establish the Americans with Disabilities Act and get us just the bare bones of what we need. We have so much further to go, and we know it. It's often hard for us to just focus. But ramps, that's it, let's just focus on ramps. We'll get to the other things later. If we all just said ramps together [that would make for a great start towards moving in a more accessible for all direction].

### Challenge

- Make a list of your activities over the course of one day. Next to each activity jot down the ways in which each one could pose an accessibility problem if you were a chair user.

### 13. Professional Physically Integrated Dancers Spotlight

- Write down 3 ways in which you see where you could affect positive changes for the disabled people in your community.

## Mary Verdi-Fletcher

Last, but certainly not least, is the phenomenal Mary Verdi-Fletcher. What an honor it was to speak with this pioneer in the integrated dance world. Mary is the president and founding artistic director of Dancing Wheels Company and School, a world-renowned, professional, integrated performing dance company and inclusive dance school. Mary opened the Dancing Wheels integrated dance company in 1980, which was the first professional integrated dance company of its kind back then. Mary followed up that accomplishment by opening the Dancing Wheels School in 1990, a world-class training center for dancers, choreographers, and educators. The school serves over 6,500 students annually, giving much-needed accessibility to the arts and dance to *all* students of *all* abilities. Self-awareness, self-confidence, and embedding lessons of equality and inclusion are the fundamental building blocks of all their programs. In addition, the school fosters personal and social growth that builds vital independent living skills. Assembly-based lecture performances and residencies in outside Pre-K through college settings are an important part of infusing the arts into the lives of students of all abilities for Mary. She offers funding in the form of scholarships to 40 percent of her students with disabilities, as well as those with socio-economic struggles.

Mary Verdi-Fletcher, Founder of Dancing Wheels Company and School of Dancing Wheels (image courtesy of the Dancing Wheels Company).

# Tap Dance for All

Whether it is through her professional company, performing over 72 shows a year with over 5 million people to date experiencing the innovative and revolutionary artistry of her Dancing Wheels performance company, or the school-based immersive assembly lecture performance presentations, Mary Verdi-Fletcher unquestionably has made an everlasting mark in the way society sees the ability and artistry of those who have disabilities.

Mary was born with spina bifida, a birth defect when the spine and spinal cord do not form properly. Her mother was a professional dancer herself, but back in the late 1950s there were zero options for physical activity for a disabled child such as Mary. Back then a child was either left to die or put in a home. Mary's mother was not going to let that happen to her daughter. So, Mary and her brother learned how to dance in their home from their mother when Mary was only three years old. At an incredibly early age Mary's focus was clear: she wanted to follow in her mother's professional footsteps. While growing up it was important to Mary's mother that she was seen as Mary, and not as handicapped (a term that was used back then, but one that is no longer appropriate to use today. More on why it is a negative word to the disabled community in Mary's interview). Mary's mother taught her to believe in the impossible, and thanks to her mother she never knew that there were things she could not do in life. As such, dance became her life force. Mary broke ground and paved the way for the disabled community, accomplishing many firsts. Before becoming the first professional wheelchair dancer and opening the first professional integrated dance company and dance school, Mary helped create the first Independent Living Center in the state of Ohio. Later she became their first development director, where she raised over $100,000 in her first year. Mary is lovingly called the "Rosa Parks of Cleveland" for her relentless advocacy in ensuring equal opportunities for the disabled people who wished to ride public transportation in Ohio. Her tenacity led to every bus nation-wide becoming accessible to all, including and especially disabled people.

In 2014 Mary was awarded the Governor's Award for Arts Education, the Ohio Dance Award for her major contributions to dance in Ohio, and the Henry Viscardi Achievement Award, which pays tribute to exemplary leaders in the disability community who have had a profound impact on shaping attitudes, raising awareness, and improving the quality of life of people with disabilities.

Mary Verdi-Fletcher has redefined what it means to be a dancer.

## 13. Professional Physically Integrated Dancers Spotlight

When asked what words she would use to describe those with disabilities, she explained that she sees disability as someone with great strength, steely determination, high creativity, and an unstoppable will "because we have to be, and because we have the right to participate."

### The Interview

**VICTORIA:** *I have watched many of the videos you have posted of you and your company members dancing together. In every video your artistry had me completely forgetting that you are in a wheelchair, and I found myself becoming thoroughly immersed in your performance, the emotion, and the story of the piece. For me it felt like a sense of freedom, a freedom of movement and expression. Is the word "freedom" an accurate description of what performing feels like for you?*

**MARY:** Actually, there've been times where I've said it's been the greatest freedom of my life, because it equates to limitless possibilities. There are no barriers on the stage for me as an artist, and I can transcend who I am depending on the piece I am doing. Any aspect of disability is removed because it's a place of freedom. It's almost like flying to me.

*I know your company has been around for over 40 years now. Considering you pioneered establishing the very first integrated dance company, how did you come to create such a new and innovative concept? And how has the company shifted, changed, and evolved over those 40 years? And lastly, where do you see it going post pandemic?*

Those are big questions. My mother was a professional dancer, so as a small child with a disability I really didn't see the limits of my disability. My mother always taught me to tell people that "I'm not handicapped, I'm Mary." They used the word "handicapped" back then, but they don't anymore. I was like, well what does she mean by that? Later, I learned that she meant she wanted people to see me for who I was, not my disability. So, for years I wanted to follow in her footsteps, to be a dancer. But of course, society wasn't ready for that. They didn't have any place [for people with disabilities] to go train. Although, she would put my brother and I together in our living room and put little dances together for us. When I was very young, I had braces and crutches. Later, I broke my leg three times, so I used a wheelchair after that. They were those big, old-fashioned wheelchairs, you know, that weigh a lot,

## Tap Dance for All

**Mary Verdi-Fletcher performing the mesmerizing *La Vie En Rose* (image courtesy of the Dancing Wheels Company).**

and I used to break the wheel off the wheelchair just moving [around]. And mind you, I'm just a little thing, like I only weigh 71 pounds!

That desire to move was always in me. The story unfolds in the disco days. There was a lot of social dancing going on then. I just innocently started to watch my friends that were dancing, and then one gentleman that was a friend of all of ours asked me to dance. I was like, "Well, I don't know, what am I going to do?" We started partnering, and from there I went into dance classes [and] started partnering with different partners. I entered those big dance competitions that were on television, like Dance Fever. There were like 2,000 people in the audience, and I just went out there with my dance partner. It was so awesome. It was complete silence when they first saw me come out, and the producer was leaning forward on his table, like, "What is a person in a wheelchair doing dancing—here?" So, we busted it out in the song "It's Raining Men" by the Weather Girls. Everyone went crazy! [My partner] took a flying leap and jumped over my head. He jumped on the armrest of the wheelchair and then jumped over my head [again]. I wasn't getting lifted out of the chair at that point because I didn't know I could, you know, [and] we needed a smash ending of course. We got a standing

## 13. Professional Physically Integrated Dancers Spotlight

ovation, and it got covered by the media. There was no social media back then, but [our performance] spread like wildfire. We were chosen as alternates to go to California to be on the show. Ironically, the producer said to me, "You know, I've never seen anything like this in my life, but I felt like if I chose you to go, they would have said that I chose you because you're disabled." And that was before the ADA or anything. From there we were on Walt Disney, and then we appeared on CNN and Good Morning America. We traveled all over. Eventually, the more people that saw us, the more they wanted to participate. So, I added more people, and it wasn't long before I became associated with Cleveland Ballet. They needed outreach and educational programs, so I created that for them. I also added more stand-up dancers to the mix. I trained [extensively] with the Cleveland Ballet, and that's where I learned a lot of translation: taking movement structure, typical movement structure, and adapting it so that it could work for a wheelchair user.

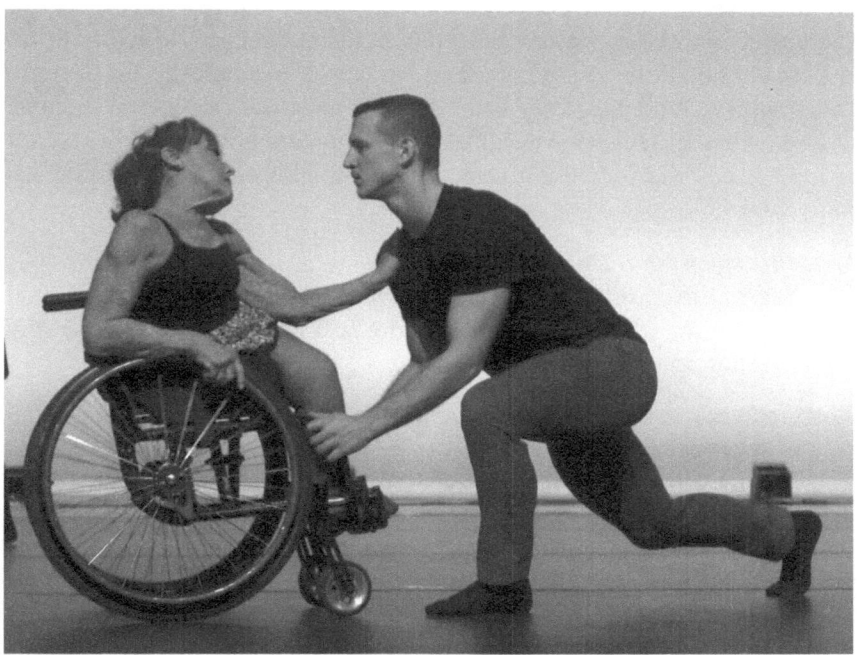

Mary Verdi-Fletcher and Matt Bowman partner in the beautiful piece titled *Neither Lost Nor Found* (image courtesy of the Dancing Wheels Company).

# Tap Dance for All

***Can you believe that one moment in time, being asked to dance, changed your entire life's trajectory?***

Yeah, although I believe that it was meant to be. I feel like the arts choose you, you don't choose it. But a lot of people don't hear the calling and follow it. I had to sacrifice a lot, obviously. I worked at the first independent living center in the state of Ohio. And at one juncture I said to my husband, "I want to do this full time." So, I had to give up my income to be able to do it. He said, "I'll give you one year, because that's all we have to live on. If you succeed, then good for you, and if you don't there's always another job to go to." So, I built a 501(c)(3) nonprofit because I wanted to take it out to a lot of assembly programs in the schools. I felt like that was the best way to change attitudes early on, before preconceived ideas about disability and dance were formed. When I became associated with Cleveland Ballet, I was able to have access to ballet dancers. So, it grew and grew from there. Then I decided that wasn't good enough. I wanted to do main-stage concerts, and I wanted to be competitive in a healthy way, competitive to my nondisabled peers in the dance world. So, we created main stage concerts, and we went on the road. I got a touring manager and an agent way before a lot of these companies had agents. They were like, "Why would you get an agent?" My answer was because we wanted to get booked and paid. We started to get booked all over the country, and before I knew it, I had a full company ensemble.

***Was this the first of its kind?***

Yes, in the country. It might be in the world even, but a professional one, you know, where we were working full time. There were people dancing, but not on a professional level.

***With all your company travel, have you found any difficulties getting to where you need to go?***

I think airlines are the worst. I have had a number of really difficult incidents with airlines. My wheelchair folds up, so it's very fragile. It's small, so it fits in the closet of the plane. The most recent ruling is that you can store your wheelchair in the closet on the plane if it fits. So, I've been on a plane where they had me strapped to their straight-back chair, [with] my wheelchair out on the jet way, and the flight attendants refused to put [my chair] in the closet because they didn't want to move their stuff. I refused to get on the plane until they moved it. Their response was, "Well, we don't have to." I replied, "Well, yes you

## 13. Professional Physically Integrated Dancers Spotlight

Left to right: Hoang Dang, Joey King, Mary Verdi-Fletcher, Sara Lawrence-Sucato and Robbie Cecil perform the gorgeously choreographed piece titled *Walls of Glass*. Integrated dance at its finest (image courtesy of the Dancing Wheels Company).

do have to. It's in the ADA law." They had to go get ground authority, who returned with the book that told them that they had to move [their belongings]. It held up the flight for like ten minutes. Basically, I was helpless because I only had my mouth accessible [because my arms were strapped down to their straight-back chair]. No passenger, at that point in time, got in front of me and got on the plane. They were all behind me waiting in the jetway. I mean, that was amazing! Finally, the exasperated flight attendants said, "Oh, okay," and begrudgingly took their bags out of the closet and put my wheelchair onboard. The captain came to me, leaned right over, and said, "I see you got your way." I responded, "It's not my way, it's the law!" We have a company dance that shows all of this [type of] discrimination that happens in society to the disabled. I was able to conquer that, but those are the kind of things that [we] have to contend with.

*That is unbelievable! Not only is that wheelchair your legs, but it's also your livelihood.*

And if they break it, and at a couple of points they did, I'm like, "So, are you going to pay for my performance? Pay not only for the chair, but the performance that I'm missing?"

*If the airlines break a piece of luggage, they must pay for it.*

They'll pay for the breakage, but we have to send it away to get it repaired. So, it's not the same.

*What was it like for you taking dance classes growing up? I know you said that you started dancing at the age of three. What was it like then?*

Well, there were no dance classes, actually. My mother taught me how to dance some, but as far as going to a dance studio there wasn't anything available for a child with a disability back then. You know, I was born in 1955, so basically there wasn't anything for any physical activity for people with disabilities way back then.

*How about when you entered your teen years?*

Basically, I just learned from nondisabled partners, dancers to experiment with, until I became connected with Cleveland Ballet. Some of the dances I did early on were more like the ballroom style of dance, so I learned those techniques from my nondisabled partners. And then I became more involved in classical training with the School of Cleveland Ballet.

*Today, things are beginning to shift for the disabled community as far as inclusivity goes. I have begun introducing my* **Tap for All** *program to studio teachers and studio owners in hopes of shifting their perspective to one of more inclusivity and encouragement, inviting and welcoming disabled people into their dance space and dance community. What advice would you give to studio owners and instructors to help facilitate that shift in perspective?*

I would say for them to get as much training as possible in how to make an inclusive studio and dance classroom environment. There are a number of manuals out [there]. Ours is on our physically-integrated dance and methodology, but if they Google [it] they will find others. It is imperative that they get this training because it will relieve them of a lot of concern, and it will allow them to have the information on "protocol." It will also open their eyes. We've had teacher certification

## 13. Professional Physically Integrated Dancers Spotlight

training where the teachers come away saying they had never put that all together [before]. So, they need to be able to translate the movement, figure out where that translation is coming from, and why it is important. Those kinds of theoretical activities are vitally important, but so is knowing the application of how to do it.

There's a great deal of fear, both from the side of the participant as well as the teacher. And if neither one of them has experience, I would say they are going to struggle through it, but they don't necessarily have to. There's still a double-edged sword, I would say, because there are a lot of disabled people who don't know that they can [dance]. So, in turn, they don't participate, or they'll say, "Well, I'm not a dancer." Or the teacher will say, "I'm afraid to have them in because I won't know what to do with them." So, there's a real double-edged sword [in play here]. I found this in my advocacy days with accessible public transportation. There was a discussion over accessibility, and they were like, "Well, how are we going to know if people are going to ride the main line transportation buses if they're in wheelchairs? We don't see any of them trying to get on buses." Well, they're not going to try to get on the buses because they're not accessible. So, our philosophy is that you open it to be inclusive for everyone, and then the doors will start to open.

**You mentioned a term earlier that is no longer being used: handicapped. Especially today, language and representation are so important. So, to help everyone reading this better understand, learn, and do better in this respect, are there other terms or words coming from the nondisabled community that are just not helpful or respectful to those with disabilities?**

We try to refer to artists with disabilities, you know, by the ADA guidelines. With that, it's "people first." I will tell you, there's a young up and coming group of artists with disabilities that want their disability to be seen first. So, they refer to themselves as disabled dancers. That's their preference, but for me I still want to be seen as me, and someone who happens to have a disability. I'm a woman first, I'm a dancer first, and then I happen to have a disability. If they feel they're proud of their disability, and they want it to be in the forefront, [that is their choice]. Often, I will slip both sentences together, like I'll say, "We're looking for a disabled artist," or "We're looking for an artist with a disability." That way I'm staying within the range of what a community is accepting. However, I will say we're associated with, or rather I'm associated with,

## Tap Dance for All

a large group that has come out of Dance USA. They meet once a month, and they're artists with disabilities, plus all the practitioners who work with artists with disabilities from all over the country. They claim there's nothing wrong, no wrong statement, but I will say that nobody uses the word handicapped anymore. Mostly, it's derivative was from "hat in hand," denoting the idea of [a] beggar. They felt that was a negative term of course. And we try to go with not disabled, like a nondisabled partner. For Dancing Wheels, we just get rid of all the politics, and we simply say stand-up and sit-down dancers. So, our stand-up dancers could be somebody who has a sensory disability, they could be deaf or blind, but they're just standing when they're moving. And our sit-down dancers are wheelchair users. We just got rid of all that political stuff.

**What do you think are the biggest misconceptions that able-bodied people have?**

I also think that using the word "able-bodied" means that they're more able, and they're not necessarily more able as an artist.

**Right. So, what would a better term be?**

Nondisabled. I feel the media, in a subtle way, often indicate what's appropriate. They don't know. They'll use words like "wheelchair bound," and I'll respond with, "We are not 'bound' to our wheelchairs." We always try to be sensitive and to teach, that's my goal.

**Do you feel that society is trying to make the shift towards being more inclusive?**

It depends on where in the community you are dealing with it. I find that there are very closed minds in academia, where they're institutionalized in their teaching. It's extremely hard to break through a different mindset. They've had curriculums and processes for years and years and years, and it's hard to break that system. I would love to have our manual in all the dance departments in universities for the students to purchase because it is something that will help them tremendously to be inclusive in the world of dance. I have so many students that come to me that want to do their papers on integrated dance, so I know there's interest out there.

**How do you feel about a disabled person finally being cast in a Broadway show and winning a Tony Award? There are so many talented disabled actors and dancers out there. Could this open the door to more opportunities for the disabled community?**

## 13. Professional Physically Integrated Dancers Spotlight

Yes, I mean let's face it, look at the Emmys, the Grammys, the film producers, and all the shows that are on TV. If you saw one person with a disability it would be unusual. And even shows like *Glee*, right? The guy wasn't really in a wheelchair. Actually, I met him. We did a big gala for somebody in Hollywood, and he was there. He said to me, "Holy cow! I wish I would have been as proficient in my wheelchair, even though I'm not disabled, to be able to dance like you." They always use a stand-in to do the wheeling work. I said to him, "I'm sure if they had a stand-in, they could've found an actor with a disability that sang and played that role for real." Even that show *Mom*, the husband is in a wheelchair, and I am almost 100 percent sure that he is not disabled. So, why [do they keep doing that]?

**There is something like one million disabled people all over the world and you are telling me the producers could not find one disabled actor?**

Ten percent of the population is disabled, and another percentage of that are wheelchair users. The disability doesn't have to be

Left to right: Hoang Dang, Mary Verdi-Fletcher, Joey King, and Robbie Cecil again show the limitless ability disabled people have in *Walls of Glass* (image courtesy of the Dancing Wheels Company).

a wheelchair user necessarily, right? It's so aggravating to me. I have heard some producers say, "They have to go with a name that draws in the audience." So, that somebody is known, but how do you ever get to that status if you are never given that opportunity? Christopher Reeve became disabled after he was famous, so everyone knew his name. I don't think he did any acting after his injuries though.

***You travel all over the world performing. How have other countries been with regards to accessibility?***

We have a tour manager, so we have guidance for the places that we go. It's not all ADA compliant because they're not American. We say that if there is even one step, they have to provide a ramp. When we went to China, the gentleman that was our producer there personally built wooden ramps so that we could get over a step. We gave him the measurements we needed to be able to get into a bathroom and close the door. I would say a lot of times in other countries they're more compassionate and want to make it work. Whereas sometimes in the United States they're like, "Well, it's not accessible so...." We know that some of the theatres are incredibly old, and sometimes we've had to use a port-o-potty off stage. Sometimes we dress in a closet versus a formal dressing room. We do what's called a "makeshift accessibility" for them (old theatres). There might be a way to get on the stage with a ramp, [or] from the audience to the stage. And then once we're on the stage, off to the side we would create our makeshift dressing room and port-o-potty. At times we've actually gone outside to a port-o-potty because that's the only way we could. I feel strongly that it's more important for me to get on the stage and perform, to change attitudes and ideas, and to break through that stereotypic view of, "Oh, we don't have artists with disabilities, so why should we make our theatres accessible?" So, sometimes we forgo the "convenience" if you will, of the ADA, to be able to make our point and know we are opening minds and conversations, versus insisting on the elegant glamour of it all.

***What would be your top three moments during your 40-year journey with Dancing Wheels?***

I think certainly the performance at the Christopher Reeve Celebration of Hope on national television. It was an amazing experience, not just because we were on national television, but because of the entire experience in general. We were there performing "I Believe I Can Fly" with James Ingram singing it live, with a full chorus behind

## 13. Professional Physically Integrated Dancers Spotlight

him singing, and an orchestra, of course. We had only rehearsed to the CD, right? So, when we got to the event we were like, "Oh my God!" And then, there were the biggest stars in Hollywood there to support Christopher Reeve. We received a standing ovation that night, and for me that experience wasn't about all the accolades of getting a standing ovation. What it said to me was that it opened their minds and hearts to the possibilities for all these people, who, you know, are tainted by Hollywood. They've seen everything, but they've never seen something like that before. In an instant our performance changed their view and their hearts. They were crying, and I was ready for a nervous breakdown. My one dance partner, well he's our artistic advisor [and] one of my favorite people of all time, was dancing with me and saw that I was so nervous in the opening part of it. We were in a circle holding hands with our heads bowed down when he said, "Honey, if you don't loosen up those little arms, you're going to break in two." I just laughed so hard. He always makes me laugh. So, that [performance] was a big one.

Gosh, there've been so many others, like going to all these countries. Like I said, it's more of a sacrifice than it is a luxury. It has been so eye opening to see how other people with disabilities live in other countries and how appreciative they were that we could bring our artistry to them. I mean it was like feeding the hungry.

Of course, I always love doing the lecture / performances of the assembly-based programs that we've done in the past. We did 75 in one year for thousands of kids. I really felt like that was so important in the mission of what we were doing. Again, it changed attitudes almost immediately for those who attended. One time I had a gentleman, he was 35, come to me and say, "I still remember when you came to my junior high school and you danced, and I have to tell you that I have never looked at another disabled person the same way since." I used to feel sorry when I saw someone with a disability. But now, if I see somebody in a wheelchair rolling down the street or have a disability I think, I wonder what they do? I wonder if they're a dancer, or a doctor, or a nurse. I said, "Thank you for sharing that. I genuinely appreciate it, but I will tell you that makes me feel awfully old, knowing that you were a kid then and are 35 now!"

And then of course you know that my husband donated his kidney [to me]. I lost both kidneys, and I also danced while I was on dialysis. Do you remember Jerry Springer? Jerry Springer had a good show at one point out of Cincinnati. There was a little girl in a wheelchair that had taken our summer program, and I don't know how this came about, but she really wanted to meet me again. So, he arranged for me and my nurse to fly to Cincinnati to be on his show to surprise this little girl. So, I went to Cincinnati and did that, and when I returned, I found out that my husband and I were a [kidney] match in 3 out of the 6 areas. He donated his kidney, and one month later [after surgery] I was out [there] performing. You just can't sit back and not do anything, right? I have many more [moments] I'm sure.

**I feel it's so important for everyone reading this book to understand that those with disabilities go on to live amazing lives, have exceptional experiences, and touch people's lives in extraordinary ways.**

I think if [all the performer was dancing for] was to just sort of—if I can use the word "grandstand," to be onstage [and] get the glory—I think that feeling eventually goes by the wayside after awhile if you don't have a mission behind it [and] you don't believe that your artistry is moving people. Whatever that means, moving them to understand better, or that it just brought so much to their heart when they saw one single dance. What is it about what you do that moves them? I try to

**Mary Verdi-Fletcher commands the stage with grace and purpose behind every move in *La Vie En Rose*. Image courtesy of the Dancing Wheels Company.**

## 13. Professional Physically Integrated Dancers Spotlight

impart that onto our younger dancers. I will say this generation is a little much to reckon with. I have dancers now that were my former dancers, who are older now, and they're [still] so passionate about their movement. Some of them still do some dancing here and there you know. You can just see the difference when a dancer moves from a place of passion. When I hear "I'm tired" from this generation, I tell them I did 8 dances, and rigorous dances, in one concert, and I did it twice in one night because we ran the whole show before the actual performance. Plus, I'm 66 years old, have spina bifida, and had a kidney transplant. So, what's your excuse?

***Once COVID-19 and the variants calm down to the point where performing and live entertainment is once again safe to attend, what does the post-COVID time look like for Dancing Wheels?***

I obviously want to ramp up our touring. We had a number of international tours that were on the docket prior to COVID. One of them is in Dubai. I would love to go to Dubai, be a missionary there, right? We, as an organization, could use more financial stability, as most every other organization today. With that stability I could add more dancers. It needs a theater system which we don't really have now. I have a couple of apprentices, but I just need that system, I need more dancers. I could use more stand-up dancers, but I definitely need more sit-down dancers. It's not even a matter of money right now for the sit-down dancers, it's just finding them. And all that weighs heavy on my mind, because I am fit and can dance now, knock on wood, but you know, in 5 years I'm going to choose what I can dance. In fact, I should be doing that now because I do all the administrative stuff too, you know.

*If you are interested in learning more about the training manual from Dancing Wheels you can find that information at www.dancingwheels.org/dancing-wheels-training-manual/. To find further information about the Dancing Wheels Physically-Integrated Dance Teacher Training Certifications, please go to www.dancingwheels.org/teacher-certification/.

Challenge

- Several principles and goals of Mary's Dancing Wheels Company and School are:
    **Enhance** integration and diversity in the arts with works uniting people of all abilities.

## Tap Dance for All

***Provide*** successful, independent, and creative role models for those with disabilities.

***Erase*** negative stereotypes about people with disabilities in professional careers, primarily in the arts.

***Instill*** greater understanding and professionalism in individuals of all ability levels.

- Using each of these four points demonstrate how you would use your creativity to promote and develop each of them.

### Quotable Quote

*"Disability is not a brave struggle or 'courage in the face of adversity.' Disability is an art. It's an ingenious way to live."*

—Neil Marcus

# 14

# The Evolution of Tap

### OBJECTIVES

- Comprehension of where tap began and how it evolved over the decades.
- Understanding how discrimination and exclusion existed back at the birth of tap and still exists today.
- Learn how to utilize tap history to stimulate cognitive function and fun for disabled people and senior populations.

Marginalization and exclusion have been a part of our culture since the dawn of America, when people from all parts of the globe arrived here with high hopes of establishing a fresh start on the North American continent. But instead of freedom and prosperity, many cultures that came here found themselves living in poverty and being denied the liberty and privileges that others were afforded. Although the actual access that was denied may have been for different issues back then when compared to today, when we take a look at the hard-fought battle of the disabled population over the past four decades for accessibility rights, it is clear that the quest for equality continues. The history of the American tap dancer was born out of slavery and those considered to be on the lowest rung of the ladder in society. The only path forward is to expand our vision beyond ourselves and our self-imposed limitations by truly seeing the beauty and worth of other human beings not like us and trying to understand others' struggles and dreams. As Mahatma Gandhi said, "Be the change that you wish to see in the world." For me and my mother, creating a more inclusive world through the art of tap dancing is our small way of tossing a pebble into the pond of exclusivity

**Tap Dance for All**

to create an inclusive diverse ripple effect. Our hope is that all who read this book will become the ripples in that pond and change it from one of exclusivity to one of inclusivity and diversity.

The following little-known facts are an integral part of tap dance's remarkable legacy and colorful history. The tap of today is a mirror of the past and a reflection of the talent, dedication, creativity, and determination of the many performers' accomplishments, which has assured tap of its rightful place in the world of dance.

## *The Roots of Tap*

The roots of tap can be traced back more than 200 years. Tap was influenced by West and Central African tribe dances dating back as far back as 1694 when European traders and travelers of that time brought fully-packed boats back to the Americas full of their newest procurement—enslaved people. The Europeans soon realized that these enslaved people did not just dance by moving and shuffling their feet, they utilized every part of their body when they danced. They seemed to be using one set of rhythms for their upper body while using an altogether different rhythm—creating a polyrhythm—with their feet and lower body. Because the enslaved people were separated and scattered once they landed in the Americas, which in turn split tribes up, little is known of the individual dances of the various tribes initially brought here. This new tribal mixture of culture created and produced multi-blended dances never seen before. Dance was one of the few pieces of African culture to survive the long, difficult voyage to the New World. In the evolution of the shoes worn for tap dance, originally the dancers danced in bare feet. To provide additional flexibility, both in sound and movement, shoes were later added. The first taps were used in the 1850s, consisting of copper pennies that were screwed to the heels of shoes or boots. This little piece of tap history is fun to test students' knowledge of tap trivia in class. Students love to try and guess which coin was first used as the taps on tap shoes. These little pieces of metal added a new unique sound for the dancers of that time, with the use of metal taps coming in later to replace pennies and adding even more dimension and sound variety for the performers. The first person credited with making tap a true art form was a free African American man named William Henry Lane, nicknamed Juba. In 1848 white minstrel

## 14. The Evolution of Tap

shows were the entertainment draw of the era, and Juba was the first and only Black performer to receive top billing.

Other dance styles, such as English and Irish, helped to add additional layers to tap as time progressed. Because of the lower-society status of these British founders of tap, there is no tangible footprint left behind to follow because they were perceived as unworthy of mention or any type of credit to the art form. The only crumbs we have to give us any indication of what their early folk dances were like come from the interpretations of the high-society dances of the time. Of course, the original dances became diluted by the addition of the upper crust's refinements to it. The use of different names for tap steps by instructors can be traced back to this era. No other dance form has ever had the vast number of names for the same step as tap. Much of this is due to steps being stolen from one dancer, having the thief mix in a bit of their own style, then renaming and claiming the step as their own creation. Flat out, carbon copy replications were never permitted between dancers and could get you physically injured. But, so long as a dancer put their own unique twist to a step, the dancer would likely get a pass on their piracy. Stealing signature steps was seen as the ultimate atrocity, because that was taking away the livelihood of another dancer. Making money as a performer was difficult enough, so to pilfer the creation of another was most definitely considered a high crime back then and not to be tolerated in the performing world. The same holds true today: to outright steal a choreographer's dance piece and call it your own is a lawsuit in the making, plus a damaged reputation to go along with it.

The clog shoe and clog dancing can be traced back to the nineteenth century and a dance called the Lancashire Clog. These loose wooden shoes were first utilized by farmers, and then a little later by mill workers during the Industrial Revolution to try and keep their feet warm and dry while standing for long hours on damp, cold factory floors. To keep their blood circulating and stay warm, the workers would bounce and knock their feet together on the floor, motivated by the rhythmic beats from the machinery they were hired to man. Clogging soon moved into the pubs, streets, and even formal competition, complete with a cake as the usual prize. In the late 19th century, the dance moved to the stage. These dancers opted for a more form-fitting clog, one that was more stylish and acceptable as high class. Once this upper-crust transformation took place, Irish step dancing became known as jigging. Arms were sternly held at the sides of the dancer and became the signature look for

## Tap Dance for All

this dance form thanks to its Irish step dance masters. The main reason for this rigid upper body was the fear that the dance would be banned by the church if it were deemed too sensual or suggestive. This tap trivia fact is another fun one to use in class. Everyone knows that Irish step dancing uses a signature position of the dancer's arms held steadfastly by their sides, but do your students know why they dance that way?

Pennsylvania and New England received Irish and Scots in large numbers in 1700, and due to agricultural deterioration and an economic depression, even more Irish made the trip to America, landing in the eastern and southern states of the U.S. first in 1814, and then two more times in the 1840s and 1850s. With the arrival of the Irish came their culture and their dance. Unfortunately, they were not greeted with a high stately status, but one of an even lower level than Black people for some of them. Since Black people could be owned as slaves they were seen as valuable to white American men. Even though the Black and the Irish could not have been further apart geographically and culturally, they both ended up living in the same poverty-stricken low-class neighborhoods, and they both cultivated their signature dances from the rhythms created by their feet.

The popularity of tap rose thanks to the introduction of minstrel shows, vaudeville and nightclubs. The popular minstrel "Jim Crow" character was first performed by Thomas Rice in 1828. Rice created the black face of a black dancer by using burnt cork and grease paint. The minstrelsy show rose to huge heights of success using satirized songs and dances. This type of atrocious portrayals of minorities would be endured in American culture for 150 years to come. Abolitionist Frederick Douglass denounced blackface performers as "the filthy scum of white society, who have stolen from us a complexion denied to them by nature, in which to make money, and to pander to the corrupt taste of their white fellow citizens."\* The most influential blackface star of the twentieth century was Al Jolson, a Jewish immigrant from New York. Even though the appeal of blackface declined by the 1930s, this toxic part of cultural racism has been seen as recently as the Oscars ceremony in 2012, various television skits, and in 2019 when Virginia Governor Ralph Northam and state attorney general Mark Herring admitted

---

\* Annika Neklason. "Blackface Was Never Harmless," *The Atlantic*, February 16, 2019, https://www.theatlantic.com/entertainment/archive/2019/02/legacy-blackface-ralph-northam-didnt-understand/582733/.

## 14. The Evolution of Tap

to wearing blackface costumes as young men in college.* Even Jimmy Kimmel, who used blackface in impressions in comedic skits about Carl Malone and Oprah Winfrey, felt compelled to apologize publicly for his hurtful, offensive words and actions.† The minstrel era was indeed a sad chapter in our country's history.

Vaudeville lasted fifty years, from the mid-1880s to the early 1930s, usually comprising ten to fifteen people performing a variety of acts—everything from acrobats, jugglers, and comedians, to magicians, singers, and dancers. These early vaudeville shows were performed in beer halls, were crass and oftentimes obscene and vulgar. Vaudeville shows became more wholesome in 1881 thanks to the minstrel singer Tony Pastor and the New York City theater he founded. He completely made over the raunchy image of vaudeville into a squeaky-clean variety show that could attract families with children. This transformation proved to be an enormous success, and nine years later vaudeville had gained the reputation as clean family fun and entertaining, providing top notch performers suitable for both young and old. This type of entertainment was in fact so popular that in the following 25 years or so, close to 300 theaters across the country played host to these new types of vaudeville acts. Powerhouse tap dancing performers such as George White, Pat Rooney, Sr., and Greenlee traveled from city to city across the country wowing audiences with their show-stopping performances. Acts that included young family members, called family acts, also became incredibly popular. George M. Cohen was one such act. The Four Cohens included his sister, mother, and father. Eddie Foy, Sr., utilized his seven tap-dancing children to showcase his act called the Seven Little Foys. The Four Covans were formed from the two Covan brothers and their wives. This foursome had the reputation for being one of the fastest tapping and most spectacular family acts ever seen. This was a glorious time for tap dancers. Whether it was Broadway, nightclubs, or vaudeville, it was the outstanding tappers of that time

---

\* Eugene Scott. "Mark Herring Said Ralph Northam Should Resign for Wearing Black Face in College. Then Herring Admitted to Doing the Same Thing." *Washington Post*, February 6, 2019, www.washingtonpost.com/politics/2019/02/06/mark-herring-said-ralph-northam-should-resign-wearing-blackface-college-then-herring-admitted-doing-the-same-thing/.

† Sonia Rao and Emily Yahr. "Jimmy Kimmel Apologizes For 'Embarrassing' Sketches as Hollywood Reckons With Its Use of Blackface," *Washington Post*, June 23, 2020, www.washingtonpost.com/arts-entertainment/2020/06/23/jimmy-kimmel-apologizes-blackface/.

that brought in the audiences and brought down the houses with thunderous ovations.

Rhythmic tap, with its elegance and flat-footed, smooth, syncopated rhythm and speed took hold and changed the style of tap in the early 1900s, with King Rastus Brown spearheading the revision. John Bubbles, aka John William Sublett, quickly recognized the brilliance in this adaptation and made it his own, becoming the true creator of rhythmic tap by adding rhythmic complexities that have become the cornerstone of the style. John Bubbles was a rhythmic tap master, and as such taught other up-and-coming tap stars of that era. One such bright star was Eleanor Powell, who was one of the greatest and most brilliantly gifted tappers of all time. Sadly, Bubbles was not acknowledged or recognized back then for his contribution thanks to the biases very much present in the culture of that time.

The next modification to tap came thanks to Bill "Bojangles" Robinson. He is known and remembered for bringing tap up onto the balls of the feet. This new style became known as Broadway tap. Robinson made such an impact on tap that he was given his own national holiday. May 25th has become National Tap Dance Day in honor of Bill "Bojangles" Robinson's birthday. His true birth date is not actually known due to the lack of documentation at the time of his birth, but historians came as close to the date of his true birthday as they could, settling on May 25th to commemorate him and the dance form he forever changed.

I often use the information about both John Bubbles and Bill "Bojangles" Robinson in my classes as a fun way of infusing a tiny bit of tap history into the hour. Young tappers usually find John Bubbles' name quite funny, which in turn helps them to remember who the father of rhythmic tap is. Most tappers know that there is a National Tap Day, but few realize Bill Robinson's connection to the day. Sharing this information not only enhances the students' knowledge of tap history, but it helps to ensure these important tap figures remain in the forefront of the dance form.

## *The Golden Age of Tap*

The Golden Age of Tap consisted of the 1920s, 1930s, and 1940s. During this era, if you were a dancer you needed to tap if you wanted to work, because every show of this period, whether a movie musical or a

## 14. The Evolution of Tap

live show, prominently featured tap dancing. The top-billing tap headliners of the 1930s and 1940s were Fred Astaire, Ginger Rogers, Gene Kelly, and Eleanor Powell. Thanks to these physically gifted dancers, tap morphed into a more athletic dance form, utilizing ballet and more powerful explosive jumps, leaps, and turns. With this metamorphosis came the need to stand out and be noticed, because if you got noticed, you got work, and if you got work, you got paid. The Berry Brothers infused acrobatics into their syncopated cane-twirling act. King, King, and King had the unusual act of dancing while wearing convict uniforms and being chained to each other. The top tap acts stayed on top by being new, creative, inventive, and original.

Wages for Black performers still did not compete or even come close to white acts of the time, but still far surpassed the going wages in almost any other profession that was open to Black people. Freedoms and opportunities were more abundant for Black performers than Black non-performers. As a bonus and benefit to those freedoms was the additional exposure they received. Places that did not welcome a non-performing Black person did, however, graciously open their doors to Black performers. The exception to this was in the South. Theatres there were still "all Black" or "all white" at that time, and segregation was completely entrenched in the Deep South. The buzz circulating through the South about the Black shows piqued the curiosity of white audiences to the point of arranging one night per week to see for themselves what all the fuss was about. To placate the sensitivities of the white audiences coming to see the shows, the theater producers had the entire all-white theater disinfected before each show. The resurgence of Black musical comedies to Broadway was spearheaded in 1921 with the success of the show *Shuffle Along*. This show established that there was money to be made in white theaters with Black musicals.

The time step is a short combination created by tap dancers, originally as a means of giving the live band playing behind the performer the time signature and rhythm the dancer wished to have maintained during their performance. Each performer had their own signature time step, their "calling card," unique to their personal performance style, yet still discernible as being a time step. Some seasoned hoofers had more than one time step in their arsenal to serve up to the band. Every tap dancer knows some form or other of the Shim Sham. The birth of this iconic tap step took place in the 1920s. Much debate has taken place with regards to who truly created the simple short combination, but

## Tap Dance for All

Leonard Reed claimed original ownership of it until the day he passed away in 2004. It was purposely created to be simple so that any tapper could execute it with ease. Some hoofers used the Shim Sham as a finale, like Reed and Willie Bryant. These two hoofers took bits and pieces from both the Rastus Brown and Jack Wiggins Shim Sham versions, then mixed up the order to avoid being discovered as thieves. Reed was a notorious tap-step thief, constantly watching and absorbing what his fellow hoofers were creating.

Also, in the mid–1920s, mass production of plates for tap shoes began. James Selva and Salvatore Capezio began producing their new line of tap shoes in 1925. Capezio's legacy carries on through the feet of dancers all over the world.

Competitiveness kept the hoofers of the 1920s producing creative new styles in response to their need to stand out from the pack. The following seven styles gave the tap performer a voice with which to make their own mark.

1. <u>Flash</u>: A style used to "wow" the audience with a big finish, typically blending acrobatics into the dance at the end of the routine to finish with a surprise.
2. <u>Novelty</u>: This style utilized expert dexterity with a variety of props integrated into the choreography. The creative use of stairs, suitcases, ropes, canes, or other props helped to set these tap dancers apart from each other.
3. <u>Eccentric, Legomania, and Comedy</u>: Distinct, quirky, and all-out wild aptly describes how dancers of these three styles used their bodies to fool the eye of the audience with their crazy rubbery-leg choreography, and over-the-top tricks and gags.
4. <u>Swing or Classical Tap</u>: This style incorporates both jazz and ballet upper body movements with rhythmically-precise tap choreography.
5. <u>Class</u>: Style, class, and impeccable dress described the tap dancers in this category.
6. <u>Military</u>: As the title suggests, military drum rhythms and marches were the signature features of this style of tap.
7. <u>Rhythm, Close Floor, Paradiddle or Paddle and Roll</u>: Rapid and rhythmic in nature, utilizing heel and toe taps almost exclusively.

For each one of those styles there were hundreds of tap dancers trying to separate themselves from the endless sea of other dancers,

## 14. The Evolution of Tap

all vying for their shot at stardom and fame. Legendary tappers such as John Bubbles, the Condos Brothers, Buddy Ebsen, Henry Williams, Hal Le Roy, and Clayton "Peg Leg" Bates were considered the brightest stars and most significant tap dancers of their time in the above seven categories. All these tap dancers were tried and true hoofers. The term "hoofer" refers to a tap dancer who has especially fast footwork—another little tap nugget I often share with my classes.

In 1925, the place in New York City where dancers spent time together and traded ideas was in a back-room rehearsal space called the Hoofer's Club, located in the Harlem Lafayette Theatre. One story of how Leonard Reed learned his wing specialty steps comes from the Hoofer's Club. A dancer named Piano (legend has it that no one knew his real name) used an upright piano to assist himself, much like a ballet barre, for the descent of his wings. Reed studied Piano then figured out how to do the same step unassisted. He then added his uncommon style and flair, resulting in a combination of specialty wing steps that he could claim as his own. In 1931 the first white male to become an honorary member of the Hoofer's Club was Hal Le Roy. Bill Robinson sponsored Hal, gaining him entrance into this elite tap dancers club. Hal went on to become an overnight success on Broadway in *The Gang's All Here*. He was one of thousands of dancers that studied with Ned Wayburn. Ned was a director, teacher, and producer who staged dozens of shows. He coined the phrase "tap and step dancing," and invented ragtime dance steps.

In 1927 a whole new avenue opened for tap dancers. *The Jazz Singer* was the vehicle that gave the "talking" motion picture acceptance, and ability to see and hear vaudevillian tap dancers on the big screen. Broadway stars now had a new medium by which to shine: the Hollywood motion picture musical. Stars such as Bill Robinson, Fred Astaire, Ginger Rogers, and Eleanor Powell reached new star-studded heights in the 1930s. During the next 30 years Fred Astaire set the standard on how dance was shot on film. He insisted the camera follow him, shooting him from head to toe, with few, if any, cutaways. In Busby Berkeley's famous swimming sequence in the 1931 film *Footlight Parade*, all the dancers / swimmers wore tap shoes in the complex artistic water formations. Tap steps were often named for real people. The Lindy was named for Charles Lindberg, the Shorty George was named for dancer Shorty Snowden, and the Tack Annie was named for a New York City pickpocket named Annie. The seniors you teach will likely remember seeing and enjoying all of the above-named movie stars. Both young and old enjoy learning how certain tap steps got their name, plus fun trivia like the dancers in *Footlight Parade*.

Nightclubs such as the Cotton Club (Harlem, New York City), the Plantation Club (Culver City, California), the Coconut Grove (Los Angeles, California), and Ciro's (Hollywood, California) are where you could find as many as 20 tap dancers in a single show. Solos, duets, trios, or even entire chorus lines performed together with singers and bands. Ruby Keeler, the Nicholas Brothers, and Louis DaPron all began their careers in these nightclubs. Integration of shows began by the 1930s and 1940s, but it would take another 30 years before actual performance opportunities would start changing for the African American performer. Ask your senior students if they ever frequented these venues and saw any of the above performers.

Shirley Temple did more for tap dancing's popularity than any other dancer of that time. In 1934, at the early age of six years old, Shirley took the film world by storm. From 1935 to 1938 she was the top box office draw, making 24 films between 1934 and 1940. How many of those 24 films have your senior students seen?

## *The Decline of Tap*

When the country was going through the Great Depression and World War II, it was tap that lifted everyone's spirits. All the major movie studios featured dancers at this time. Gene Kelly and Vera Ellen were at MGM. Ruby Keeler and Gene Nelson were at Warner Brothers. The Nicholas Brothers, Dan Daily, and Betty Grable were at Twentieth Century-Fox. Several studios employed both Ann Miller and Donald O'Connor.

Tap dancers performed with many well-known orchestras in the big band era. Bunny Briggs danced with the bands of Duke Ellington and Earl Hines, while Ralph Brown was the feature performer for bands such as Count Basie, Dizzy Gillespie, and Charlie Parker. Thanks to the Broadway show *Oklahoma*, tap was caught in an unfair false competition with ballet. That along with a drop in nightclub attendance created a decline in the popularity of tap. Las Vegas and television were the redeeming feature for the dance form at that time. The most popular shows on TV were variety shows that included tap dancers and other

### 14. *The Evolution of Tap*

acts. Las Vegas provided tap dancers with new opportunities to showcase their talent because it had been developed as an entertainment resort. Casino showrooms provided a place for older tap dancers to perform and retire. Even with these new venues to dance in, the art form was struggling to survive.

## *Rebirth*

The Newport Jazz Festival in 1963 was a crucial factor in the new renaissance of tap due to the performances of many famous tap dancers of the past. In the 1970s several tap companies were formed in hopes of cultivating a younger tap audience. The Jazz Tap Ensemble was formed in 1979 by Lynn Dally. Linda Sohl-Ellison and Tony Relin co-founded Rhapsody in Taps in 1981. Brenda Bufalino, Tony Waag, and Honi Coles founded the American Tap Dance Orchestra in 1986. Tap's revival period brought many exciting female tap dancers to the forefront. The collaboration of women like Jane Goldberg, Carol Hess, Gail Conrad, Andrea Lewis, and Lynn Dolly with prominent tap legends of the past helped assure tap's preservation.

Broadway also helped the resurgence of tap with shows like *42nd Street*, *Black and Blue*, and the revival of *No No Nanette* in 1971 with the original star, Ruby Keeler. All three shows prominently featured tap dance throughout. This had an instant impact on tap's renewed popularity. Suddenly tap classes sprung up and enrollment soared. But it is thanks to the late Gregory Hines that tap secured its place in the twentieth century. With the 1989 film *Tap*, Hines updated tap's image with a fresh new take on the dance form using more modern music and a masculine, dynamic style. In 1984 a ten-year-old phenom was about to take tap to the next level. Savion Glover's precise lightning-fast footwork impressed everyone. As Savion grew, so did his talent, developing his own unique style that he called "free-form hardcore." Hip-hop and funk rhythms were the basis of his style. As the dawn of a new century was approaching, tap saw a whole new generation appreciating the excitement of creating rhythms and learning its history from its masters thanks to Savion Glover, Gregory Hines, and the people who formed tap companies.\*

---

\* Brian Seibert, *What the Eye Hears—A History of Tap Dancing*, Farrer, Straus and Giroux, 2015.

### Tap Dance for All

A special saying exists in the history of tap, one with which all dancers seem to agree: "Like cabaret singers, tap dancers seem to get better with age!"

CHALLENGE

Create a family tree for tap's lineage utilizing the history given in this chapter. By constructing this tree, you will have a wonderful tool to use in your senior classes.

QUOTABLE QUOTE

*"A tap dancer is really a frustrated drummer."—Eleanor Powell*

# Appendix
## Tap Glove / Mitten and Tap Board Instructions

### OBJECTIVE

- Understand what materials are needed and how to create your own tap gloves and boards.

## Tap Glove / Mitten

If you want to offer classes to assisted living centers and senior centers, you will want to make gloves or mittens with removable taps so that you will be able to easily wash them after class. Do not count on the location to take care of the gloves for you—they simply do not have the time or means. Look at making the mittens as part of your business start-up cost. I have made 18 sets of mittens in each size—extra small, small, medium, and large—using a sewing machine. Since I am not a professional tailor, it took time to make 72 sets of mittens, or 144 individual mittens, but I got better and quicker as I went along. By the end, at my fastest, I was able to complete four pairs (eight single mittens) in one full day of work and I am now ready to go anywhere and teach this fun class. I chose to make mittens rather than gloves because it was the easier sewing option, being the sewing novice that I am. The extra-small size worked extremely well when I taught the program in a studio setting with younger students that were around 8 years old. Seniors tend to have tiny hands as well, so those extra small mittens really came in handy.

# Appendix

## Materials Needed

Lyrca: each mitten will need either a 7" × 8" (extra small), 8" × 9" (small / medium), or a 9" × 10" (large) square of fabric for the body of the mitten. Cut out two squares at a time, place right sides together, and pin the pattern to the fabric. To gauge how much fabric you will need, first figure out how many pairs of mittens you want to make and calculate the amount with the understanding that one yard of fabric yields 36" of material in length. The typical width of most fabrics is 54".

Yes, it is now time for a math equation. If I want to make 10 pairs of small mittens (20 single mittens), how much fabric do I need? Each single mitten will need two 8" × 9" squares of fabric. Nine inches divides into 54 six times, so you will yield 6 squares, or 3 single mittens across the width of the fabric. By doubling over the fabric, you will be cutting out double the squares (12) and double the number of single mittens (6 instead of 3), plus reducing the time it takes to cut out the squares. But we still need to know how many yards to buy. I need 16" of fabric to make one mitten (8" × 2 = 16"), so if I want to make 20 single mittens, I will need 160" (16" × 10) of fabric length. If you divide 160" by the number of inches in one yard you will end up needing 4½ yards of fabric (160 / 36 = 4.4).

You will also need fabric to make cuffs for the mittens. What I have found helpful is to make a Velcro tab extension on the end of the cuff so that the student will be able to adjust the fit as needed. For the extra small size, you will need a 3" × 8½" piece of fabric for each mitten. For the small and medium sizes, you need a 3" × 9½" piece of fabric for each mitten. For the large size mitten, you will need 3" × 10" pieces of fabric. An additional 12" or ⅓ of a yard of fabric for the 10 cuffs should suffice.

Velcro: As of drafting this book, www.uline.com has the best online price on Velcro. You will need both hook and loop Velcro. A 1" wide strip is advisable, and the taps will need roughly 10" of adhesive hook Velcro per glove. So, for 10 sets of gloves you will roughly need 16' of adhesive hook Velcro. Two sets of sew-on patches were used for each mitten I made. I sewed two 2" strips together for the toe tap, and three 2¼" strips together for the heel tap. The cuff took 1" of loop sew on Velcro for the cuff tab, and 3" of hook sew on Velcro for the inside wrist section of the cuff. For 10 sets of mittens, you will need 25' of loop sew-on Velcro, and 5' of hook sew on Velcro.

Taps: As of this writing, www.DiscountDance.com has the best

## Appendix

prices on taps. Their Super H-3 heel tap was the best size to use for the toe tap of the mitten, and their Super D toe tap worked best for the mitten's heel tap. If you sign up with the teacher program at Discount Dance, you will receive a discount on all your purchases.

Pattern: You can simply trace your own hand or mitten that fits you well onto paper, cut it out to use as your pattern, and use the measurements I provided for the cuff above to complete the mitten. Another option is to look online for free mitten patterns from websites such as www.seekatesew.com.

Miscellaneous: Straight pins, thread, measuring tape, sewing machine.

The following is the order and the steps that I used to make the process of making the tap mittens the most streamlined and efficient. If using a sewing machine, do not forget to adjust the tension of the thread and presser foot when shifting from medium-weight Lycra fabric to heavy-weight Velcro. Your presser foot for each will be different as well.

1. Cut out all squares: Cut squares from the fabric, pinning sets of right sides together.
2. Pin pattern: Pin pattern to a set of fabric squares and cut along the pattern shape. Repeat with all sets of squares.
3. Cut out all cuffs.
4. Pin together the pinky side of the mitten: Stop about 2" from the top. Repeat with all gloves.
5. Pin together cuff: Pin right side of fabric to the inside. Repeat with all cuffs.
6. Sew outside of mitten: Start at the bottom and travel up the mitten. Repeat with all mittens.
7. Sew the cuff together: Leave one of the short ends open. Trim excess material. Turn the cuff right side out. Repeat with all cuffs.
8. Press all mittens and cuffs: Press seams open so they lay flat.
9. Sew cuff onto mitten: Attach the seam of the cuff to the bottom of the right side of the mitten. Here is where you need to decide if you are making a right or left mitten. If you are making a right mitten the extra tab will be on the left when looking down at it to pin together. Once you have sewn the seam and flip it over to have the inside of the mitten facing up, the tab should be on the thumb

## Appendix

side of your right hand. Reverse this procedure so that the tab on the left mitten is on the thumb side of your left hand. Repeat for all mittens.

10. <u>Press</u>: Press the cuff seam open on all mittens.
11. <u>Make Velcro patches</u>: Cut all Velcro: two 2" strips of sew-on loop Velcro for each individual mitten for the toe tap, and three 2¼" strips of sew-on loop Velcro for each mitten for the heel tap. These measurements are the same for all mitten sizes.
12. <u>Sew Velcro patches</u>: You will need to adjust your sewing machine to work on heavy fabric. For my machine, I set it to its leather setting. Sew the two 2" strips together so that they are side by side. Repeat to complete all toe patches. Sew the three 2¼" strips together so that you have three strips side by side for the heel tap. Place the Super D tap onto the triple patch and cut around the tap so it is the shape of the tap. Repeat to complete all heel patches.
13. <u>Sew on patches</u>: Place the double-strip patch in the center at the top of the right side of the palm side of the mitten, about ½" from the top of the mitten. Sew into place. Place the triple-strip patch

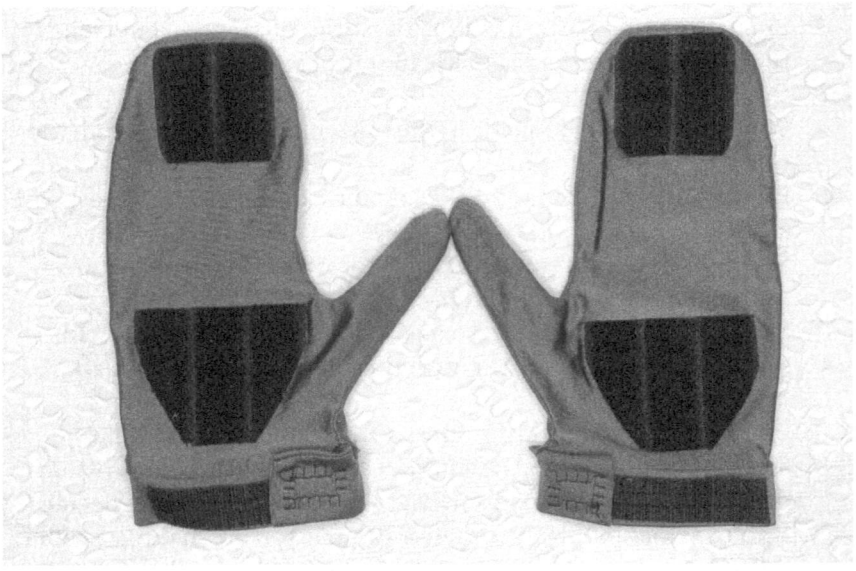

**Tap mittens created by the author, shown here to exhibit the use of the Velcro patches for both the taps and cuff (photograph by the author).**

*Appendix*

in the center of the heel of the mitten, above the cuff. Sew into place. Repeat for all other mittens.

14. Cut cuff Velcro: Cut one 3" strip of sew-on hook Velcro and one 1" strip of sew-on loop Velcro for each mitten.
15. Sew on cuff Velcro: Sew the 3" hook Velcro onto the cuff, below the heel Velcro patch. Fold over the Lycra tab and sew the 1" strip of loop Velcro onto the tab of the cuff. If necessary, trim down the hook and loop Velcro to better fit the cuff band. Repeat with all mittens.
16. Sew up mitten seam: Pin together the mitten seam with the right sides facing and wrong sides out, keeping in mind that you will begin sewing at the base below the thumb, regardless of whether it is a right or left mitten. Repeat with all mittens. Sew the mitten, taking your time when sewing around the inside of the thumb. Stop and adjust every few stitches when sewing the top of the

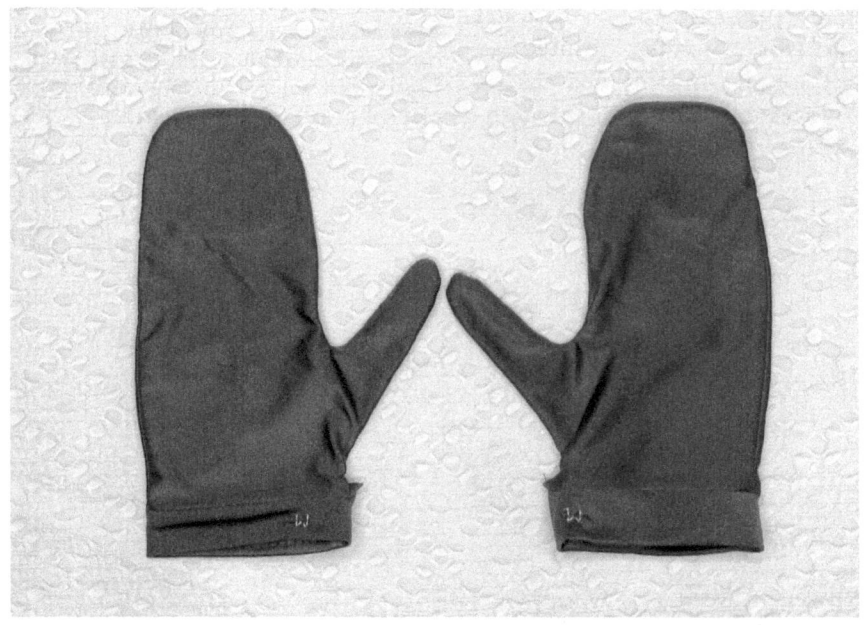

Back side of tap mittens created by the author. These are a medium sized set of mittens, denoted by the "M" embroidered on the cuff. Since her sewing machine had the capability to embroider, she dug out the instruction manual and set out to learn how to do it. The size label assists when having to separate the gloves after washing them (photograph by the author).

# Appendix

thumb together. Trim excess material and turn the right side out. Repeat with all mittens.
17. <u>Taps</u>: Cut self-adhesive hook Velcro to the shape of each tap and attach.

Congratulations! You now have tap mittens!

<u>Special Note</u>: When making a pair of mittens for myself I made sure to not cover the entire thumb of my right hand with the mitten, like a fingerless glove, or rather a thumbless mitten. I did this so that I could easily start and stop my music on my iPad without having to keep taking the mitten off and on throughout the class.

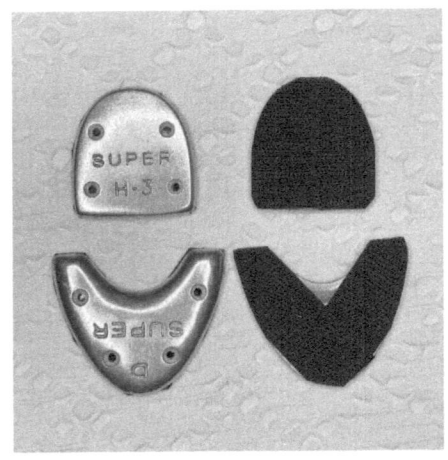

**Front and back of taps. Here you can see how the self-adhesive Velcro is used on the back side of the taps, and how you could also simply sew on the taps if opting not to sew them yourself (photograph by the author).**

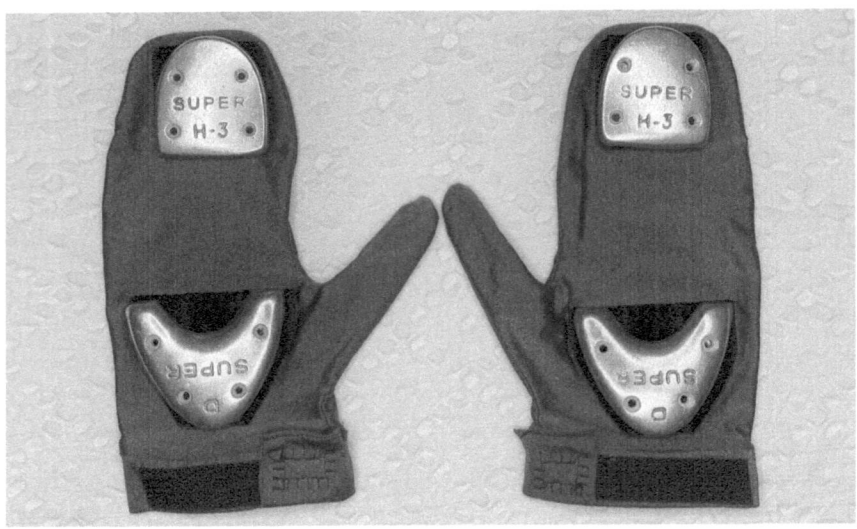

**Tap mittens assembled and ready for hand tap class (photograph by the author).**

*Appendix*

# Tap Board Bag

Honestly, I made up the bag as I went along for my 18 tap boards. There was no specific pattern for such a thing that I could find, so I winged it, taking it one step at a time. The following is how I did it, and so far, it is holding up well, as is my back because of being able to easily remove the boards from the main bag. I used a faux leather material, as I thought it would be the most sturdy and inexpensive material.

1. <u>Measure</u>: Stack your finished boards and measure the length, width, and depth for all sides.
2. <u>Determine Amount of Material Needed</u>: Add up the measurements to give you the amount of material you will need, adding ½" to each piece for a seam allowance. You should end up with 6 pieces in total: 2 large pieces for the top and bottom of the boards, and 4 pieces for around each of the four sides. On one of the short ends, I split the material in half so that I could run a sew-on Velcro strip to use as the opening of the bag. On one of

**Finished tap bag (photograph by the author).**

# Appendix

the long ends, I fashioned a carrying handle from woven cloth accessory trim I found at Michaels craft store.
3. Additional Support: Reinforce the top strip by cutting and sewing an extra piece of the material where you want the handle to be.
4. Handle: Cut and sew handle material onto the top piece.
5. Sew 1st two sides together: With right sides facing, sew the bottom strip to the long side of one of the large pieces.
6. Sew on 3rd piece: Sew the non-opening short side to the short side of the long piece.
7. Sew on 4th piece: Sew the side piece to the other short side.
8. Sew on 5th piece: Sew top piece with the handle to three sides that have been sewn together.

**Finished tap bag from the side to show the Velcro opening (photograph by the author).**

## *Appendix*

9. <u>6th piece</u>: Cut and sew Velcro hook and loop to the final side piece that has been cut into two pieces.
10. <u>Sew opening Velcro on</u>: Sew each Velcro piece to the final split side.

Drop in your boards, and away you go!

### QUOTABLE QUOTE

*"When I make with my hands, I give of my heart."—Unknown*

**Open tap bag with 18 tap boards inside (photograph by the author).**

# Glossary

**Accelerando**: A gradual increasing of speed or tempo in music

**Accent**: A stress or special emphasis on a sound

**Active Foot**: The free or working foot, with the weight on the opposite or supporting foot

**Back Flap**: Brush (back) - Step (ball, weighted)

**Ball Change**: Ball - Step (executed front, side, back, or across)

**Bombershay**: Flap - Back Flap (twisting)

**Buffalo (Single)**: Jump (out) - Shuffle - Jump (behind)

**Buffalo (Double)**: Flap (out) - Shuffle - Jump (behind)

**Chug (Single)**: Slide (weighted foot) - Heel (drop)

**Chug (Double)**: Slide (weighted foot) - Heel (drop), R-L (counts: &1)

**Cincinnati**: Brush (back) - Hop - Shuffle - Step, Reverse All, Flap 3× Alt, Step - Stomp

**Cramp Roll (Same Side & Alternating)**: Ball - Ball, Heel - Heel

**Dig**: Heel or Toe

**Drawback (Regular & Crossing)**: Brush (back) - Heel (drop) - Step

**Essence (Back)**: Brush (back), Step - Step - Step (back - out - center)

**Essence (Front - Single)**: Step - Step - Step (center - cross - center)

**Essence (Front - Double)**: Flap - Flap (center - cross) - Step

**Essence (Front - Break)**: Flap - Flap (center - cross) - Step, Back Flap - Step, Flap (cross) - Step

**Flap (Single)**: Brush - Step (transfer weight)

**Flap (Double)**: Brush - Step 2× Alt (counts: e&a1)

**Grab Off (Single Foot or Double Feet)**: Hop - Brush (back or front) - Land

**Grapevine**: Step 4× (side - cross back - side - cross front)

## *Glossary*

**Heel**: Drop or Dig

**Hop**: Stays on same side (on one foot)

**Irish**: Shuffle - Hop - Step (front or back)

**Jump**: Changing feet (from one foot to the other foot)

**Maxie Ford**: Shuffle - Jump - Toe Back

**Maxie Ford (With a Heel Drop)**: Shuffle - Jump - Heel - Toe Back

**Maxie Ford (With a Swap Pullback)**: Shuffle - Swap Pullback - Land - Toe Back

**Maxie Ford (With a Swap Pullback & Heel Drop**: Shuffle - Swap Pullback Land - Heel - Toe Back

**Nerve Tap**: Toe or Heel (rapid strikes to board)

**Paradiddle or Paddle & Roll (Single)**: Heel Dig - Brush (back) - Ball - Heel

**Paradiddle or Paddle & Roll (Double)**: Heel Dig - Brush (back) 2×, Ball - Heel

**Pickup / Pullback (Single)**: Jump - Brush (back) - Land (done on one foot)

**Pickup / Pullback (Swap)**: Jump - Brush (back) - Land (opposite foot)

**Pullback (Double - Two Feet Together)**: Jump - Brush (back) - Land (both feet at the same time)

**Pullback (Double - Two Feet Separated)**: Brush - Brush (back, off ground), Land - Land

**Pullback (Crossing Double - Two Feet Separated**: Brush - Brush (back, off ground), Land - Land (cross over 2nd Land)

**Riff (2 Count)**: Toe (inside edge) - Heel (strike)

**Riff (3 Count)**: Toe (inside edge) - Heel (strike) - Heel (bounce)

**Riff (4 Count)**: Toe (inside edge) - Heel (strike) - Heel Dig - Toe (drop)

**Riff (5 Count - One Foot)**: Toe (inside edge) - Heel (strike) - Heel Dig - Toe (drop) - Heel (bounce)

**Riff (5 Count - Two Feet)**: Toe (inside edge) - Heel (strike) - Heel (bounce) - Heel Dig - Toe (drop)

**Riff (6 Count)**: Toe (inside edge) - Heel (strike) - Heel (bounce) - Heel Dig - Toe (drop), Heel (bounce)

**Riff (7 Count)**: Toe (inside edge) - Heel (strike) - Heel (bounce) - Heel Dig - Toe (drop), Heel - Heel (bounces: back - front)

**Riff (8 Count)**: Toe (inside edge) - Heel (strike) - Heel (bounce) - Heel Dig - Toe (drop), Heel - Heel (bounces: back - front), Toe (lift)

**Riff (12 Count)**: Toe (inside edge) - Heel (strike) - Heel (bounce) 3× (out-cross-out), Heel Dig - Toe (drop) - Heel (bounce)

# Glossary

**Riff (24 Count)**: Toe (inside edge) - Heel (strike) - Heel (bounce) 6× (out - cross - out - back - out - cross - out), Heel Dig - Toe (drop) - Heel (bounce)

**Riffle**: Toe (inside edge) - Heel (strike) - Brush (back)

**Riffle - Heel**: Toe (inside edge) - Heel (strike) - Brush (back) - Heel (bounce)

**Scuff**: Heel strike (back edge with a forward leg swing)

**Scuffle (Single)**: Heel (dig) - Brush (back)

**Scuffle (Double)**: Heel (dig) - Brush (back) 2×

**Shag**: Flap 3× - Single Chug

**Shim Sham**: Stomp - Brush (back) - Step 2×, Stomp - Brush (back) - Ball Change, Stomp - Brush (back) - Step

**Shim Sham (Scuffle)**: Scuffle - Step 2×, Scuffle - Ball Change, Scuffle - Step

**Shim Sham (Shuffle)**: Shuffle - Step 2×, Shuffle - Ball Change, Shuffle - Step

**Shuffle**: Brush (forward) - Brush (back)

**Slap**: Brush (forward) - Tap (toe, no weight transfer)

**Stamp**: Step (whole foot, transfer weight)

**Stomp**: Step (whole foot, no weight)

**Time Step (Advanced Waltz)**: Flap - Shuffle - Step, Heel - Heel (drops)

**Time Step (Bombershay)**: Brush (back) - Hop 2×, Shuffle - Step - Stamp - Heel Dig, Flap, Brush - Step - Step 3×

**Time Step (Buck - Single)**: Shuffle - Hop, Step - Flap - Step

**Time Step (Buck - Double I)**: Shuffle - Hop - Toe Back, Step - Flap

**Time Step (Buck Double II)**: Shuffle - Hop - Flap, Flap - Step

**Time Step (Buck Triple I)**: Shuffle - Hop, Shuffle - Step, Flap - Step

**Time Step (Buck Triple II)**: Shuffle - Hop - Toe Back - Heel (drop) - Step, Flap - Step

**Time Step (Cramp Roll - Single)**: Brush (back) - Hop - Step, Flap - Step (ball) - Heel – Heel Dig

**Time Step (Cramp Roll - Double)**: Brush (back) - Hop, Flap 2×, Step (ball) - Heel - Heel Dig

**Time Step (Cramp Roll - Triple)**: Brush (back) - Hop, Shuffle - Step, Flap - Step (ball) - Heel - Heel Dig

**Time Step (Cramp Roll - Double / Triple)**: Brush (back) - Hop, Shuffle - Step 2×, Step (ball) - Heel, Heel Dig

## *Glossary*

**Time Step (Cramp Roll - Advanced)**: Brush (back), Hop 2×, Shuffle - Step - Stamp - Heel Dig, Brush (back) - Hop - Flap, Flap Cramp Roll

**Time Step (Double / Triple)**: Shuffle - Hop, Shuffle - Step, Shuffle - Step - Step

**Time Step (Double Wing - Single)**: Brush (back) - Hop - Step - Step, Double Wing - Tap (forward)

**Time Step (Double Wing - Double)**: Brush (back) - Hop - Flap - Step, Double Wing - Tap (forward)

**Time Step (Fundamental - Single)**: Hop - Shuffle - Step, Flap - Step - Stomp

**Time Step (Fundamental - Double)**: Brush (back) - Hop, Shuffle - Step, Flap - Step - Stomp

**Time Step (Mock Wing)**: Brush (back) - Hop - Shuffle - Step, Flap & Brush (out), Brush (in), Step - Heel Dig

**Time Step (Traveling Regular or Offbeat - Single)**: Shuffle - Step, Shuffle - Ball Change 2×, Brush (back) - Hop - Step, Shuffle - Step, Hold

**Time Step (Traveling Regular or Offbeat - Double I)**: Shuffle - Step, Shuffle, Ball Change 2×, Brush (back) - Hop - Toe Back - Step, Shuffle - Step, Hold

**Time Step (Traveling Regular or Offbeat - Double II)**: Shuffle - Step, Shuffle, Ball Change 2×, Brush (back) - Hop - Flap L, Shuffle - Step, Hold

**Time Step (Traveling Regular or Offbeat - Triple)**: Shuffle - Step, Shuffle, Ball Change 2×, Brush (back) - Hop, Shuffle - Step 2×, Hold

**Time Step (Traveling Offbeat - Double / Triple)**: Brush - Hop, Shuffle - Step, Shuffle, Step - Step - Step (no weight on last Step)

**Time Step (Waltz Clog - Single)**: Jump - Shuffle - Ball Change

**Time Step (Waltz Clog - Double)**: Flap - Shuffle - Ball Change

**Toe Back**: Toe Strike (top of tap, behind other heel)

**Toe Lift**: Toe (lift then drop, heel remains down)

**Waltz Clog**: Jump - Shuffle - Ball Change (3/4 time)

**Wings (Double)**: Jump & Scrape (out, both at same time), Brush (inside edge of front tap, both at same time), Land (both at same time)

**Wings (Single)**: Jump & Scrape (out, one side only), Brush (inside edge of front tap), Land

**Wing (Single + Toe Back)**: Jump & Scrape (out, one side only), Brush (inside edge of front tap), Land, Toe Back (non-working side)

# Bibliography

Alzheimer's Association. "Can Alzheimer's Disease Be Prevented?" 2021. https://www.alz.org/alzheimers-dementia/research_progress/prevention.

Carmeli, E.E. "The Aging Hand." *The Journals of Gerontology: Series A*, 2003, M146-M152.

Duberg, A.E. "Influencing Self-rated Health Among Adolescent Girls with Dance Intervention." *JAMA Network*, 2013, pp. 27–31.

Eckstein, H. "Just Dance: The Physical and Mental Benefits of Dancing." 2014. *HC at Notre Dame*. https://www.hercampus.com/school/notre-dame/just-dance-physical-and-mental-benefits-dancing/.

Hoogandam, Y.Y."Older Age Relates to Worsening of Fine Motor Skills: A Population-Based Study of Middle-Aged and Elderly Persons." 2014. *Frontiers in Aging Neuroscience*.

Jansheski, G. "What Is Cerebral Palsy?" 2020. Syracuse: Cerebral Palsy Guidance. https://www.cerebralpalsyguidance.com/cerebral-palsy/.

Jimison, R."5 Reasons Why Dancing Is Good for Your Health." 2017. *CNN Health*. https://www.cnn.com/2017/06/08/health/health-benefits-of-dancing/index.html

Lanzito, C. "The Healing Powers of Dance." *AARP the Magazine*. https://www.aarp.org/health/fitness/info-03-2011/dance-for-health.html.

Neklason, A. "Blackface Was Never Harmless." February 19, 2019. *The Atlantic*. https://www.theatlantic.com/entertainment/archive/2019/02/legacy-blackface-ralph-northam-didnt-understand/582733/.

Parkinson's Foundation. "What Is Parkinson's?" 2021. https://www.parkinson.org/understanding-parkinsons/what-is-parkinsons.

Rao, S.E. "Jimmy Kimmel Apologizes for 'Embarrassing' Sketches as Hollywood Reckons with Its Use of Blackface." June 23, 2020. *The Washington Post*. https://www.washingtonpost.com/arts-entertainment/2020/06/23/jimmy-kimmel-apologizes-blackface/.

Scott, E. "Mark Herring Said Ralph Northam Should Resign for Wearing Black Face in College. Then Herring Admitted to Doing the Same Thing." February 6, 2019. *The Washington Post*. https://www.washingtonpost.com/politics/2019/02/06/mark-herring-said-ralph-northam-should-resign-wearing-blackface-college-then-herring-admitted-doing-same-thing/.

Seibert, B. *What The Eye Hears: A History of Tap Dancing*. New York: Farrar, Straus, and Giroux, 2019.

Toder, F.P. "6 Reasons Why the Brain Loves Dancers Over 60." 2013. *HuffPost*. https://www.huffpost.com/entry/tap-dancing_b_3749600.

Verghese, E.A. "Leisure Activities and the Risk of Dementia in the Elderly." 2003. *The New England Journal of Medicine*.

# Index

Access Dance 162
Access Living 162, 163
Alzheimer's 5, 12, 14–15, 18, 22, 29, 32, 35, 42, 45–48, 51, 63
Alzheimer's Association 32
American Dance Therapy Association 24
American Heart Association 14, 49
American Medical Association 23
American Stroke Association 37
American Tap Dance Orchestra 219
Americans with Disabilities Act (ADA) 160, 191–192, 197, 199, 201, 204
Arpino, Gerry 162
arthritis 12, 14, 18, 25, 29, 35–36, 45; osteoarthritis 35–36; rheumatoid 35–36
Arthritis Foundation 36
Astaire, Fred 54, 215

ball-heel combination 140
Bates, Clayton (Peg Leg) 217
The Berry Brothers 215
blind 8, 185, 202
bombershay combination 105
Briggs, Bunny 218
Brown, King Rastus 214
Brown, Ralph 218
Bryant, Willie 216
Bubbles, John 214, 217
Buffalino, Brenda 58, 219
Buffalo: 45; combination 73; double 85
Burzynska, Aga 23

Capezio 216
Casel, Ayodel 8, 53
cerbral palsy 1, 11–12, 18, 25, 29, 33–35, 42, 45; ataxic 34; dyskinetic 34; mixed 34; spastic 33
Cerebral Palsy Guidance 33

Chace, Marian 24
choreography 3, 6, 11, 16–17, 23, 27, 40–41, 51, 54–58, 63–64, 158
Cincinnati 116
Ciro's 218
Clemens, Stephanie 163
Cleveland Ballet 197–198, 200
Coconut Club 218
Cohen, George M. 213
Coles, Honi 219
Collins, Leon 58
Condo Brothers 217
Conrad, Gail 219
Conte, Lou 43
Cotton Club 218
cramp roll 61, 68; flap combination 100, 115; military 88; riffle-heel combination 133; scuffle combination 132; shuffle combination 102
crossing brushes: 65; heels 69; combination 79
Crossman, Zoe (Laryssa) 186, 188
CounterBalance 163

Daily, Dan 218
Dally, Lynn 219
Dance for All Bodies 169, 171
Dance for Communication 24
Dancing Wheels Company 193–194, 202, 207
Dancing Wheels School 193
Dannelly, Lindy viii, 173–193
deaf 8, 39–40, 185, 202
dementia 5, 12, 14–15, 22, 32–33, 47–48, 51
diversity 3, 8, 19
Dolly, Lynn 219
Douglass, Frederick 212
Draper, Paul 54
drawbacks 88; combination 98, 114

# Index

Duffy, Barbara viii, 58, 60–63
Du Pron, Louis 218

Ebsen, Buddy 217
Ellen, Vera 54
essence 45; back 89; back combination 125; double front 81; single front 81

flap, double 104; back 112; combination 132; front 112
flap-heels, traveling double 87–88, 122; grapevine 88; single 87; triple 88
The Four Cohens 213
The Four Covans 213
Foy, Eddie, Sr. 213
froggy 45, 101
Frontiers in Aging Neuroscience 23
Full Radius Dance 173–174, 176, 178–179, 181, 183, 186, 188–189

Glover, Savion 8, 53, 219
Goldberg, Jane 219
The Golden Age of Tap 214
Grable, Betty 54, 218
grapevine: 45, 71; combination 71
gum off the shoe 45; combination 97, 122

handicapped 194–195, 201–202
Hayworth, Rita 54
hearing impaired 8, 29, 38–40, 46; impairment 12
Hess, Carol 219
Hines, Gregory 8, 219
hoofers 215–217
Hoofers Club 217
Hubbard Street Dance 43

improvisation 3, 6, 56–59, 62–64
inclusivity 2–3, 8, 19, 157, 200, 210
Irish 45; combination 80, 84; dance style 211–212

jazz square 74
The Jazz Tap Ensemble 219
jigging 211
Joffrey Ballet 162
Jolson, Al 212
Jordan, Michael 16

Keeler, Ruby 218–219
Kelly, Gene 9, 53–54, 215
Kim, Mindy viii, 167–173
King, King, and King 215

Lancashire Clog 211
Lane, Ginger viii, 8, 158–167
Lane, William Henry (Juba) 210–211
Le Roy, Hal 217
Lewis, Andrea 219
Lindberg, Charles 217; see also Lindy
Lindy 45, 74, 217; see also Lindberg, Charles
lupus 25

Master Tap Tips 43
Maxie Ford 45, 66; combination 79, 84, 132
McKrae, Edna 162
Miller, Ann 54, 218
Minstel era 213; show 212
Momenta Dance Company 163
mononeuritis multiplex 175
multiple sclerosis 25
My Gimpy Life 183
myotonic dystrophy 167–168, 170

National Tap Dance Day 214
Nelson, Gene 218
neuroplasticity 23
New England Journal of Medicine 22, 33
The Newport Jazz Festival 219
Nicholas Brothers 218

O'Connor, Donald 9, 54, 218

paddle and roll, paradiddle 16, 61, 65; combination 79, 87, 94, 110, 116, 117, 120
Parkinson's 11–12, 18, 25, 29, 30–31, 33, 35, 45–46, 63
Pastor, Tony 213
pick up 103; combination 140
Plantation Club 218
Powell, Eleanor 53–54, 214–215, 217, 219
pullbacks: 61, 103; combination 132, 135; shuffle double 112

quadruple combination 131

Reed, Leonard 216–217
Reeve, Christopher 204–205
Reich, Sarah 8
Relin Tony 219
Rhapsody in Taps 219
Rice, Thomas (Jim Crow) 212
riff 61; 5 count (1 foot) 75; 5 count (2 feet) 76; 4 count 75; 4 count

# Index

combination 81; 7 count 76; 7 count combination 124; 6 count 76; 6 count combination 100, 108, 123; 3 count 69; 3 count combination 81, 124; 12 count 99; 24 count 99; 2 count 69
riffle combination 102
Robinson, Bill "Bojangles" 214, 217
Rogers, Ginger 54, 215
Rooney, Mickey 54
Rooney, Pat, Sr. 213

sacroiliac joint 175; dysfunction 175
scissors 45; slow 75; fast 75, 91
Scott, Douglas 176–177, 179, 181–182, 185
scuffles 69
sentimental journey 125
7–7combination 95
shag 73; combination 86
Sherer, Teal 183
Shim Sham 45, 75, 215–216; with breaks 84; with hard break 111
Shorty George 217
shuffle, combination 87, 90, 98; double 87; 5 count 112; rolling combination 91, 109, 113, 124
*Shuffle Along* 215
slap 67; progression I 67; progression II 68
slicing combination 100
Snowden, Shorty 217
Sohl-Ellison, Linda 219
Specificity of Training 27
spina bifida 194, 207
Stocker, Ali 192
stroll 109
stroke 12, 14–15, 18, 25, 29, 37–38, 45, 47, 49, 51, 63; hemorrhagic 37; ischemic 37, transient ischemic attack (TIA) 37
Susie Q 45
Swing and Sway 45, 84, with break 101
syncopated combination 129

Tack Annie 45, 79, 217
tap: Broadway 3, 52–53, 55; chair 8–11, 14, 17, 29, 33, 35–36, 38, 43, 45, 56, 58, 169, 170–173; hand 8–11, 14, 29, 35, 38, 40–41, 43, 56, 58, 171, 173; history 3; rhythmic 3, 52–53, 55, 214; stand-up 9, 11, 20, 41, 56, 58, 169, 171, 173, styles 216
Tap for All (program) ix, 5, 7–9, 12, 18, 20, 31–32, 38, 40, 200
*Tap Into Improv* viii, 58
Temple, Shirley 218
time steps 62, 215; advanced waltz clog 150; bombershay 151; buck 145, 146; cramp roll 150; double heel 151–152; double / triple 149, 151; double / triple cramp roll 150–151; double wing 151; fundamental 146–147; mock wing 149; mock wing combination 137; off beat traveling 148–149; stomp 15, 146; traveling 147–148; waltz clog 75, 149–150
time step breaks advanced cramp roll 155; bombershay 155; buck 152; cramp roll 154–155; double heel 156; double / triple 154; fundamental 153; mock wing 154; off beat traveling 154; soft shoe 155–156; stomp 152–153; traveling 153–154
train 45; train style 110
triplet combination 92

vaudeville 212–213
Verdi-Fletcher, Mary viii, 8, 193–207
visually impaired 8, 29, 38, 40–41, 46; impairment 12

Waag, Tony 219
Walker, Dianne 58
waltz clog double 89; single 89
warm up 14, 25, 36, 38, 41
Wayburn, Ned 217
Weave combination 110, 122
White, George 213
Wiggins, Jack 216
Williams, Henry 217
Wings combination 105; crossing double 104; double 104; pendulum 105; single 104; swap 105

www.ingramcontent.com/pod-product-compliance
Lightning Source LLC
Chambersburg PA
CBHW032038300426
44117CB00009B/1100